D0421895

Tales from Kentucky Lawyers

TALES FROM
KENTUCKY
LAWYERS

WILLIAM LYNWOOD MONTELL

THE UNIVERSITY PRESS OF KENTUCKY

Publication of this volume was made possible in part by a grant
from the National Endowment for the Humanities.

Editorial and Sales Offices: The University Press of Kentucky
663 South Limestone Street, Lexington, Kentucky 40508-4008

03 04 05 06 07   5 4 3 2 1

Library of Congress Cataloging-in-Publication Data

Montell, William Lynwood, 1931-
Tales from Kentucky lawyers / William Lynwood Montell.
p. cm.
Includes descriptive accounts, provided in conjunction
with stories told during interviews.
ISBN 0-8131-2294-5 (hardcover : alk. paper)
1. Law—Kentucky—Anecdotes. I. Title.
K184.M66 2003
349.769—dc21
2003011395

This book is printed on acid-free recycled paper meeting
the requirements of the American National Standard
for Permanence in Paper for Printed Library Materials.

∞ ♻

Manufactured in the United States of America.

 Member of the Association of
American University Presses

Dedicated to my wife, Linda

CONTENTS

INTRODUCTION

Lawyers know how to spin a good yarn. They also know how to fascinate an audience. My announcement in early 2000 that I would collect stories from lawyers and judges was met with great enthusiasm by members of the legal profession, by academicians, and especially by the general public. Fortunately, many lawyers expressed great interest in participating—getting them to set aside time for a storytelling session and general interview was another matter. All those who found time, however, recounted wonderful stories: sometimes funny, sometimes sad or frightening, sometimes thought-provoking, but always interesting.

Many people have had experiences with lawyers that they would rather not discuss, but over the past few months of traveling and interviewing lawyers and judges, I have found dedicated, sincere, and concerned professional individuals who, without lengthy hesitation, willingly shared their many stories and insights concerning the legal system. They were especially willing to trust me upon learning that I have authored numerous scholarly books over the years about local life and culture.

I certainly wished to preserve the wonderful stories in this volume, but I also wanted to preserve some part of the storytellers themselves. The stories speak for themselves; it is my hope that the reader also will see the humor, seriousness, and wisdom that are part and parcel of these great storytellers.

Two primary criteria were established prior to contacting anyone about a storytelling session. First, the teller should generally be a middle-aged or older lawyer practicing alone or as a member of a small firm.

The rationale for this was that such lawyers would most likely have interesting memories from which to draw, since younger attorneys and those practicing in larger firms around the state tend rather to specialize in a particular aspect of the law.

This led naturally to a second criterion: the law offices of these storytellers should typically be located in small to medium-sized towns or cities across the commonwealth. Practices in these locales would tend to guarantee both a greater diversity of clients with varying socio-economic backgrounds and a wider range of interesting and illuminating cases. Thanks to references and frequent contacts made by other lawyers on my behalf, I was fortunate to be able to record stories told by lawyers and judges in every geographic region of Kentucky, including the Jackson Purchase, Pennyroyal Region, Western Coal Field, Bluegrass Region, and Eastern Coal Field. (It should be pointed out that the Cumberland Plateau and Outer Bluegrass also were included by name in these categories for many, many years.) Moving from west to east, persons interviewed lived and/or practiced in the following towns and cities: South Fulton, Mayfield, Paducah, Murray, Eddyville, Princeton, Cadiz, Madisonville, Hopkinsville, Greenville, Owensboro, Franklin, Bowling Green, Leitchfield, Louisville, Edmonton, Shelbyville, Carrollton, Russell Springs, Jamestown, Lexington, Williamsburg, London, Stanton, Manchester, Maysville, Beattyville, Frenchburg, Morehead, Harlan, Hazard, Hindman, Prestonsburg, and Pikeville.

The kinds of stories chosen for the collection fall into one of a dozen or so broad categories or tale types chosen specifically because of their human-interest potential. As I listened to and recorded these stories, many sub-categories or tale types emerged from four overarching categories—humorous, dramatic, intriguing, and challenging—thus resulting in the many group classifications that are included herein. The initial four categories eventually gave way to twenty-four all together. But sex, theft, court procedures, illegitimacy, blunders, animals in court, mental and physical disability, politics, domestic disputes, and murder came out again and again in virtually all the interviews. That these themes emerged frequently should come as no surprise to anyone.

Nor should we be surprised that lawyers and judges are almost always central to these accounts. Nevertheless, note that personal actions and interactions, and not points of law, are central to each story. While the essence of these accounts may deal with certain legal themes, the focus of these stories is always people. Folklorists stress the fact that people everywhere build their lives in accordance with folk beliefs, customs, practices, and stories heard on a daily basis. It takes thematic stories and tales to assist people in dividing their daily lives along meaningful lines.

The actual interviews took place without a set script. All told, I interviewed thirty-nine lawyers and judges. After we sat down to talk, I enthusiastically strove to put the subject at ease by gathering some background personal and professional information, then gradually worked into the lengthy interview, asking, for example, "What is a chief difference in the legal profession then and now?" After a brief period spent on that subject, I used follow-up, open-ended questions such as "What is one of your favorite memories of a lawyer friend during your early years?" so as to encourage them to tell me more. Each of the thirty-nine interview sessions was recorded on either a battery-powered or an electric tape recorder. I then transcribed the interview tapes at home, a task typically requiring a minimum of nine to eleven hours for each hour of taped interview. Portions of all the interviews have been used, but not all the stories recorded during each interview have been used.

In reading the stories herein, it will become immediately apparent that this is not a collection of lawyer jokes. Many of the stories are very funny, but many of them are also poignant in that they keenly affect people's senses. Others are painful, even horrifying. The courts and the state's legal system do not always see people at their best. In fact, by the time a legal situation has found its way to court, the plaintiffs and defendants are often at their wits' end. If the problem they are confronting could easily have been solved, a satisfactory pre-court solution would already have been accomplished. Lawyers and judges must often deal with people at their very worst and try to find or effect solutions to problems that are basically unsolvable. Is it any wonder that being a lawyer is so stressful?

If we should not be surprised to shed a tear at some of these stories, we likewise should not be surprised to laugh aloud at some. Humor is, and probably always will be, nature's Prozac. How else could caring people survive day-in and day-out trying to solve the unsolvable and love the unlovable in order to keep the social fabric from unraveling or tearing irreparably? Lawyers and judges, like the police, are on society's front lines.

It is not likely that all the events described in this book actually occurred within the commonwealth. Everyone loves to hear a good story, and everyone likes to tell a good story. And no one likes a good story better than a small-town lawyer who has to make a living with wit and charm and the ability to influence and move a jury. It also will be apparent (especially to trained folklorists) that various universal narratives, tale types, and motifs recur within the pages of this book. Some tales found in such categories as blunders, adultery, miscellaneous, and other story categories were told to the author as being true. Some probably are true, and some most likely are not. Whether true or not, such stories have been reported as true for hundreds of years elsewhere in the United States and even in Europe. Telling a few nonpersonal stories does not mean that the narrators meant to deceive the hearer or the readers, but sharing them does show us that these tale types are very important to people, otherwise, they would not have been repeated so faithfully from generation to generation.

It was Stith Thompson, internationally known folklorist and native of Washington County, Kentucky, who told the world about the importance of tale types. As a student at Indiana University in the early 1960s, I never had a class from Dr. Thompson. He had already retired before I went there to study folklore, cultural geography, social and cultural history, and oral history methodology, but I did get to know him on a personal level. One of Thompson's outstanding works is *The Types of the Folktale*, published in revised format in 1961.[1] Although it excludes consideration of all varieties of legends, it does contain reference to local stories about eccentric characters that are told to be true. Consulting Thompson's tale type index may help a local historian know whether or not to print a story for truth just because it was told about a local figure. Some of the stories presented here may well be tale types, but the bulk of these lawyer stories do not fit the tale type categories. These stories are typically more personal and presented as humorous events that really took place.

Longer stories told about persons who lived in the distant past are often referred to as legends. The stories in this volume are typically brief narratives, typically set in the recent past, and are always told as true accounts. And many of them are indeed true. Legends serve to elevate the self-esteem of a person or persons by emphasizing desirable features and characteristics of personal history and ancestry. And while legends may be based in true accounts, they are often polished somewhat by numerous retellings across the years.

The smallest narrative element found in stories identified by folklorists and some oral historians is a motif. These brief story elements have the power to persist in the oral tradition of various cultures for decades, sometimes centuries. A motif may be thought of as the smallest divisible narrative unit of a story. Although universal motifs in the stories in this book have not been identified, to do so would be an easy task. Stith Thompson's *Motif Index of Folk Literature* includes the following lawyer story categories: law costs, laws, law breakers, lawlessness, lawsuits, lawyers, and lawyer's dog.[2]

If these stories told by lawyers and judges are not personal, but are about someone else in the legal profession, they are folktales; i.e., they are told by someone other than the person to whom the described event occurred. Some may be true and others not necessarily true. For example, in the adultery category in this book, read "Everybody Has Got to Be Somewhere." Likely, this is a universal narrative told by and among legal professional colleagues. If the event described happened to the narrator firsthand, the account is referred to by folklorists and oral historians as a personal folk narrative.

Another example of a potentially universal folktale is included in the "Moonshining" category under the title "Whiskey, or Something Else?" This story and the one above may be true stories, but they have universal similarities to stories told elsewhere.

The terms "folklore" and "oral history" often carry ambiguous meanings and connotations. For example, the word "folklore" is sometimes used incorrectly to designate unverified rumor, falsehood, and hearsay. When people hear something that is unverifiable, perhaps doubtful, they will likely remark, "Oh, that's just folklore." The fact that information is passed along from one person to another orally during face-to-face conversation, rather than being abstracted from written sources, is a significant feature for persons interested in conducting local history research.

The term "oral history" is used in two ways. It may refer to the method by which oral historical information about the past is collected and recorded, and it can also mean a body of knowledge that exists only in people's memories and will be lost at their deaths and at the passing of others of that same generation. Oral history is thus not only a method of gathering valuable information, it is also a body of knowledge about the past that is uniquely different from the information contained in written records. There is little to no difference between the methodology employed to collect oral history and folkloristic materials containing historical content. Nonetheless, it can be stated that not all oral history is folklore nor is all folklore oral history. However, there is a great deal of overlap between these two academic fields.

Finally, it should be noted that one of the main recurring themes in the lawyer stories in this book focus on the changes in the legal system itself over the past thirty to forty years. Some of this important information can be attributed to the natural human tendency to long for the way things used to be, but some of it also seems to reflect a genuine worry within the legal community that something worthwhile has been lost in the march of progress. Most of the persons interviewed by me seemed to feel that there was something smaller and more intimate in the way law was practiced "in the good old days." Whether their longing is correct or not cannot be proven. Perhaps they merely project a more rosy past because they are not comfortable with everything in the current, more impersonal, legal situation.

I didn't want the legacy of the southern small-town/city trial lawyer to become entirely forgotten. Such lawyers are certainly an endangered species and have almost disappeared from the scene. Even if the stories hadn't been so interesting in themselves, I felt they needed to be recorded so that future generations could understand how the current legal system came to be. The lawyers depicted in this book are apparently giving way now to a new generation for whom the profession seems to be more of a business than a way of life, but I think this volume will help preserve this legacy of the southern trial lawyer. The fact that this tradition has been preserved in the oral history of the legal profession; the fact that these are the stories lawyers tell each other; and the fact that these are the stories that lawyers recount to outsiders as well prove that this customary tradition is important to how lawyers see themselves. That this legacy can be preserved through the sharing of stories that can be enjoyed by readers of many ages, backgrounds, and professions is the greatest satisfaction the author can derive from this type of academic work.

Tales of Kentucky Lawyers is not intended to be primarily a scholarly work, though it is hoped that scholars will read the book with the same interest as those who read for pleasure and that older lawyers will reminisce right along with their colleagues who narrate the stories. It is also hoped that young lawyers might read and benefit from the experiences and insights of their predecessors, and that high school and college students in various academic disciplines who read the stories in this book will know now and in the forthcoming years the importance of those persons in the legal profession who care about the well-being of the general populace.

Although Kentucky possesses the latest recording and transmitting technology, oral stories about lawyers, judges, and relative facets of the legal profession will continue to be in popular demand by these professionals, and by those who cherish memories of these persons. The lawyers, judges, and many other persons described in these oral accounts are immortal.

I want to express deep gratitude to the men and women of the Kentucky legal community who took the time to share memories from their distinguished careers. During the research for this book I developed special respect for those individuals who have put in many years of education and practice to see that everyone receives fair representation in court. Truly, they are, as Harry M. Caudill said, "the building blocks and mortar of history." [3]

NOTES

1. Aarne, Antti. *The Types of the Folktale: A Classification and Bibliography. Translated and Enlarged by Stith Thompson* (Helsinki: Academia Scientiarium Fennica, 1961).

2. Stith Thompson, *Motif Index of Folk Literature: A Classification of Narrative Elements in Folktales, Ballads, Myths, Fables, Mediaeval Romances, Exempla, Fabliaux, Jest-books, and Local Legends*, vol. 6 (Bloomington: Indiana University Press, 1955–1958), 454.

3. Harry M. Caudill, *Slender Is the Thread: Tales from a Country Law Office* (Lexington: University Press of Kentucky, 1987), xii.

1

Kentucky Courts, Past and Present

Many of the stories in this book illustrate how Kentucky's hardworking common people, the public personnel on all levels, and the occasional villains and rascals feel about peers, relatives, judges, and lawyers during periods of tension-filled social stress. Some lawyers and judges, in addition to sharing their favorite stories regarding courtroom confrontations, willingly expressed their personal views about changes in the legal profession over the years.

While the following accounts are not like the stories in subsequent chapters, they will help readers better understand Kentucky's court system, as well as the viewpoints, feelings, and assessments of contemporary lawyers and judges. In addition, many of the themes discussed here—caseloads, clashes between men and women, collegiality, fines and penalties, legal ethics, and the use of humor—appear repeatedly throughout the book

One of the most significant changes commented upon has been the increase in court fees, regarded by many of those interviewed as a rather exorbitant burden and a source of additional stress on people called into court.

1. "It's a Hard Tax"

The typical legal fee that lawyers charge for services rendered is affected by inflation. It has really gone up. When I started practicing law in 1971, there were 3,500 lawyers in the state of Kentucky. Now there are over 13,000 lawyers in the state. So from 1971 to 2001, the growth is about 10,000 over this thirty-year period. The lawyers' fees, due to competition, should go down, but they haven't. They've gone up tremendously. We used to do divorces and a lot of things and got a fee of $150 to $200. Deeds and wills were $10 or $15. We all made a living, took vacations, and raised families on that. Nowadays, a will is $200 to $300, a divorce is $1,000 to $1,500, and fees have just gone up tremendously.

It's the contemporary court costs that really get to me, because most of the people that come to my court—a district court—are working people, young people, or people on welfare, and while we can waive costs if these people are truly indigent, it's basically a really hard tax on them. We have to give them time to pay, but if they don't pay it, ultimately they'll be arrested and will go to jail for it. I try to be as liberal with them as I can, but not all judges do. It's a hard tax.

The state legislature is what determines all of this, and they just keep tacking on five dollars here and ten dollars there. Some counties will impose costs for the fiscal court, while others won't. Some go halfway, while others go the maximum. You would have to do a survey every month to determine what the court costs are. So each county has its own lists.

Stan Billingsley, Carrollton, March 20, 2001

2. "It Costs Everybody Too Much Money"

Court costs are now out of sight. I can't recall exactly, but it seems like when I first started practicing law, a filing fee was only $35 to file a case. Today, I don't really know what the filing fees are, but it seems to me that if we're talking about a civil suit, it costs $160 to $165. However, the biggest problem that I see with the court system now, and I really find a lot of problems with this, is that it costs everybody too much money to go to court.

The state legislature is responsible for a lot of it, and all the special interest groups are responsible for it, like they add on five dollars for this cost and that cost. Well, the criminals ought to pay these costs. They're not all criminals, but they add a lot of costs on to traffic violators and other people. Now, they've come up with the idea that a person ought to pay for incarceration. Why, hell, if they could pay for their incarceration, they wouldn't be stealing to go to the pen anyway. How smart is that? That's stupid. I mean, what are you going to do?

You say, "Let the criminal pay for their own incarceration." How are they going to pay for it? Let's assume a guy goes to jail, he then gets out, but who's going to give him a job? Would anyone give a man like that a job to enable him to pay for his jail time? Of course not. To me, that's just as dumb as a fence post. A lot of judges enforce it, but most of them have enough sense not to. And as for those who enforce the law in this regard, I don't know where the criminal gets the money to pay. I don't know how these costs are collected. I don't know that they can be collected.

John O. Hardin, III, Cadiz, March 21, 2001

3. "POOR GO TO JAIL, RICH GO HOME"

There are a lot more fines in Kentucky than there were when I first started practicing in 1950. The reason for that is the State of Kentucky spends a lot of money on a lot of things, and in recent years they have tried to use the court as a taxing system so as to tax the people. And the fines do not take into consideration the wealth of the person. If a person has a lot of money, if they give him a $1,000 fine and a $200 cost, he just writes a check and goes home. A poor person has to go to jail and sit there for a long time, which is basically unfair because the court fine should be in relation to the financial wealth of the individual to be affected.

Edward Jackson, Beattyville, July 20, 2001

4. "JUDGES ARE BUSY ALL THE TIME"

Years ago, when I first started practicing law, you could get into court quick, you could get a hearing quick, you could do what your client needed you to do within a reasonable period of time. Of course, the economy has changed, the standard of living has changed, and the cost of living has changed. But you didn't have so many different courts back then. You had a county court, a city court, and a circuit court. Well, in circuit court, you tried circuit court cases, but you didn't have continuous sessions of court like they do now. The population has grown, and now there are too many factors for getting in court, such as theft.

I practiced a lot of domestic relations law and I used to be able to draw up petitions for many things and file them in court. Within thirty minutes I could get it resolved. I could go to the judge and get it signed and have it in the sheriff's office within an hour's time. Admittedly, I was faster than most lawyers back then. Nowadays, you're lucky if you can find a circuit judge because they are so busy these days. They're in court all the time. I think the court schedule on certain judges is totally unreasonable. I think there needs to be a lot more circuit judges than there currently is. But in certain portions of the state, there are some circuit judges that have very small courts.

But in other areas, the judges are busy all the time. Judge Cunningham does an amazing job in four counties. I don't see how he does it. He's got domestic relations commissioners, too. That's a step that supposedly saves time for the judges, but it makes it more difficult in my opinion for the clients, because instead of going to a judge, you have to go to a domestic relations commissioner. Then you go through the same process of having a hearing. Then the domestic relations commissioner has to write an opinion. You have to go through the same appeals process that you do in order to get to a circuit judge whom you could have gone on to in earlier years.

You've got to pay an attorney to go through all of that, plus you've got to pay commissioner's fees, and the fees just go on and on.

John O. Hardin, III, Cadiz, March 21, 2001

5. "An Informal Setting Back Then"

The pace in legal practice began to change by the time I began practicing back in 1963. The motion hour depended on the court once a week, every two weeks, or once a month. . . . In some other places it is called "docket call," but it's the same procedural concept. It's a gathering of lawyers with the judge. During most every motion hour now, the judge wears a robe. Nowadays, lawyers are told where to stand, how to address the court; the judge wears a robe and is friendly. The judge is excellent and does a good job. But it was much more relaxed when I began practicing law. I don't know of any judge back then who wore his robe to motion hour. Most of them would have a list of cases with matters pending and begin reading from the top down and calling the case. The lawyers would stand up in place where they were, and if there was something funny to be said, another lawyer felt sort of free to wisecrack. We also had some very intelligent, good lawyers who would comment on what was happening, whether it was that lawyer's case or not, then advise the judge how to rule. There was always a wisecrack or two, but nothing really disrespectful and non-courteous. It was just fun, just a much more relaxed atmosphere than now.

I remember Judge Jim Lassiter who, in Calloway and Marshall counties, did not formally call a docket. He had what I call an "at home" setup. On Friday mornings, he was sitting in the grand jury room at a table with cases. There was a pot of coffee there. Lawyers would walk in, get his attention, talk about what they had on the docket, how to handle it. A lawyer from another county would show up. I could drive over there from Paducah, for example, and he would say, "Dick, who is on the other side?"

I might name a Murray lawyer, and the judge would turn to his clerk and say, "Call Mr. Jones. Tell him Dick is here." Then the other lawyer would come over and we would talk about the case then.

It was just an informal setting back then. We knew each other better. Collegiality was easier, and there was more time for lawyers to sit around and tell stories—talk about what had happened within recent times and those kinds of things.

Richard Roberts, Paducah, November 2, 2001

6. "Cold, Calculating Individuals"

I've held legal office, and for the past number of years I find it very saddening that in the last thirty to forty years, and it's more as time goes along, that the lawyers are only interested in how much money they can make out of the law. As a result, the law is sacrificed. My daddy, who was a lawyer, said, "I love the law and I want to see the law administered properly." He was a strong-willed man. Some lawyers now are cold, calculating individuals. Even back in my earlier days, and before that, these people that you represented, a lot of times were your friends, not your enemies. And you cared something for those people. Now, they don't care. What they want is the money.

B. Robert Stivers, Manchester, July 19, 2001

7. "A Slower Pace"

In my early legal years, there were less lawyers in number, and they practiced at a slower pace. They worked hard, but the number of cases and the way the cases progressed was at a more leisurely pace. And there was more time for interaction among the lawyers. Nowadays, I see lawyers come into the courthouse, and while they are waiting for their case to be called, they are all on their cell phones, so there is very little interaction between them. They are working on their own caseload, and they are doing their own business—don't have much interrelationship with each other. Thus, the lawyers don't know each other. And with the increase in the number of lawyers, they don't have the opportunity to know each other and establish friendships, or even animosities, like they used to do.

I learned a long time ago that if the judge laughs aloud in court during a criminal case, that affects the decision of the jury. And also, if jurors get to laughing, they will probably decide in favor of the defendant. Good criminal defense lawyers know that, and the really good ones know that if they're perceived as trying to clown, then that will probably blow up in their face. But if the defense lawyer can avoid the perception that they're trying to work the jury, and if they can interject a little humor into it, and get the jury laughing a little at the appropriate things, then they've got a better chance of prevailing. As I heard an old lawyer say one time, "Laughing jurors don't send people to prison." But if laughter is inappropriate, it would probably have just a reverse effect. So part of the skill of a good trial lawyer is knowing whether or not to do it, and if so, how to go about doing it.

William R. Harris, Franklin, August 22, 2001

8. "Greater Demands upon Lawyers"

Both lawyers and judges are better than they ever were. Lawyers are better, and judges make better decisions. However, we live in a much more complex society, which makes their job a lot harder. . . . And one of the biggest problems today is that lawyers charge too much a lot of times. The problem you run into is that because of greater demands upon lawyers—on their time, they constantly have to acquire additional personnel, equipment, machinery, and technology to process the cases.

Bill Cunningham, Eddyville, January 21, 2001

9. "Low Attendance in Court"

Local residents don't go to county court sessions like they once did. I'll often have a courtroom full of jurors with an interesting case coming up, and once I select the jurors and tell the rest that they're always welcome to stay, they almost never do stay. They get out of there as quick as they can. I feel like we do some great work and the public never sees it.

It used to be that you would always have a courtroom full of visitors, but that's not the case around here anymore.

Stan Billingsley, Carrollton, March 20, 2001

10. "Lost Credibility"

Family court is so rough these days. The worst part about the judiciary system today is that they are asking us to solve societal problems that we are all ill-equipped to solve—that are unsolvable to a great extent, and in fact would be better off to be left to some other vehicle. That's one of the weaknesses as to why the judiciary and the court systems are less and less written about in newspapers these days. You do read about the high-profile cases, but most of what we do is the day-to-day and mundane matters. . . . It's no longer interesting and reportable. And I think to some extent that we've lost our credibility. The judiciary is not as well respected as it used to be. Many people, especially the poor, look upon the court system as being unjust.

Boyce Martin Jr., Louisville, December 7, 2001

11. "Location, Location, Location"

In terms of my own work, I feel that in eastern Kentucky the plaintiff (my side of the case) does better. The area there is more economically depressed. The more depressed our society is, the more sympathetic it is to other persons. The better the times, the less sympathetic we are and the tighter we become. I feel that anyone else in my business would confirm that there is a direct correlation between good economic times and bad economic times in terms of the recovery that we are able to make for our clients. During good economic times, for whatever reason, we tighten up our hold on our pocketbooks, when actually you would think that we would be more benevolent. And in depressed economic times, we loosen the hold on our pocketbooks, at least in jury verdicts that are issued. So really, thirty years ago, even twenty years ago, you might have gotten a better award in a particular case than you would today.

That's the way it was when President Carter was in office and times seemed so poor economically. And now there's a direct reflection of that. We've got Bush in the White House. Kentucky has either five or six of its congressional representatives who are Republicans. And without regard to what your politics are, the Republicans are tighter with the pocketbook than the Democrats, and that gets reflected in most aspects of my work. In other words, the jury will be less likely to grant a favorable decision. But they are more likely to in eastern Kentucky where it's been us against them, the coal miner against the company, for a long, long time. Usually, if you had an appropriate corporate defendant there, in any kind of case at all, you could anticipate some pretty good success. The further west you went, the less favorable to the client. . . .

Most every county is getting a new courthouse these days, but it is fun to try different cases in different places. I'll never forget a case I tried in Marion County. There, they had the jury box in the center of the courtroom facing the judge's bench. And between the judge's bench and the jury box was the witness stand right at the foot of the judge there in the center, facing that jury box. And it had that witness so close that you almost couldn't walk between the witness stand and the jury box. You were on top of one another. That's probably the most unusual place in which I ever tried a case. Whether or not they've still got that courthouse, I don't know.

When you go to a new place to try a court case, one of the first things you try to do is to meet the court staff. You want to be their friend, and you want them to be your friend. You want to find out the first name of the bailiff, who is a deputy sheriff. You want to know him by his first name, and you want him to call you by your first name. The same thing is true with the court clerk. That way, you break down that hometown barrier. If the jurors happen to hear the sheriff's bailiff call you by your first name, that can't be anything but good for you. That way they know that I'm not such a bad guy, even if I am from Louisville.

At the same time, being from Louisville is good for me. When I was in western Kentucky, I tried a few cases that turned out well. Since then, just about all my business comes by referral from other attorneys. So when an attorney from that part of the state refers a client to me here in Louisville, they think they're getting the big dog: "He's out of Louisville!"

I'm no better lawyer than I was when I was there, but my location carries a little different weight.

Peter Ervin, Louisville, April 26, 2001

12. "Lover of the Jury System"

In my experience, I have not encountered a conscious effort in which judges tried to influence the jurors. But what I have seen happen, and what good lawyers try to avoid, is to irritate the judge through their own conduct, or perhaps having one of your witnesses irritate the judge to where the jury picks up on the vibes of a disliking of the judge toward you or your side. . . . I don't recall ever being in a circumstance in which I thought the judge was positively trying to influence the jury for one side or another. I am a great lover of our jury system and would hate to see anything happen to it. And I think that most of our judges feel that way. Most of them are credible. . . .

Peter Ervin, Louisville, April 26, 2001

13. "Jury Rigging"

In my fifty-three years of practicing law in court, I've seen what I thought were bad decisions on the part of the judge, both pro and con, but as far as ever having any evidence at all that a judge was paid to decide a case a certain way, I never did find any. But I have been in cases where a juror had been accused of taking money. Of course, in a criminal case the jury's verdict has to be unanimous. Thus, if just one fellow takes a bribe and refuses to go along with the rest of the jury, this will effectually stalemate the accused's conviction. I do know of instances when that took place, and I suspect that jury rigging and jury tampering might, in some sections of the country, be more prevalent than we realize.

John L. Cox Jr., Stanton, November 26, 2001

14. "Too Much Authority"

I think the federal courts are unconstitutional because the U.S. Constitution provides for the trial by jury, and when they come along and provide for the federal judge [the power of authority] with the power to give you a fifty-dollar fine, plus court costs, or can put you in jail for twenty-one years, so he elects to put you in for twenty-one years. If we are going to have a democracy, that's too much authority for one person to have.

In federal courts, most of the defendants I've been associated with had rather be in a state court than a federal court, and that's because they're afraid of the judge.

The judge is nothing but a person who has been through law school and got a license. They don't have to be a lawyer, but they are. Even in the Supreme Court of the United States, they don't have to be a lawyer.

A judge is nothing but another lawyer who has known a governor or a senator and got to be a judge. State judges have to be appointed by the people. Federal judges are appointed for life. The attorney general is the only person who can sign a petition to remove federal judges from office. Nobody else can sign it.

Edward Jackson, Beattyville, July 20, 2001

15. "Television Advertisements"

I despise their practice of having advertisements on television. The Supreme Court says they can do it, so they can do it, but I find it distasteful. I wish it didn't happen. And truth of the matter is, I hardly ever see a client represented by lawyers who advertise their services, especially in those instances in which I suspect that the client has more than a high school education. I think they appeal to a market of people who don't have any access to the legal profession. That is, they don't know any lawyers; they don't know anybody who's got a lawyer in the family. This is partly the legal profession's fault because a lot of lawyers have defaulted in their obligation as citizens. When I was growing up, lawyers were scout masters, little-league coaches. They were active in the community and people kind of knew who they were. They were respected. That was how they advertised back then. Nowadays, it's probably a by-product of the pressure on the lawyers to handle more cases and make more money to meet their expenses and pay off their student loans. It seems as if the legal profession doesn't make itself as available to the public these days, thus when people need an attorney, they don't have any way of accessing one. All they've got to rely on is the advertisements they've seen on TV. As I said, I thoroughly despise it.

William R. Harris, Franklin, August 22, 2001

16. "Just Put Out a Little Sign"

I don't like television commercials sponsored by lawyers. Melbourne Mills is one of the first to start that practice, at least he was the first one I ever knew that advertised, and that has been several years ago. If I'm not mistaken, the Federal Trade Commission ruled that you could not prohibit a lawyer from advertising, so it snowballed under the federal level and came down to the state level.

When I first started practicing, you just put out a little sign. You didn't advertise, or anything. But now, in present times, they're just full of television, etc.

Asa R. Little Jr., Frenchburg

17. "ADS DEMEANING"

If we had a responsible media that was going to use court-recorded TV tapes, that would be different, but these thirty-second commercials never express what is going on in the court proceedings. In the same sense, I think that a televised ad for a lawyer is demeaning. These ads demean the legal institution. It's a little like religion: a good preacher and a good lawyer are both trying to sell someone on their position. . . .

Boyce Martin Jr., Louisville, December 7, 2001

18. "WORD-OF-MOUTH ADVERTISEMENTS"

I personally don't like television commercials that lawyers sponsor in their own behalf. It has degraded the profession. I practice in a small town where people tend to know who we are; thus, we have a lot of word-of-mouth advertisements. Television commercials are part of the reason people tend to look down on lawyers these days."

Sue Brammer, Maysville, February 20, 2002

19. "THE BEST ADVERTISEMENT"

My law firm doesn't advertise. We believe word-of-mouth is the best advertisement. When I was in law school, advertising as an attorney was still looked down on. We've avoided TV commercials because our impression is that the general public already has a bad impression of attorneys in general. And when they see the commercials that are out right now, I think it lends to that feeling.

Melanie Rolley, Madisonville, April 15, 2002

20. "IT'S A DISGRACE"

I hate lawyer commercials on television the worst in the world. I think it's a disgrace, and I've said that when the Supreme Court allowed it, they played hell. It makes me sick at my stomach listening to those people. It's terrible and ought to be stopped. If they can't make it on their own like we did back then, then they shouldn't be in the legal profession.

Robert Stivers, Manchester, July 19, 2001

21. "Less Laughter"

There was a lot more laughter by judges during the pre-1990s. It's not that way now. Back then, in a court proceeding, judges would just throw their heads back and laugh about something. In a case I was in yesterday, it involved nine judges, and the only one that said anything funny was me. And I did that just trying to keep the argument moving, and to lighten it up a little bit, because everybody was taking themselves so damn seriously.

Boyce Martin Jr., December 7, 2001

22. "Decline in Good Storytelling"

Lawyers don't tell stories like they used to for a number of reasons. We are much more homogenized than we used to be because of television, mass media, and computers. I saw a decline in good storytelling and joke telling with the advent of television.

Richard Roberts, Paducah, November 2, 2001

23. "Best and Worst"

When lawyers get together over a cup of coffee or for a meal, they usually tell about what they did best or what they did worst. They would describe their biggest blunder, or perhaps talk about their most troublesome client.

Keith McCormick, Morehead, June 22, 2000

24. "Judges' Conversations"

They [lawyers] just appear before us [appellate judges] in court, and go on. But judges sitting around with each other at lunch talk about local politics and also national politics, because we are all appointed since we have some qualification that allows the president to appoint us. As much as we say we drop our political points of view, we still tend to talk about them during our conversations. Many of the things we talk about are big issues between Republicans and Democrats.

Boyce Martin Jr., Louisville, December 7, 2001

25. "STORYTELLING DYING OUT"

Back in the 1940s to 1950s, lawyers truly liked just sitting around and telling about big trials they'd had. They liked to tell about big fees they charged. And a whole lot of what they talked about was just made up. When a lawyer told a story, you'd try to match it with one of your own; take away a little, or add a little to it. But lawyers don't do that very much now. A lot of lawyers are in a court that isn't in their hometown, so they are in a hurry to get home when court is over for the day. They don't have time to sit around and talk very much anymore. Nowadays, storytelling has just about died out.

Cass Walden, Edmonton, June 8, 2000

26. "FINDING TIME FOR STORIES"

What happens is the judge sets eight cases for trial in the morning, and all the lawyers show up at 8:30, and from 8:30 until 10:00 we're all hanging out together in the halls or in the rooms, drinking coffee, talking, awaiting to see which case gets tried.

While we're together, we share stories—legal stories in the sense that they're in the context of what we know to talk about. Legal stories are about all we know and can talk about. This lends itself to the passage back and forth of stories and tales, and these naturally get embellished a little bit each time they are told.

Lawrence Webster, Pikeville, November 9, 2000

27. "MORE FEMALE LAWYERS"

When I graduated in 1984, almost one-half of our class was female, and I feel that the trend is continuing. Most of the time, the attorneys with whom I worked typically bent over backwards to be fair with women lawyers. And the judges never seem to consider the fact of whether a lawyer is male or female. But there were a few older male attorneys who would call us women lawyers "Honey." I don't think they meant anything by the use of that word, nor realized it was somewhat demeaning to be in court and be referred to as "Honey." Actually, I was pleasantly pleased that during my times in court that no prejudice was leveled against me for being a female attorney. However, a concern of mine when I began practicing law was that prejudice might indeed be directed at me. However, that did happen with clients. When I first began practicing law, I did a fair amount of divorce work. Being a woman lawyer helped in some ways because I had women clients come in who wanted a divorce, and they felt more comfortable talking to a woman lawyer. On the other hand, I think there were some men who didn't want a woman representing them.

Sue Brammer, Maysville, February 20, 2002

28. "A LOT OF TESTING"

I think female attorneys are generally well accepted. I've had several men come in and state that they have chosen me because they thought it would look better to the court if they had a female attorney. That may be because our commissioner here is a female. In my 1993 graduating class at Chase College of Law, Northern Kentucky University, the number of men and the number of women was about fifty percent each.

Everything has gone well with me as a female attorney. In dealing with other attorneys, men who are my age just accept me outright. But some of the older men lawyers make me prove myself. I think they do a lot of testing to see if I really know what I am doing.

Melanie A. Rolley, Madisonville, April 15, 2002

2

THEFT

Most attorneys consider theft to be one of the most difficult crimes to defend, as the jury typically consists of persons who value honesty. Yet, on occasion a few jury members themselves might suffer lingering feelings of guilt for having stolen items in times past; to deny the reality of their own conduct and to condemn such behavior by others, even these jurors will likely find the defendant guilty of the accused theft.

Stories in the theft category are not about jurors per se. Instead, these accounts tend to be on the humorous side, especially when the accused gives unexpected responses to questions posed by lawyers and judges.

29. "CONVICTED THREE TIMES"

When I was county attorney during the 1940s, one day I read in the *Courier-Journal* where the county court clerk had shortcut the Kentucky Department of Revenue for more than thirty-five thousand dollars for fishing and hunting licenses and various other state taxes. So I thought it my job to throw him out of office. So I got an order from the county judge, and we took his keys and put him out. The commonwealth attorney at that time didn't want to prosecute him as he liked him pretty well. It turned out that this county clerk had spent all of the stolen money gambling on a riverboat, a shantyboat on the banks of the Ohio River here at Maysville.

He had one of the most important lawyers in Maysville as his defense counsel, and I got him indicted on three different charges. I tried him on the first charge, convicted him, and then his attorney appealed it to the court of appeals, which meant it would be hung up for two to three years.

The next term of court, I tried him on the second indictment and convicted him. His attorney likewise appealed that decision, and then the next term of court, I tried him the third time. After I tried him and convicted him the third time, his attorney gave up; thus he went to the penitentiary for three or four years.

John H. Clarke, Maysville, February 20, 2002

30. "THE CLASSIC THIEF"

When I was public defender, when I first started practicing law, I was defending this guy, Charles Nelson. Charles was doing time in prison for some kind of theft. He had a terrible record. He had a rap sheet a mile long, but it was all property crime. There wasn't a violent offense on the list. He wasn't violent. He was just a con artist and a thief. He was about forty-five years old. He got word to me that he wanted to file a motion for shock probation in his latest conviction.

Shock probation was passed by the legislature about 1970. The concept is that usually when a judge sentences someone to the penitentiary, that person loses all jurisdiction. They then become a ward of the State Department of Corrections. The legislature said maybe the judges should retain some jurisdiction so that when a young offender goes in there and sees the penitentiary for the first time, he is shocked into appreciating the seriousness of his crime, so they ought to let him out. Maybe do just 30 to 60 days, or something like that. So they are setting shock probation. If you file a shock probation now, no sooner than 30 days after you sentence him, and no longer than 180 days.

Well, Charles Nelson wanted to file shock probation, but he had been convicted so many times and been to the penitentiary so many times that I knew that the judge wouldn't grant it. I said, "Charlie, you don't have a prayer. The judge is going to look at your record and he is not going to grant you shock probation."

Charlie said, "Well, I want you to do it anyway. It will give me something to do, something to think about while I'm in here."

I said, "Okay." So I got my pen and said, "This is going to be embarrassing, I've got to tell the judge why Charlie Nelson, who has got a long criminal record of theft and this kind of stuff, should be granted shock probation, which is usually for first-time offenders. So I want you to give me some explanation about your crime, about your situation, that might be convincing to the judge."

He sat there for a minute, then said, "Hmmm, how do you explain just downright greed?"

He was one of these convicts that had a crisp denim jacket, shirt, and all that stuff. This was probably the first time he was ever confronted with the real reason for his life of crime.

Bill Cunningham, Eddyville, January 21, 2002

31. "Thief Didn't Have Money to Pay for a Lawyer"

I met a couple of lawyers coming back from court one afternoon. I was going to the courthouse for some reason. These two lawyers were coming back, and they said to me, "John, you should have been in court this morning."

I said, "Why?"

They told me that this guy, I never knew what his name was, was charged with stealing something like twenty-five hundred dollars worth of either merchandise or money.

The judge asked the man charged with theft, "How do you plead?"

He responded, "Not guilty."

The judge said, "Do you have a lawyer?"

He said, "No, the court is going to have to appoint me a lawyer."

The judge said to him, "Look, you've been accused of stealing twenty-five hundred dollars. Why can't you pay to hire you a lawyer?"

The man said to the judge, "Hell, Judge, if I had stole twenty-five hundred dollars, I'd hired John Hardin [the lawyer who is telling the story]. That way, I wouldn't have needed for you to appoint me a lawyer."

I don't know what happened to him in court. I didn't represent him! But I assume he didn't steal the money.

John O. Hardin III, Cadiz, March 21, 2001

32. "Window Shopping inside Store"

A burglary suspect was arrested inside a department store at 3 A.M. He pleaded not guilty and asked for a jury trial. Being really foolish, he decided to take the stand and be examined.

The prosecutor asked him the bottom-line question, "Well, if you weren't committing burglary, just what were you doing inside the Ben Franklin store at 3 A.M.?"

The defendant replied dumbly, "Well, I was just window shopping on the inside."

Stan Billingsley, Carrollton, March 20, 2001

33. "MAN CAUGHT STEALING STOLEN TIRES"

I remember a fellow one time who was out in the country hunting, and he came across a little shed that was full of stolen tires. Well, he decided to take some of the tires. Well, he was inside the building, and about that time he heard some people coming. He thought they were hunters or something, so he hid inside the building in the middle of those tires. The people who came in were the thieves that stole the tires and put them in there. They came back because they were afraid somebody would steal a bunch of their stolen tires, and they had a bunch of lumber and they nailed up all the windows and doors and nailed him in there.

He was afraid to say anything because he didn't know what they would do to him. But he couldn't get out because he was sealed up in there. He stayed in there for three days. Finally, some people came by and he hollered at them, and the sheriff came and got him and, of course, arrested him for having all these stolen tires.

He finally told the sheriff what he was going to do was go in the building and steal the tires. But these were stolen tires all along. So he was planning to steal tires that had been stolen already.

I think he was sentenced to two years in prison for a conspiracy to steal tires.

Morris Lowe, Bowling Green, March 9, 2001

34. "THE CLASSY CROOK"

I remember one kind of amusing story. There was a drugstore up at Smiths Grove. I think the man that ran it was named Decker. He lived next door to the drugstore, and he devised his own homemade burglar alarm. He had a phone in the drugstore, and he had a phone to that same line in his house. When he closed the drugstore at night, he would take the phone off the hook and lay it down, then he would go in beside his bed and take that phone off the hook. That way, if anybody came into the store, he would be able to hear it because it was right beside his bed.

It was Christmas Eve, and these two men came down from Louisville and they were going to burglarize his store. They parked their car about a block away, and so they wouldn't lose their pocketbooks with their identity cards and other things in them, they both took their wallets out and put them under the front seat of that car. Then they went to that drugstore, and went up on the roof and they cut a hole in the roof. Well, the noise that came down through that open hole could be heard by Mr. Decker on his phone, so he knew someone was breaking into his store.

He got his shotgun and went out to the store. The men saw him, and one of the men jumped off the roof and got away, but Decker caught the other one. Then, he called the only policeman in town, and they found this strange car parked a block away. The hood was still warm, and the car was licensed to the man that got away. And both their wallets with all their identification was under the seat! It was easy to convict the man that he caught coming off the roof, but Decker never saw the one that got away. We ended up trying the man that got away, for we had his car with the warm motor parked a block away with all the identifying things under the seat. It was his brother-in-law we had caught.

So when I got ready to argue the case, knowing it had been Christmas Eve, I argued that

> It was Christmas Eve, and all through his house
> Not a creature was stirring, not even a mouse
> When suddenly upon the roof, there was a clatter
> And he got up to see what was the matter

And that story, or song, about Santa Claus, I adapted that. And when I got through, the fellow's defendant got up and said, "Hey, I liked that argument. It was very clever and very good."

I said, "I thought he had some class about him. He was a classy crook."

Morris Lowe, Bowling Green, March 9, 2001

35. "IT'S OKAY TO KILL BUT NOT TO STEAL"

I heard this homicide story from Judge Douglas Graham over in Wolfe County. If he'd just told it one time, I wouldn't have paid any attention to it, but he said it many times. They had a fellow there in court for murdering somebody. And they had somebody there for stealing something. He was very hard on anybody that stole, but he was kind of sympathetic to somebody who maybe got into a racket with somebody and killed them. He wanted them to have a fair and impartial trial, and he would let in a little evidence that maybe he should have kept out.

Here's Judge Graham's expression: There's a lot of people who need killing, but there is nothing that needs to be stolen. He would say that in open court! Of course, there was no jury present in the case.

Edward Jackson, Beattyville, July 20, 2001

36. "Scrap Metal Thieves"

I was once appointed to represent two rough looking men from Louisville who were charged with stealing copper pipes out of a schoolhouse. They were said to have been caught inside at night with tools, ripping the copper pipes out of the wall. They pled not guilty and said they had only gone into the building to get out of the rain.

On the day of the trial, I was stunned to see them both show up in the courtroom in front of the jury with work shirts on that had the embroidered sign of "Louisville Scrap Metal Company" on them. These fellows were, of course, found guilty.

Stan Billingsley, Carrollton, March 20, 2001

37. "The Juvenile Thief"

I was in front of Judge Clay with a young juvenile who had picked up some small trinket at a store. It was nevertheless shoplifting. Even though he was a minor, they do have court for juveniles. This young fellow was appropriately grieved by what he had done. He apologized and said that it would never happen again. Well, the judge put him on probation and sent him out the front door. And it wasn't but about two minutes later that through the back door of the courtroom came the sheriff with my client by the scruff of the neck, and said, "Judge, this young fellow just come from this court?"

The judge said, "Yes, he did."

He said, "Well, I caught him stealing stuff from cars in the parking lot."

The judge asked, "What was he stealing?"

The sheriff said, "Well, lo and behold, who owns this red Datsun?"

The judge says, "Well, that's my car! What was he stealing?"

He'd picked up this red baseball cap that says on it, *United States Marine Corps, World War II*.

The judge says, "That's my hat. Maybe I was a little hasty about that probation thing. Let's reconsider."

Keith McCormick, Morehead, June 22, 2000

38. "SHERIFF WHO HAD THE RIGHT WORDS"

Sheriff Wendell Wilson was quite a brave fellow. They had a bank robbery in Russell Springs. These two desperados went in at gunpoint and robbed the bank. They made their way out of there, and they had a manhunt everywhere for them. They got up into the edge of Russell and Casey County, and had been chased all up in the hills there. Their car broke down and they abandoned it, so they took to the woods on foot. Wendell took after one of them. And Carl Meece, the sheriff of Casey County, who was very short and stocky, was standing in the road there with Wendell. The FBI had a helicopter and were in charge of the case. They were planning their strategy there in the road.

Wendell and Carl started talking, and Wendell told Carl, said, "Well, Carl, I don't know much about this helicopter and all the way they are searching, but it appears to me that them fellers that robbed the bank is in the woods, and the only way to get them out of the woods is to go in and fetch them out."

So Carl went one way, and Wendell went the other. Wendell got the drop on this fellow. But the fellow had a gun on Wendell, too. They had a gun drawn at each other. Wendell, who had no officer training and very little education, but who was still intelligent, instead of firing, said to this fellow, said, "Now, fellow, one of us is going to die right here. I've got my life right, but I still don't want to die. You may not have your life right, so why don't you just put that gun down?" And this fellow did put his gun down.

This fellow told this story in district court in Bowling Green where they was tried for bank robbery.

Robert L. Wilson, Jamestown, April 19, 2002

3

Court Fines

Court costs and fines, both past and present, are described in the first chapter. All who commented on this facet of the judicial system agree that legal fees and court costs have skyrocketed in recent times and will likely continue to do so. The three following humorous accounts about court fines take the reader back many years when fines were minimal and times were not so fast.

39. "Unequal Fines Assigned to Rapists"

When lawyers sat around and talked in earlier times, they talked about different cases. I remember a story they told about my father, John Hardin Jr., who was a circuit judge, and who practiced law for fifty years.

I was told that he represented three men who were accused of rape. The judge, or jury, found them guilty of something—I don't know just what—and fined them one hundred dollars, fifty dollars, and twenty-five dollars. The story claims that he was asked why he fined this one man just twenty-five dollars.

My father responded, "Because he was third."

The second man got a fifty-dollar fine, and the first one was fined one hundred dollars.

I wasn't involved in that case, but that's the story I've heard told about my father.

John O. Hardin III, Cadiz, March 21, 2001

40. "Judge Fines Himself for Being Late"

Here's a story to tell you how rough my daddy really was. He was late for court in Jackson County one day, and he got in there and he rapped the bench and he hit it. He said, "I'm late for court and I'm fining myself fifteen dollars." He said, "Mr. Clerk, you make a record of it." And he paid the fifteen dollars. What he did that day is right in the court books over there.

People came to court [for years after that], and they didn't fool around when they saw what he was doing.

B. Robert Stivers, Manchester, July 19, 2001

41. "Judge Fines Himself for Drunkenness"

Back in the 1930s, a lawyer named Calvert was appointed Special Judge to preside over a term of circuit court in Harlan County. One morning, he ascended the bench, red-faced and trembling, and with a bang of the gavel he fined himself for drunkenness, and then adjourned the court. That incident was featured in newspapers all over the United States.

Eugene Goss, Harlan, May 22, 2002

42. "Whistle Bird Fined for Not Swimming the River"

My daddy was a very strict, retired army man; very strict on us boys and everybody else. When he spoke, he didn't have to speak twice. And when he was circuit judge, he was the same way. One time, he subpoenaed an old friend of mine and some others to come to court. His name was Whistle Bird Davidson. He violated every game law in the country. He never had any license, but he just hunted at any time and all the time; out of season or in season, it didn't make any difference.

Whistle Bird didn't come to court. A day or two later, he didn't come in, and Franklin P. Stivers sent the sheriff after him. The sheriff arrested him and brought him back, put him in jail. Daddy called him out. He said to him, "Whistle Bird, you were subpoenaed to come to court weren't you?"

He said, "Yes, yes, Judge, I was."

"Well, why didn't you come to court?"

"I couldn't get here."

"Well, why couldn't you get here," Daddy asked.

Whistle Bird said, "There's a tide in the river."

Daddy said to him, "Did you have a boat, Whistle Bird?"

He said, "No, I didn't have a boat, so I couldn't get across the river."

Daddy said, "Whistle Bird, can you swim?"

He said, "Yes, I can swim."

My daddy said, "Well, fine him twenty-five dollars for not swimming the river and coming to court."

Whistle Bird got really mad. Years later, I hunted with him and it took him a long time to get over that to where he and I could joke about it. Every time I'd see him, I'd ask him, "Whistle Bird, can you swim?" He never did answer me; just mumbled under his breath. See, when Daddy fined him for not swimming the river, it was wintertime, too!

That was at Oneida, where the Red Bud River and Goose Creek come together and form the South Fork of the Kentucky River.

B. Robert Stivers, Manchester, July 19, 2001

43. "Buckets Full of Pennies in Courtroom"

In Owen County, two young men from eastern Kentucky were charged with hunting deer without a license. They appeared in the clerk's office to pay their fines and court costs. Each owed about $250.00. The clerk came upstairs to the courtroom and was quite mad because they showed up with two five-gallon plastic buckets full of pennies with which to pay their fines. The clerk had no capability to easily count out fifty thousand pennies, and she was steaming.

It occurred to me that pennies are legal tender and that we couldn't refuse to accept legal tender. So I told her to send them up to the courtroom. The courtroom was only accessed by climbing the longest flight of stairs in the world, as there was no elevator in the building at that time.

They came to the courtroom, which was full of people. I asked them where their pennies were, and they had left them downstairs. I then told them to go get their pennies. They struggled up the stairs and set them in front of the tall bench on which I was sitting. I told them I couldn't see them, and to lift them up to the bench. They struggled to do this but complied. I told them that pennies were legal tender and that I would be glad to accept them, but they could go across the street to a bank and have the pennies counted on a machine and save us all a lot of trouble.

They refused to do so, wanting to make a political statement. I told them fine, to sit at a table in the courtroom and count each penny in my presence and then they would have to swear under oath that the amount was exactly correct, not short or long. And if they were wrong, I would hold them in contempt of court, and if they made any noise and disrupted the court which was continuing, I would hold them in contempt and send them to jail.

They sat down and started counting. After about half an hour, they raised their hands in surrender and asked if I would let them take the pennies to the bank. I said, "Yes, of course."

They left, and everyone in the courtroom got a chuckle. But when they got to the top of the stairs, one of the buckets broke from its heavy load and twenty-five thousand pennies tumbled down the thirty feet of stairs. It was an awful racket! The whole courtroom burst into laughter, as they all knew from the awful sound what had happened. An hour or so of penny plucking ensued and they finally paid the clerk with paper money!

Stan Billingsley, Carrollton, March 20, 2001

44. "Real Big Court Fine"

Several years ago there was a man going through western Kentucky, who was a native Alaskan. I think he was of Eskimo descent. Here in western Kentucky he was charged with DUI. The fine and court cost was $487. His blood alcohol content was well above the minimum for DUI.

The judge told him, said, "You can either serve time in jail here in lieu of the fine, or you can pay $487 and go on."

This fellow said, "Judge, as high as that fine and cost is, you might as well *hang* me."

Ken S. Dean, Madisonville, April 15, 2002

4

ANIMAL STORIES

The following animal stories include separate accounts of an owl, a hog, a cow, a cat, a mule, horses, chickens, and dogs. Interestingly enough, men were typically the owners of these animals. The animals in these stories were almost always treated like family members.

The charges include theft, death by shooting, and, in two stories, the use of animals for sex purposes. The bulk of these narratives reflect the importance that owners place on the friendship they have with their animals, a truism for past and present times. Domesticated animals, often treated as family, have been a part of Kentucky life and times across the years.

45. "THE GREAT HORNED OWL STORY"

There was a case I was sitting on in district court in Grant County. This man had a stuffed owl—a horned owl. He had reported to the police that it was stolen, and he found out who stole it from him. So the prosecutor filed a charge for theft against this man and we had the trial. There wasn't any jury. The case was tried before me. Well, the prosecutor put on the worst case I had ever seen. The victim was called to the stand. He said, "I've learned that the person that took the owl from my house is a good friend of mine, and I think I must have given him permission to come in and take it."

Well, obviously at this point the case was going nowhere. And the prosecutor was pretty good; a hard-nosed fellow. I couldn't see where this case was going, and I thought he must have gone loony by putting on a case like this. He knew I was going to have to find the fellow not guilty, because even the victim said that he gave this fellow permission to have that owl.

Well, there was a fellow in a nice suit sitting in the back of the courtroom. I had never seen him before over there. He was the only one watching this trial, except the clerk and the attorneys. I couldn't figure out when they was going to call him as a witness. I assumed that he was a witness, but they never called him. The prosecutor didn't call him; defense didn't call him. They rested and submitted the case, so I obviously had to find the man not guilty. There was no question about it. It was an open and shut case of innocence. They proved nothing. The prosecutor didn't seem upset. He didn't seem embarrassed. So, I was kind of scratching my head, thinking that's kinda strange.

When the defendant got up to leave the courtroom, the fellow in the back of the room stood up and showed his credentials. He was a federal wildlife officer who then arrested him for possession of an endangered species—a stuffed, horned owl. It was illegal! The prosecutor was just using this to get it out who was the owner of the thing. It was kinda funny, but I thought it was clever on his part.

He just loaned the great horned owl to his friend and had forgotten all about it.

Stan Billingsley, Carrollton, March 20, 2001

46. "Judge's Blind Dog in the Courtroom"

One funny story I like to tell is this one. There was a lawyer here named Reed Caudill. His son is Mike Caudill, the county attorney here now. Reed lived on Wakefield, which is about a mile from the courthouse. He had a blind dog named Gabe. After Reed would come down to his law office, Gabe would follow him downtown. I guess he smelled his leg. Sometimes, he would follow Reed to the courthouse.

One day I was prosecuting a case as commonwealth attorney. Reed was defending this fellow. The presiding judge was John B. Rhodes, who was a tall, erect man, ninety-three years old. He looked like Robert E. Lee; had a goatee, a beard, and moustache. He was very distinguished looking, very proper. He was a good judge with a great sense of humor. He always told me that the greatest attribute a judge could have would be a good sense of humor.

We were trying this case in front of a jury, and Reed's blind dog,

Gabe, followed him downtown; followed him upstairs into the courtroom. He came in through the swinging doors.

He began trying the case. The jury was sitting there, and a man was testifying. The dog walked into the courtroom, walked in front of the jury wagging its tail, and walked over to where Reed was and just laid down under his feet, under the defense attorney's table.

Reed started patting his dog. It was just killing me, but I could not ask that the dog be thrown out of the courtroom, as I thought that the jury would just become enraged. So I asked the judge if I could approach the bench.

The judge said, "Yes."

Well, I went up to the bench and whispered, "Judge, there is a dog in the courtroom."

He said, "I know it, but he ain't bothering nobody."

I said, "He's bothering *me*."

He asks, "What do you want me to do?"

I said, "I guess nothing." So I went back and sat down. I don't know what a judge would do today if a dog walked into the courtroom.

Morris Lowe, Bowling Green, March 9, 2001

47. "Man Has Sex with Ugly Hog"

There used to be a crime called "buggery." It had to do with having sex with animals. A fellow was in court for having sex with a hog, and he was being prosecuted for it. Of course, his mind wasn't real good.

This real old, little lady was an eyewitness to what he was charged with. She took the stand in front of the jury and she told about him having sex with the hog. When she got through testifying, she got off the witness stand and started to leave the courtroom, and she looked as if she wanted to say something else. She paused. Not knowing what the answer would be, I said, "Ma'am, is there something else that you witnessed that the jury should hear?"

She said, "I just wanted to tell them that it was the *ugliest* hog in the lot."

The jury just died laughing.

Morris Lowe, Bowling Green, March 9, 2001

48. "Man Arrested While Having Sex with a Dog"

I was out to dinner here in Carrollton with a former county attorney two weeks ago. During our conversation, the name of a character came up, and it happened to be the same name as the character in this story. It's a little rough, but it's a true story. It happened sometime in the 1970s before I came to Carrollton.

There was a fellow, and I won't use his name, that lived here and he wasn't real swift. The sheriff got a call telling him that there was a man downtown on the courthouse lawn having sex with a dog. The sheriff goes down there, and sure enough this fellow is with the dog. The sheriff arrested him, but the fellow says, "Damn it, Sheriff, do I have to stop before I'm finished?"

That really happened. I can name the man.

Stan Billingsley, Carrollton, March 20, 2001

49. "ARSON CASE SETTLED BY CHALK CATS"

Sid Trivett and I were defending a family charged with arson. This is a difficult case to convict anybody of in the mountains. The theory seems to be that if you're willing to burn your own house down, they ought to have to pay you. In this particular case, this family called in all the neighbors and told them, "If you want anything out of that damn place, you'd better get it. She's a-going up this afternoon at five fifteen."

So a bunch of the neighbors came up. One of the members of the family went down to the local gas station and bought a five-gallon can of gas, and told them that that house was a-going up. He come back, and the neighbors gathered around and watched this family set the house on fire. The kid with the gas can spilled some gas on his arm and accidentally caught his arm on fire and ran into the mountains screaming in pain with his arm being on fire, but he got it put out.

The house burned. They indicted them for arson, and the arson investigator claimed that one of his elements of proof was that he had found a picture in this house of what I would call a chalk cat—one of these chalky little trinkets like you get along the side of the road. It's about a foot and a half tall. It was a chessy cat, spotted and with a big smile on its face. The arson investigator said that he knew they had such a cat, and that he had found that cat after the fire where they were then living, which proved they had taken their stuff out of the house.

Well, this was after all these neighbors came in and testified that they watched them burn this house down. But the arson investigator penned his case, in large part, on this chalk cat.

The trial started on the Friday before Labor Day, and recessed until the following Tuesday. Sid Trivett, the attorney for some of the defendants, went out over the weekend somewhere and bought about thirty of those chalk cats identical to the one like the picture was. When the jury got back in the courtroom the following Tuesday after Labor Day, he had the walls of that courtroom lined with chalk cats smiling at the jury.

The jury found those people not guilty, notwithstanding the fact that the fellow who had run to the hills with his arm on fire appeared in court with this huge burned scar on his arm right where they had described it.

Bristol Haile, a local character around here, used to talk about juries finding people not guilty when the defendant got up and swore that he did it, but the jury didn't believe him. So that's about what happened here.

Lawrence Webster, Pikeville, November , 2000

50. "HORSES BROUGHT INTO THE COURTROOM"

Pelham McMurray, who died a couple of years ago, had a very successful law practice here for a number of years. Early on in his career he was county attorney. At that point in time, paternity suits were a big part of what the county attorney did because a paternity suit had to be adjudicated not only for child support, but also in regard of eligibility for various kinds of state support. And that was before the very sophisticated blood tests, which now have basically ended paternity suits, or litigation, because you know who he father is. Back then, you didn't. And a lot of it back then was bringing in a six-person jury and letting them look at the parents, and look at the child, hearing the testimony and this kind of thing. Well, that was Pelham's background.

He said during that time a fellow came to see him with a lawsuit. These two farmers had been negotiating a stud fee for a stallion, and while they were arguing about it, the stallion jumped the fence and took care of the business anyway. So after that they were having a lawsuit as to whether the one farmer owed a stud fee to the other farmer.

Pelham said they treated it just like a paternity suit. They brought the horses in and brought the foal in for the jury to look at. I don't know how it came out, but Pelham said, "We tried it just like a paternity suit."

Richard Roberts, Paducah, November 2, 2001

51. "Blind Mule Story"

This is a story told to me by Attorney Lige Coffey. He was one of my best, closest friends. He had a fellow working for him by the name of Calvin Cape. Calvin did farm work for Lige and was quite a character. Well, Lige was different from most everybody I've ever met. He wouldn't put on any pretense; he was just as plain as he could be, but an intelligent attorney. But he never had any ambition to be really successful financially. But he was very successful from the amount of friends he had. He'd give away more than he ever charged.

He told me a story once and I used it several times in closing arguments in court. The story goes that Lige was at his home one morning and Calvin come over and said, "Lige, I want you to carry me down to the river. I hear that Pim Spencer has got a mule down there for sale."

Lige said, "Why yeah, I'll carry you down there." Naturally he was referring to the word "take," to take him down there. So they went down to see Pim, and Pim was an old man who lived on the Cumberland River. Lige said he was setting up on his porch in a rocking chair, smoking a pipe. Said they stopped and hollered at him, said, "Pim, have you got a mule for sale?"

He said, "I shore do, and a good'un, too. He's out at the barn in the first stall you come to. Go on out there and check him out."

Said they went out to the barn and saw this big sorrel mule out there. Looked good. So they opened the stall gate and rustled the mule out of the stall. The mule came out and was trotting around in the barnyard and ran square into a tree. Didn't slow down, just ran square into that tree. So they went back up to the house, and said, "Pim, we can't use that mule."

He said, "Well, why not? That's a good mule."

Lige said, "Well, Pim, your mule is blind. Can't see nothing. We turned him out and he run right square into a tree and didn't even slow down; didn't even see it. He's blind."

Pim said, "Lige, that mule's not blind, he just don't give a darn."

We were trying a case in Louisville, and I told that story. It just fit the facts extra good. After it was over, one of the jurors came around and said, "We kept telling that story over and over in the jury room." Said, "That fellow on the other side of Wilson's case was just like Pim's mule. He didn't care!"

Robert L. Wilson, Jamestown, April 19, 2002

52. "Was the Farmer in Danger Also?"

This old farmer was leading his cow down the road, and a big semi-trailer truck came flying down the road and forced this old farmer and his cow over into the ditch. The farmer then sued the trucking company. So, he was testifying in court, and the defense lawyer for the semi-trailer truck company got up and said, "Isn't it true that right after this accident, you told the truck driver that you were not hurt?"

The farmer says, "Yes, it was like this. I was leading old bossy down the road and here comes this semi down the road doing ninety miles an hour and kind of clipped old bossy and knocked her over in a ditch and drug me over there. The truck driver got out and . . ."

The defense lawyer says, "Objection judge; just answer my question."

The judge tells the farmer, "Answer the question." Then he tells the defense lawyer to ask his question again.

The lawyer says, "Isn't it true that right after this accident you told the defendant truck driver that you were not hurt?"

The old farmer says, "Well, it's like this. I was leading old bossy down the road; here comes this truck down the road; it took old bossy and knocked her over into the ditch."

The defense lawyer said, "Object, Judge, he's not answering my question."

The judge says, "Well, just let him go on and answer."

Then the old farmer says, "Well, it was like this Judge. I was leading old bossy down the road and here came this semi down the road doing ninety miles an hour and it hit old bossy and knocked her over into the ditch, and pulled her over there with me. This fellow jumped out of the truck and came back up the road and he looked over at bossy and says, 'Is she hurt?' And I said, 'Oh, you just don't know what you've done to my cow. Just look at her there.' Well, the driver ran back up to his truck and got his gun, brought it back with him, and went to old bossy and shot and killed her. Then he looked at me and said, 'Are you hurt?'"

And that was the end of the case. The judge just let him [the trucker] go.

Charles English, Bowling Green, May 27, 2002

53. "Monetary Value of Coondog"

A suit was filed in Harlan Circuit Court over the ownership of an old coondog. The case gained wide notoriety, and the trial attracted a courtroom full of people. Experts were called on both sides, and both sides offered convincing arguments that the dog was a certain man's property, not the property of his adversary.

With the wisdom of Solomon, Circuit Judge Edward G. Hill declared, "I can't tell who this dog belongs to under the evidence, so I am going to order the dog sold and the proceeds of the sale divided between the two litigants."

In spite of the fact that each party had spent hundreds of dollars on legal fees and expenses, at auction the dog fetched the great sum of ten dollars and fifty cents.

Eugene Goss, Harlan, May 22, 2002

54. "THE PET ROOSTER"

I remember one time back in the 1950s when I was County Judge, we had a fellow here who was kind of a drunk and a ne'er do well. His name was Joe Red Higdon. He had a pet rooster, and when he went anywhere he'd put that rooster on his shoulder, and the rooster would ride there on his shoulder. One night, they called me from jail and said, "Kenneth, we've got Joe Red Higdon and four or five others here in jail, and all of them are drunk. And Joe Red has got that rooster with him, and the rooster is drunk, too. What do you want to do with the rooster?"

Well, they'd been feeding that rooster whiskey, too, you know. When they said, "What do you want to do with that rooster?" I said, "Just lock him up, too!!"

And they did lock it up. That's a true story.

Kenneth Goff, Leitchfield, May 8, 2002

55. "MAN HAS SEX WITH A DOG"

Certain deviants in our society have had sex with animals from the beginning of time. It's covered in the Scriptures. But as county attorney and commonwealth attorney, I never had but one case of that. It involved this young man, twenty-four or twenty-five years of age, and he did it regularly, and had several witnesses. As I understood from the case, when a female dog is in heat it will submit to a man and have sex with him. But otherwise, I guess they would growl and bite him.

This case I had was way back there, I guess about 1960. The courtroom was full of people. He was really open about what he had done. They had a house built on this hill with a dirt floor underneath it. The dog slept under the floor. This fellow would just go under there and have sex, and there were several witnesses to the fact that he had.

When the case came to court, the sheriff at that time was a very thoughtful, intelligent man, and he wanted to talk with me and the judge. He said that he thought it would do more harm to the county to try the case than to not try it. He said that it would put ideas in the minds of some of these young boys and so forth. So the judge said, "Well, we'll dismiss the case."

I said to the judge, "I prefer not to dismiss it. I prefer to reassign it about two months from now, then we can dismiss it quietly." So that's what we did, and the best I can tell from the information that I received, other than having sex over the top of the dog, sex was very much like two humans having it.

I think they worked out something that said he was supposed to leave and go to Ohio. That used to be a very prevalent thing when I first started practicing back in the 1950s. A fellow could get out of a case by going to Ohio or some other state, not when it was murder or robbery, but in the other cases when it was a felony, the person could get out of the prison term by agreeing to leave the state and never coming back. That is something like the Russians had by putting them in Siberia, or like the English had by sending them into exile. I've read stories where in England they used to exile a lot of people, and these fellows would get so homesick they'd slip back into England, but the law would catch them and hang them. . . .

When our recent president was having trouble about his sexual life, I said, "What he should have done is come down here in the country and got me as a country lawyer, and I would have got him out of all that trouble."

Edward Jackson, Beattyville, July 20, 2001

5

UGLY WORDS IN COURT

Ugly words are taboo in the courtroom, and are thus rarely used there by attorneys and judges. However, some bad words and off-color stories are said to be in vogue in the chamber, which is where judge and lawyers gather in the courthouse. Edward Jackson of Beattyville states that if someone uses an ugly word in an average testimony in court, the judge will tell them that if they know better words to use, then use them. But if they don't, then go ahead and use the word(s) they just uttered. If a fellow says, "I saw him f——ing that girl," the judge might say, "Well, if you are talking about sexual intercourse, then say it that way."

In the following stories, both women and men, including a judge and lawyer, use dirty words. In two instances, the dirty words were written and not verbalized.

56. "DIRTY, GRAPHIC WORDING ON MONETARY CHECK"

I was sitting on the bench one day in Williamstown, over in Grant County. The clerk came in with tears in her eyes. She was really mad. I asked her, "What's the matter?"

She said, "Do we have to take this check?"

Some lady from Flint, Michigan, had come through Grant County. They've got a state police barracks there, and they must have twenty troopers coming and going through Dry Ridge, where the post is located. They get a lot of speeders on I-75. That's the worst place to drive on I-75 if you are going to speed, I guess. So this woman got caught.

She pled guilty, and I think she sent her check in by mail, but on the check where it says "for" on the bottom, she wrote "fuck you."

This clerk was a very sweet old lady, and she was the one that was going to have to take the check across the street to the bank and deposit it. But she didn't want to be associated with that gross profanity. So she asked me if she had to take that check.

I said, "No, we'll figure something out."

So I wrote the lady in Michigan and told her that we found her words unacceptable, and that I wasn't going to order my clerk to go publish this check to any other person. I said, "If you want to make that statement, I guess free speech is your business, but I'm not going to force someone else to publish it by showing it to the third party." So I went on to say, "We consider that you have not paid your ticket, and I'll give you two weeks to pay the ticket off."

Finally, she sent in another check. Then about a month later, I got a newspaper clipping. A columnist in Flint, Michigan, wrote this article about me and my speed-trap county. It was a ravaging story, just ripping us real good calling this a free speech issue.

I always thought that was funny, and whenever I've gone on a vacation in Michigan, I've tried to stay away from Flint for I might get arrested there!

They didn't use the dirty word in the news article. They just used "profanity" when they referred to it. But the article was pretty graphic.

But since the writing on the check was such a hostile thing, I didn't see the need to make the clerk publish it to a third party.

Stan Billingsley, Carrollton, March 20, 2001

57. "THE SLANT-LEGGED WHORE"

We were trying a case in which the essence of it was that this woman was accusing her boyfriend or husband of abusing her. And she was quite a talker. She was on the witness stand, and her lawyer was just leading her right into it. He said, "Well, did your husband mistreat you?"

"Oh, yes, sir. He mistreated me all the time."

"Well, did he criticize you?"

"Yes, he criticized me all the time."

"Did he ever hit you?"

"Yes, he hit me. He was always hitting me and kicking me and strangling me and throwing me to the ground. He just abused me all the time."

"Did he call you names?"

"Oh, yes, Judge. He called me everything. You wouldn't believe the names that he called me."

She then proceeded to name them all off, and she didn't miss a single one of them. These were vulgar names. "He called me this and that and that." Each word was a little more vulgar than the other. Then she kind of paused and turned and focused right in on me. This was a non-jury case. She looked at me and said, "And Judge, the worst thing of all, he came home half-drunk one night and he called me a 'slant-legged whore.'"

Then she looked at me again and said, "And I don't want no man calling me a name that I don't know what it means."

That was probably ten years ago, and I've asked a hundred people what that term means, but no one has offered to define what it means. And she didn't know what it meant, but she was terribly offended by him calling her a slant-legged whore.

William R. Harris, Franklin, August 22, 2001

58. "LAWYER USED DIRTY WORD IN COURT"

I had a client named Snag Tackett, and this is a true story, but nobody will believe it is true. Snag stayed in all kinds of trouble, and the judge kept giving him probation. Finally, he just got into more trouble than the judge could tolerate.

They were going to revoke his probation. So we got over there in the chamber and we begged and we pleaded. Finally, the judge decided to give him one more chance, and he started laying out the terms and conditions of the probation. He said to Snag, "First of all, you've got to get a job." Snag's eyes got kind of big.

The judge continued, "And you've always got to keep your child support current and never get behind."

Snag's mouth dropped down a little bit.

The judge went on, "You can't drink; you can't do drugs; you're going to be tested frequently."

Snag started shaking his head "no," like, "My God, what am I hearing?"

I said, "Judge, are you going to let him fuck?"

Snag yelled, "*Take me away*!!!"

Now, that's a true story!

Lawrence Webster, Pikeville, November 9, 2000

59. "FEMALE RAPE VICTIM WAS BLATANTLY HONEST"

This story is a little crude, and is not one that I know personally. It involved a Jefferson County assistant attorney. He was in the Jefferson District Court putting on evidence for a probable cause hearing in a rape case, which is a felony. When a person is charged with a felony, it is first charged in a district court and arraigned there, and before it goes on to the circuit court that actually has jurisdiction to try felony cases, the defendant is entitled to a probable cause hearing. The court is required to determine that there is probable cause to believe that the crime charged occurred, and sufficient evidence for an indictment to be had for it to go to the circuit court for trial. This case involved a charge of rape. An African American woman charged this man, I guess an African American assailant, with raping her. This assistant county attorney had this young woman on the stand. And to establish probable cause in a rape case, the most important thing to establish is that there was penetration. There was forcible intercourse. So he began to ask those questions to establish this. So he asked the woman, "Is it true that the defendant forced you to have intercourse?"

"Huh?" was the response.

"Isn't it true that the defendant forced and caused you to have sexual intercourse with him by force"?

"Huh?"

Well, in this room full of lawyers, the assistant county attorney's face is beginning to turn red in front of the judge. He's asked the question twice, and he's got a witness who's going to require that he explain further what he's talking about. So he asked her the third time, "Did this defendant, by force, cause his penis to penetrate your vagina?"

After a long pause, the witness looks at him and says, "If you mean did he fuck me, he did."

That really did happen. I wasn't there, but a good friend of mine who was public defender at the time was present when that occurred.

Peter Ervin, Louisville, April 26, 2001

60. "THE MISWORDED BRIEF"

Jerry Rhoads and Tom Rhoads do a lot of workers' compensation work. I remember somebody telling me about a humorous typographical error they had. Somebody had a medical condition that was causing them some pain and they had to take pain shots three times a day or whatever. When they wrote the brief, it unfortunately came out that this person had to have "three shits a day" rather than "three shots a day."

Nobody caught the typo error until it went on to the workers' comp office. I think the workers' comp board had a little fun with it. In their opinion, they recognized that it might have been somewhat inconvenient to have to have "three shits a day," but they didn't think that this constituted a compensable injury.

Tom or Jerry Rhoads could tell you about that one. It may be an apocryphal story. You never know. At least it was attributed to them.

Joe Evans III, Madisonville, July 28, 2000

61. "JUDGE TELLS LAWYER TO SHUT UP"

I'll have to admit that I used some ugly words in court. I had a case not too long ago involving a securities fraud case, and the lawyers were from California. I was presiding as judge when this took place. There were two relatively senior judges who were also in service that day. Between the three of us, we probably had more than forty years of service as judges.

One of the lawyers just kept saying, "You just don't understand Delaware law."

And I kept saying, "Well, yes, we do understand Delaware law. I wish you would just proceed to explain what your dispute is about."

Well, that went back and forth, and I was real tired. That's the one thing about being chief judge. You've got to worry about everything but parking places and toilet paper. That was the very day that somebody complained about the rough toilet paper there in the courthouse.

After I had given the man another blessing out, as they would say, I then said, "This is ridiculous; tell us what you are talking about. We're not here as children. We don't want to be lectured to."

Well, nearing the end of his argument, he just got blubbery, saying, "Oh, it is such a great honor to be here, and I just have never been in court before more learned judges than we have here." He just went on and on, until I was finally just fed up, so I said, "All right, let's cut out the bullshit and get back to the case."

Of course, that ended up on the Internet!

Boyce Martin Jr., Louisville, December 7, 2001

62. "Putting a Stop to That S——t"

I had a client named Bim Smallwood, who had been convicted in trafficking in hard drugs, but he was married to a woman of such a bad character that he, a convicted cocaine dealer, was about to be awarded custody of a newborn child by the judge. That's how bad this woman was. She was so sorry that the judge was going to give him custody of a newborn, one-month-old child.

There we were in court. I was representing him. We were about to get that baby. All of a sudden, she stood up in front of Honorable Will T. Scott, who was circuit judge at the time, and these are her exact words. She said, "Judge, Your Honor, I'll put a stop this s——t right now."

Somebody, I think it was the judge, said, "What do you mean?"

She said, "That baby ain't his'n."

The judge said, "Whose is it?"

She turned around and pointed to the back of the courtroom, and says, "It's his'n."

My client jumped up and said, "By God, I knowed it!"

I said, "Bim, do you want custody of a child that's not yours?"

He said, "Hell, no."

And that was the end of that court case, that she would put a stop to that "s——t."

Lawrence Webster, Pikeville, November 9, 2000

63. "Defendant Uses Ugly Words"

I won't say these ugly words, but we had a case one time and I was in the courtroom, the district courtroom. A man had shot and killed his estranged wife on July 4, at the strip pit over on the north end of Muhlenberg County. He was charged with murder and was in jail waiting for the trial. Meanwhile, the sister of the dead woman came into district court on a petition asking the district judge to award her custody of the children of these parties. They had two or three minor children.

The sheriff had to bring over this defendant because he was a party to the proceedings and had certain rights. So, he came in and, of course, objected to his estranged wife, who was now dead, having her sister to take care of the kids. He wanted somebody in his family.

The courtroom was packed with people—little old ladies coming in having their husbands' wills probated, and others like that. They were on the front row and there were police officers everywhere, and the courtroom was rather small.

The district judge—Judge Ehlschide—made his ruling awarding custody to the woman. As the defendant was leaving the courtroom, he turned to the judge and called him several ugly names in a row. I'll not repeat the words, but I'll never forget what happened. Everybody had some buzz conversation going on, but virtually everybody heard what he said to the judge.

The judge looked at him and asked, "What did you say?"

Well, when he said that, the courtroom just got deadly silent, and the guy turned around and repeated it. So, the judge ordered him out, and told them to take him to the jail. Then the judge said, "You know, I heard him the first time. I don't know why I asked him to say that again."

David Jernigan, Greenville, May 17, 2002

64. "Lawyer Cussed the Judge"

Here's a story about Alvie Holland from Hazard. Back during the '70s, he got really upset with Judge Bernard T. Moynahan, who was the federal judge here in Pikeville. They got into a big argument in court. Of course, as you might suspect, the judge always wins those arguments. So Alvie went back to Hazard, and the next time he saw his client, he said, "Buddy, you would have been real proud of me the other day." Said, "I got mad at that federal judge down in Pikeville, and I cussed him and called him every name in the book, and gave him a piece of my mind."

The client said, "Alvie, where did you do that?"

Alvie said, "Oh, about ten miles out of Hazard."

He'd done it on the way home!

Lawrence Webster, Pikeville, November 9, 2000

6

ADULTERY

Kentucky residents have a double standard on sexual conduct and other forms of behavior. Many persons think it is perfectly all right for two adults to have sex with one another without the benefit of clergy. Most states, including Kentucky, have eliminated adultery and fornication as crimes. For example, if a married man and a married woman not married to each other are caught having sexual intercourse in a parking lot, they may be charged with disorderly conduct, but they cannot be charged with any form of adultery. Thus, adultery never comes to court anymore.

The stories in this category imply, or testify to, the act of adultery. However, the person(s) involved, if brought to court, were there on another charge. Thus, some of the following stories are rather humorous when sexual activity is brought into focus.

65. "He's My Man"

I had a lady appear before me in court in Clinton County awhile back. She wasn't used to coming to court. I don't guess she'd ever been to court. She was around thirty years old, very muscularly built; had great big broad shoulders—a big woman. She was charged with criminal mischief, specifically for breaking down a door in an apartment house.

The courtroom was full. She came up before me before I called her name. I said, "You are charged with criminal mischief for breaking the door down at this apartment house. How do you plead?"

She said, "I'm going to plead guilty, Judge. I done it. I broke that door down, but I've already paid for the damages, so I'll just plead guilty."

I said, "Well, before I pass sentence on you, I want to know why you broke it down."

She said, "Judge, that old bitch had my man in there, and I went in after him."

And I said, "Well, did you get him?"

She said, "I shore did, and I'm going to keep him, because *he's my man!*"

I said, "Well, lady, I'm going to dismiss your case. Go on home and take care of that man."

She didn't hit the other woman. As far as I know, she just went in and got her man. She got him by the hair of the head and dragged him out of there. I guess she took care of him well after that, as I never saw them in court anymore.

Robert L. Wilson, Jamestown, April 19, 2002

66. "Mother's Son Was a Woods Colt"

I had another moonshine case under Judge Ford just after we'd had the one about the blind deputy. The revenue agents were chasing this moonshiner, a fellow who wasn't too bright. But they caught him and brought him in. His mother got up and testified. She was testifying that this wasn't his moonshine still; he was just up there. She said, "He's just a woods colt [the progeny of unwed parents]." Judge Ford raised up in his seat, said, "What did you say, woman?"

"I said he's a woods colt."

Judge Ford said, "Well, tell me what a woods colt is."

By that time the whole courtroom in Breathitt County knew what a woods colt was. They were breaking up!

Then she told him, said, "He's the one that was born out in the bushes out there, and no daddy."

Judge Ford really didn't know what she meant by "woods colt."

I got the laugh on Judge Ford for that.

B. Robert Stivers, Manchester, July 19, 2001

67. "The Iron Rod Story"

I had a food stamp case one time. We call it the Iron Rod Case. This poor fellow came to me who was depressed and considering suicide. He was a pretty simple fellow. He was from another county, but he

wanted to talk to somebody about his sad condition in life. I think he
had been in jail and had tried to kill himself. They asked me to talk with
him.

I asked him, "Son, what's your problem?"

He said, "My life is all messed up. I've slept with this other woman,
and I'm married and just having these problems." He pulled some letters out of his pocket, said, "Here, look at this."

So I took this handwritten letter. It wasn't very good handwriting.
It was a letter from his lover over in another county. In this letter, she
referred to him by the name of Iron Rod. She said something to the
effect like, "If you will come back over and bring some more food stamps
with you, I would really appreciate it and would love to see your iron
rod again."

Well, I assured him that with a complimentary letter like that, he
had nothing to worry about, and he went on with his life. I never found
out whether or not he ever went back to see her, but he did live though.

She was trading out for his food stamps. I didn't know you could
trade food stamps for sex—an iron rod!

Stan Billingsley, Carrollton, March 20, 2001

68. "Eyewitness Identification Not Always Accurate"

When you are serving as prosecutor, you always wonder if you have
sent an innocent person to prison. I never had that feeling during the
thirty-two years I served, except one time. One time there was a lady in
a store and she had a little baby in the store with her. And the man
remembered that some woman with a baby about a year ago had come
in and passed a forged check for about two hundred dollars. He called
the police and said that that lady was in the store now again, and they
came down and arrested her. It turned out that the year before that, a
woman had passed a check like that to nineteen different stores. And
she was carrying a little baby each time. In court, this woman said, "I
didn't do it." But she didn't know where she was at on that day. Every
one of these nineteen store owners identified her, positively, absolutely,
as passing forged checks, so she was put in jail. She was sentenced to
nineteen years—one year each, and the judge ran them consecutively.

I said to the detective that worked on the case, "Did you notice
that her husband was present during the trial, but he never, ever, spoke
to her, or came up?" He never tried to make her bond. The normal

thing a husband will try to do is get his wife out on bond. He never talked to her lawyer. He never tried to get her out on bond, or help her in any way. That's very unusual.

Well, that bothered me. She was sentenced and sent to prison. I began to ask something about her husband, and some people that knew him said, "Well, he was going with another woman at that time that had a small baby."

So, me and the detective began to investigate that case. We ended up in Nashville hunting this woman that he knew with a baby. We ended up at a nightclub there named Printer's Alley, and we finally found this other woman.

By that time, we had gotten her driver's license, and she looked just like this man's wife that we had sent to prison. And she had a record of passing bad checks. After we found her, we sat down at the table with her. She didn't want to talk to us.

I told her, I said, "I want to tell you what, we may have sent a woman to prison for some crimes that you committed. But I'll tell you what. We don't want to send you to prison, but I don't want an innocent woman to be in prison. If you will admit that you did this, and come back and plead guilty, we will probate you."

So she said that she did do it, and she wrote her handwriting out for us, and it was her handwriting [on the checks]. So we didn't arrest her. We said, "If you'll come to court and appear before the judge and tell him you did it, we'll get you probated." And she did.

Then we sent an order to the prison to release that woman. And she never even said, "Thank you." Didn't even speak to us when she came back to the judge.

Both women did look alike. I have always figured that eyewitness identification is the worst kind of identification, because it is possible for a person to be mistaken about somebody. Out of the thousands that I've helped send to prison, that was the only person that I ever had a bad feeling about.

Morris Lowe, Bowling Green, March 9, 2001

69. "Husband Catches Milkman in Bed with His Wife"

When I was in law school at the University of Kentucky back 1970 during my senior year, we were called one day into the large courtroom—the mock trial room. Harry B. Miller was to speak to us. At that time, Miller, a real short man, was the premier defense lawyer in central Kentucky. He was with this big law firm in Lexington and was an excellent lawyer. He had a way with words and could command a room.

After he talked, he threw the group open to questions. One of the law students in my class raised his hand and said, "Mr. Miller, what do you do when you know your client is guilty?"

Well, Harry Miller stood up at the podium. I'll bet he wasn't five feet tall, but he stood up as tall as he could and said, "Son, it's like the milkman. It reminds me of the milkman who was visiting this lady. He went upstairs and she invited him into the bedroom. He undressed and got in bed with her and they were having sex.

"Her husband got to feeling ill on his way to work, so he turned his car around and come home unexpectedly. He walked into the bedroom and saw them and was totally stunned. Just totally stunned. Couldn't say anything, or do anything.

"The milkman got up out of bed and put his socks on, his pants on, and his shirt on. He had one of those little plastic neckties and he put that on. He put his hat on and picked up his carton of milk bottles— a little metal carton of glass bottles, then looked the husband in the eye and said, 'It's a goddamned lie.'"

Miller ended his response to the student by saying, "Sometimes you have to be direct."

Stan Billingsley, Carrollton, March 20, 2001

70. "Everybody Has Got to Be Somewhere"

When I was a law student down in South Carolina, a judge told this story and I always thought it was funny. He said that back when he practiced divorce law he had a client come in and tell him this story. Said that he came home a little early one night and he was surprised when he looked at his wife. She was getting up and getting dressed. The bed was all disheveled and he couldn't quite figure out what was going on. He said he opened the door to his bedroom closet to hang up his coat, and there was his best friend standing there stark naked. And he said, "Sam, what are *you* doing here?"

The guy looked at him with a straight face, and said, "Well, everybody has got to be somewhere!"

Randy Teague, Madisonville, July 28, 2000

71. "ADULTERY LEADS TO HOMICIDE"

One time I had a case in which my client was charged with murder. He'd been out with a woman that he shouldn't have been out with, and he took her back to her house. There was a man in her bed—another boyfriend in her bed waiting on her. So my client went and got his gun and came back and shot the fellow. My client was a big fellow, weighed probably 240 pounds. The guy that he shot was a little fellow, like 150 pounds, who smoked marijuana. He couldn't hurt a fly. So my client was charged with murder.

After the shooting, he got in his car and took off running. He went across the river into Indiana. He was arrested over there shortly thereafter. His wife called me. She was a sweet woman, for whom I had done some legal work before this. As it came out, she had the money to pay for the lawyer, while her husband didn't have any. So she hired me to defend him.

There was an audio tape he made for the police when they caught him. They asked him, "Where were you going?"

He said, "I was going to my ex-wife's house in Indiana."

Well, his current wife would not appreciate that had she known it. She was the one paying for his defense. He was quite concerned, and I'll admit that I was a little concerned that she might withdraw her funding for this enterprise. But what he said to the police was on this tape, and we knew it was going to be played at the trial. So I took that tape and I timed it, timed it, timed it, and wrote down the exact point when this offensive statement came up on the tape. Just exactly at that point, my client and I were seated at the defense table and we came up with a serious case of coughing until what he said about the other woman was over. His wife never heard it! He got away with that, but he was still convicted.

So if you see an attorney coughing, you'll know he's probably up to something!

Stan Billingsley, Carrollton, March 20, 2001

72. "ASSAULT"

A man showed up in court one day with his face all black and blue and bandaged, and with a broken nose. He was charging another man with assault.

The aggressor was much smaller than the victim, and the defense attorney asked him why the little man did so much damage to him. The fellow responded that it was because he had something in his hands at the time. The defense attorney then asked him what he had in his hands at the time he was assaulted. Being under oath, the accused had to admit that it was the defendant's wife that he had in his hands.

Stan Billingsley, Carrollton, March 20, 2001

73. "Lawyer's Son Runs Off with a Married Woman"

Mr. Simpson [pseudonym] was my law partner here in Edmonton. He had a boy, Tommy [pseudonym], that lived on one of his farms here in Metcalfe County. Well, one day one of his other tenants from one of the farms come to the office and told him that a fellow had run off with his wife, and he wanted to know what he could do with him.

Simpson said, "Well, get a warrant for him and send him to the penitentiary. Who was it?"

The fellow told him, says, "It's your son, Tommy."

Simpson said, "Oh, he'll bring her back!"

He found out it was his son, so that's what he said to him.

Cass Walden, Edmonton, June 6, 2000

7

Homicide

The following tales, which recount homicidal actions and the perpetrators' motivations, number among the most truly bizarre stories in the book. The stories describe deadly family feuds; murders fueled by drugs, alcohol, and affairs; spousal killings; and numerous other accounts of victims and their killers.

74. "Husband Convicted of Killing Wife"

I tried a murder case last summer, the only one I've tried in my career. I was disappointed but not surprised that we lost the trial. My client was convicted of murder. The case involved the death of one spouse by the other. My client shot his wife—shot her through the head. However, his defense was that it was an accidental shooting, that he accidentally shot her with a .32 caliber Smith & Wesson revolver. And that's probably why we lost the case. It's hard to discharge a revolver by accident, even though in terms of the mechanics of the operation of the gun and the angle of the travel of this bullet, I think that to some extent he was telling the truth. It may have happened just as he said.

What he said was that he was getting ready to go to the barn to clean two pistols, one of which he had recently fired and one of which he had not fired in quite some time. So he went to the bedroom to get the one he had not fired in some time. While walking back down the hall to go out the back door to the barn, he apparently was cocking the hammer on that revolver and letting it back down. Or likely, if what he said is the truth, he'd cocked the hammer and had forgotten to let it go back down. And he may have. I'll explain that in just a minute.

But when he passed the living room, where his wife was reading the paper and watching the TV, she, who apparently had nagged him for years about this or that, made some sort of a nagging comment to him. He stopped and stuck his head in the door and saw that she was sitting eight or nine feet away from where he was standing. "What was that you said?" he wanted to know.

She made the comment again, then he, with his hands above his shoulders, in a blowing off gesture with pistol in hand folds his hands forward as if to say, "The heck with you." In one of his hands he had the cocked pistol. When he brought his hands forward, the gun slid, causing the trigger to hit his finger and the gun to fire.

This is sort of a preposterous story, except that the angle the bullet traveled and the distance involved suggested fully that at least that's where the bullet came from. . . . I hired a firearms specialist to demonstrate that. . . .

He had also been drinking alcohol that day. But the worst recording in that case was his 911 call to the police. "Well, I shot my wife," he said over 911.

"Well, when did you shoot your wife?"

"Oh, just a couple of minutes ago."

To listen to that message, he sounds intoxicated.

"Where did you shoot your wife?"

"*In the head-d-d-d.*"

"Well, is she still alive? We need to send an ambulance over there?"

"Nope. Don't need an ambulance."

When the police arrived, he was calmly on the carport leaning against his Cadillac and smoking a cigarette.

"Where's your wife?"

"Well, she's inside."

Actually, she wasn't dead, but she died within about forty-eight hours.

That situation was sort of odd; a little different. But he was convicted and is now a resident at the Kentucky State Reformatory at La Grange.

Peter Ervin, Louisville, April 26, 2001

75. "Murderer's Son Accused of Murder"

I had a fellow call me from Hazard asking me to defend him for murder. I told him that he could get a cheaper lawyer there, as I couldn't come up there for less than twenty thousand dollars.

He said, "Money is no question. Come on up and I'll give you the twenty thousand dollars. About thirty years ago, you represented my father in a murder case and the jury found him not guilty."

Well, at that point, I stepped aside and was out of his case because he thought I could make a repeat performance, but you can't do that in the law business. So I didn't take his case.

Edward Jackson, Beattyville, July 20, 2001

76. "BELIEF IN LIE DETECTORS"

In one of our adjacent counties there was an actual shooting and a killing. The deceased was certainly not a gem, nor a much-missed member of the community. He was nevertheless a human on the planet who ended up shot and killed. As an unfortunate twist, we ended up representing the fellow who was charged in the case. The police were really struggling with this, although they seemingly had their case put together fairly well. Nobody saw what happened, although there were enough indicators that something happened and that our guy did it. They brought a charge, and we went to trial.

The police were sort of concerned because this fellow had taken the lie detector test twice and passed. We started trying that case, and we were about three days into the trial. Our client leans over to me and says, "I want to take the deal."

Of course, the "deal" means a plea bargain, which is an offer that is less than what you might get at the trial. In this case, it was substantially less, and I leaned over and said, "You know, this trial isn't going too badly and on top of that you've passed this lie detector twice."

He leaned back over and asked me, "Do you *believe* in lie detectors?"

Keith McCormick, Morehead, June 22, 2000

77. "HOMICIDES"

There's a number of accounts that could be told about killings in this area, and I'm the last man alive that knows them. A few years ago, my first cousin Joe Burchell was a game warden. He is two to three years older than I am. Another of my cousins was John "Flint" Lytle, a lawyer. We decided to get together and tell what we knew about what had taken place here in the last seventy-five to eighty years. Between the three of us, we could tell you anything that happened in here back sixty-five to seventy years ago. A lot of the things we talked about were the killings that things were never done about. It wasn't long after we'd got together and talked about getting together that Flint Lytle had a heart attack and died. He knew who was involved in a lot of killings, bushwhackings, burning of the courthouses, and things that we talked about.

We had feuds all the time. My family was involved in some of them, and some were killed. In fact, my uncle who was police judge in Manchester back in the 1930s was killed when some family members drove up behind him and shot him all to pieces. And they indicted four or five of my Stivers uncles for killing Frank Baker, who was the commonwealth attorney up here, but nothing was ever done about it. Nothing was ever done because they couldn't prove a darn thing. They killed all the witnesses when Uncle Pit was the last one that testified about them killing Alf Neal. He was the police judge.

Joe Burchell and I talked about getting together, but for some reason we never did. About four years ago, he died, leaving only me. About two years ago, I dictated what took place in this country and had it typed up, and both the typing and the tape are in the bank vault. I told them to take it out of the vault ten years after I die, because there's some people still living and it would affect them, and I didn't want to do that.

The reason I did that was because historian Dr. Tom Clark asked me to do it. He said, "You must dictate that, write that."

The next time I'd see him, he'd talk about it again, but I still hadn't done it. But finally I did. It's not a good piece of history for a lot of people, including my family, but that's the way it was, so it's now tape-recorded and transcribed.

B. Robert Stivers, Manchester, July 19, 2001

78. "Son Tried for Killing Both Parents"

This was told to me by Alvie Hollon in Hazard, who died two to three years ago. He was a very famous lawyer. I worked for him for one year. I was very fortunate, because he taught me how to handle a lot of stuff that I wouldn't have learned in law school.

He wasn't in a case concerning a county that joined Perry, but the lawyer there was a very famous criminal lawyer. Of course, if you get very famous as a criminal lawyer, you get some high fees paid to you. Hollon told me about this case in which he was defending this young champ for killing his father and mother. He talked this case around Hazard, which is proper if what you say is benefitting your client, but if you are revealing confidential information, it is not. But according to Hollon, he won every case he ever tried.

The day of this young man's trial, the court got full of people who were wondering what kind of defense Hollon would make. So when he made his defense, in his final argument, he said, "For God's sake, have mercy on this poor orphan."

He had killed his father and mother, so that made him an orphan!

Edward Jackson, Beattyville, July 20, 2001

79. "MANSLAUGHTER"

I defended an elderly man for manslaughter. He's dead now, and was in his seventies when this happened back in 1983. His son had custody of his children—the defendant's grandchildren. The son's ex-wife came over with a man from another state and stopped at the end of the road out in the country where they lived. They cut the telephone wires and the pedestal poles so there would not be any phone calls like there had been in the past when they came up there to try to get the kids. This way, they couldn't call the sheriff.

So this man who was with this woman drove up into the yard, and the woman ran up and grabbed the child and ran to the vehicle. Then the grandfather, who was a very small, wiry fellow, and was a ginseng hunter, came out and grabbed the child, and this other man pulled a knife. Well, the grandfather had a little nine-shot .22 pistol. This younger guy, who was only twenty-nine or thirty at the time, flung the man around and held him down on the ground and shouted, "You old SOB."

The old man pulled out his pistol and shot this fellow in the shoulder five times, then on the sixth shot he shot him through the lungs and heart, then had to take his foot and push him off of him. Actually, he should have never been indicted.

I was sitting in my office that morning and somebody called me, said, "Get out here, my dad just killed somebody." So I went out there, and the life squad had just removed the body and the blood was still on the ground.

This mother, who had come over to try to kidnap her child, of whom my client had custody, had said, "Somebody will have to call the life squad." Somebody told her, said, "You can't call them, you'll have to go get them." I didn't realize what that meant till later, because in the past they had always called the sheriff. What that meant was that she [the mother] knew that these telephone wires had been cut, thus they could not use the telephone to call anyone. That was significant in the trial.

After a four-day trial, the jury was out for less than half an hour, came back in and acquitted the old man for killing this fellow. Somebody asked me later, "How did you get him acquitted when he shot the man *six* times in self-defense? Why did he shoot him six times?"

My response was, "Because he ran out of bullets." He actually had to push this fellow off of himself with his foot after he shot him six times. And only the last shot was the lethal shot.

That was a very hard, very trying case. Unfortunately, the young man lost his life because the elderly man did kill him.

Ken S. Dean, Madisonville, April 15, 2002

80. "Real Reason for Man Buying a Gun"

I had a client, Leonard Adkins, who was charged with shooting at some boys. Leonard had some pretty daughters that are all the time attracting attention in the community. Boys would come around at night, sneak around his house. Well, Leonard would get exasperated and go out and fire shots in the air. Every now and then he would go a little farther.

One of those boys said Leonard Adkins shot at him, so the police were investigating Leonard. There in court they interviewed Leonard, so he explained that he had took his pistol out that night because he heard some disturbance. When he heard somebody running, he shot in the air. And Leonard was scared to death because he just about knew he was going to be charged with a felony.

He told them what happened, and that seemed to satisfy the state police detective who kind of closed his little notebook and said, "Well, I don't think this is going to amount to anything, Leonard."

Leonard let out a big sigh, reared back, and said, "Boy, I'm glad to hear that. You know, they say that I bought that gun to kill that boy, but that's not so at all. I bought that gun to kill ——— ———."

He went on to name someone else!

Lawrence Webster, Pikeville, November 9, 2000

81. "UNKNOWN CAUSE OF WOMEN'S DEATHS"

These men I'll tell about are still alive. Two women, Chelsea Graham and Rachel Farley [pseudonyms], locally had been living with these men named Tony Simmons and Frank Stanton [pseudonyms]. These women had fallen out with them. I think one of the men had knocked one of the women's teeth out. They turned it in to the insurance company as an automobile accident and got the insurance company to pay for the dental work.

They had a falling-out, and the women threatened to tell the police or tell the sheriff about this insurance fraud. Apparently, the falling-out got pretty rough because one of the girls came into the sheriff's office and said, "If I'm found dead, Tony Simmons is the one that did it."

In about a week, both women disappeared. Of course, everybody figured these two men had done it, but they didn't find the bodies. They got various tips that the bodies were at one place or another, then checked them out but the bodies weren't there—couldn't find them.

So one day, some teenage guys stole some guns from Mt. Sterling, Kentucky, at the American Legion Armory. The police found out who had stolen them, and one of these boys made the statement that they had thrown some of the rifles off the Maysville-Aberdeen Bridge into the river.

So, in investigating that case, they sent some divers down into the river to find these rifles. The divers went down and came back up, said, "We can't find any rifles, but there is a Cadillac down there." One of the state policemen, Hershel Shouse, investigated. He said, "Yeah, you'll find a couple of dead whores in there."

They got a wrecker and pulled the car out and there were two skeletons in there. They had been dead over a year there in the water. Nothing was left but the bones. We traced them to a place here in town called, I think, the Country-City Bar. Somehow another, the girls and these fellows had gotten back together, and the girls had gotten into the cars with these two men. They went to a place called The Ranch House over in Ohio, and that was the last time the girls were seen. The car belonged to Frank Stanton. Strangely enough, nobody thought Frank did it, even though our case was stronger against him. Frank liked to kill people by shooting them, and these girls had been shot. His story was that they had been to The Ranch House, and that he and the girls had driven to Ripley, Ohio, and he'd gotten out to buy something, an ice cream cone or something to drink, and while he was there the girls drove off and left him there. He walked back to Maysville.

I never did think of a way I could get in the information about the girl telling the sheriff, "If I'm found dead, Tony Simmons did it." But we tried the men and they were both acquitted. We never did find out who did the shooting.

Woodson Wood, Maysville, February 20, 2002

82. "Strange Homicide Case"

One of the most interesting cases I ever had involved a fellow by the name of Russell Brammer, who was convicted of murder. The case started when the circuit judge at that time, John Breslin, came by the courthouse and said that they had found a man burned up in his car up in Springdale and asked me if I wanted to go up with him. So, I said, "Sure, I'll go with you."

We found a body that had been burned up in a burned-up car. The body was thirty to forty feet from the car, badly charred. There was something red, something very bright red, and something yellow. Something, I don't know whether it was internal organs, whether it was liver, or what it was, stood out against the black skin of the blackened corpse. I looked at the body, and said, "I don't think that man burned up in the car." There was no sign of fire between the car and where this man's body was located.

They checked everything out and found a wallet next to the body with identification that it belonged to Russell Brammer. They checked the car license and it also belonged to one Russell Brammer, so they identified the body as that of Russell Brammer. I told them that didn't look right to me. You get an instinct about these things after so many years. I asked them to take fingerprints off the body, whatever else they could do, to check to be sure that it was him. We had his wife and brother look at the body and they identified it as him in spite of the fact that the corpse had all its fingers and Russell was missing one of his. The corpse also had Russell's ring on the body. So I had them issue a warrant for Russell. They checked and found that it was not his body. Russell was described to me as being about six-foot-two and weighed about 220–230 pounds, maybe more than that. But the charred body looked very small, more like a 150–pound man. So, they did issue a warrant for him and he was found hiding down on the riverbank under some driftwood. That was in the winter. They brought him down here. He wasn't in very good shape.

We put him in jail. It turned out that he was wanted in Ohio, and they had already set a trial for him on another charge over there. I believe he got out on bond here in Mason County, so when he went back to Ohio they arrested him and put him in jail over there because he skipped bond for not showing up for trial. They disposed of him. We finally were able to extradite him under an agreement that we have between the states that says we can get him back and try him, but then we have to send him back to Ohio to serve his time. Then when he was finished over there, he would come back over here to serve his time.

So we got ready for the trial, and I called the prosecutor in Ohio because I wanted to try to be able to prove what Russell's motive was for killing this man. Proof was a little skimpy at that point. I mean, here was a guy with his ring on, and his wallet burned up by this car, but that doesn't really prove that Russell killed him. We didn't have any direct proof or motive, so I called the Ohio prosecutor and told him that we would like to have him testify that Russell Brammer and his car burned up and wanted to prove that he was wanted over there in Ohio. And the Ohio prosecutor told me that he had gotten two telephone calls . . . that Russell Brammer had been in an accident and had burned up in his car on December 1. So the car didn't burn up until December 1. So we had a witness who said he'd seen Russell Brammer and somebody else driving down the road near where this car burned the night before. To my surmise, he took him down there and tried to kill him on November 30, but couldn't get him out. We found a whiskey bottle there, by the way, which contained whiskey and scopolamine, which is a knockout drop called the Mickey Finn drop, and another drug, and plaster of paris, all mixed in with the whiskey. I asked the pathologist, who was involved in the case from the state police. He said he didn't know why they would put plaster of paris in there, as it was just used in construction and in roach powder, where the roaches would eat the plaster of paris and drink water, and it would kill them, but it is not poisonous. They came to the conclusion that when they couldn't get him out with Librium and scopolamine and the other drug, the guilty person had put roach powder in there, thinking that would poison him.

We were able to extradite Russell and bring him back to trial. He jerked us around for awhile, but finally pleaded guilty, so we had to take him back to Ohio. The judge here called his case to sentence him so that we could send him back, and the jailer said that Russell was sick.

And, in good humor, the judge said, "Why, that's fine. We'll get him back in two weeks from now." But in just about an hour the jailer came to bring Russell over. The jailer was on one side and one of the turnkeys on the other side. And this guy's head was just swinging back and forth just like he was ready to go at any time. The judge said, "My Lord, take him to the hospital," and they did. Local doctors examined him and said he had tuberculosis of the spine.

We asked if he could travel, and they said, "Oh, yes, as long as he's got a nurse with him and in an ambulance." So I called the Ohio State Penitentiary and asked if they had any hospital wards—that we had one of their prisoners and didn't want to keep him here in our hospital with the sheriff outside the door for two or three weeks. So I asked if they had a hospital ward they could put him in. They said, "Yes, we can take care of him."

So we put him in an ambulance and rolled the ambulance in front of the courthouse. The judge came out; the lawyers came out. I asked if there was any reason why the sentence should not be imposed. Of course, Brammer couldn't have said anything at that point. The judge sentenced him to twenty years in the penitentiary. Then, the ambulance took off to Columbus, Ohio, to the penitentiary, at eighty to ninety miles an hour and rolled into the penitentiary just at the exact time that Russell rolled over and died.

I was afraid to go back into Ohio for several years after that, as I thought they were probably under the opinion that I had intentionally sent them a dead man. But I didn't. I didn't know the man was dying. It turned out that he had consumed some toilet bowl cleaner—had a very painful death, but he never showed that much distress. He looked like he was in bad shape, but didn't show that much distress.

In any event, we never did find out who the other man was that was burned by the car. Russell told us for several weeks that if we'd leave him here in jail in Mason County that he would get the name of that victim, and that he would come back and tell us who it was. He killed that man, but claimed that he didn't know who it was. He actually hit him with a rock. It's my opinion that he fed him this whiskey and all these drugs, knockout drops, and everything, and probably got him comatose. But when he started to pour gasoline on him, the fellow came to and could see that good ol' Russell, who was bringing him free whiskey, was not good ol' Russell after all. So when he tried to get away, Russell followed him with a rock that he found there and hit him in the head with it and killed him, or at least knocked him out. Then he poured gasoline on him and set him on fire. We never knew who the man was. The pathologist I mentioned earlier said that he personally used to be a coroner down at New Orleans and said they found floaters every few days. Those were people that nobody ever knew who they were. They just had no families. So I'm sure that Russell met this alcoholic guy in a bar, and he didn't have any family and didn't know where he was.

By the way, I didn't think this man could be Russell because he was too little, but it turned out he was. The pathologist said that fellow was about six-two and weighed about 225 pounds. See, the fire shrunk the tissues. I guess Russell Brammer put his ring on this fellow so that we would think it was he who was dead.

That account made the detective magazines. They stated in these articles that I personally flew down to Frankfort to personally assist in the investigation. That's not true, however. They just saw that I was commonwealth attorney, so they thought that was a state job instead of it just being a local job.

Woodson Wood, Maysville, February 20, 2002

83. "A Mean Murderer"

I tried this murder case about a fellow named Earl Doyle. He was one who drank a little bit, and he had a friend named Leo King who ran a filling station at Mays Lick, Kentucky. He also drank a little. Earl stopped in at Leo's filling station one day and asked how much he owed him. He had an account there. As I understand it, Leo told him, said, "I'm too drunk. You'll have to add it up yourself."

So Earl added it up and paid him whatever the amount came to. Earl then went on home and his wife looked over the tickets and said, "Earl, he cheated you. He charged you too much." She didn't know Earl had been the one that added it up.

So being a little drunk and a little mean, Earl stuck his pistol in his pocket and drove back to the filling station and shot Leo for something Leo had nothing to do with. So we tried him and we qualified a death jury. A lot of people, when they serve on a death jury, say they will not hesitate to inflict the death penalty, but that's a real tough jury. But some of them are pretty tough, but some of them will not convict anybody of anything. They're just marching to a different drummer.

We tried Earl, then I thought I was working along pretty well and he talked about how Leo was a mean man, but I don't think Leo was a mean man, so I asked, "Why do you say he was a mean man? Did you ever see him do anything mean?"

I thought Earl wasn't very smart. He said, "Yeah, one time I saw him pick up a little puppy and beat his brains out against a telephone post."

But I never did find out whether that was true or not, or whether he thought he pulled a smart one on me. I had asked one too many questions. I think they gave Earl something like four to six years in prison for what I thought was a cold-blooded murder. He went to the penitentiary, served his time, then got out. So he didn't get much of a prison sentence, but that's not unusual.

He'd been out of prison several years. When the sheriff went to arrest him, he shot at the sheriff. He was out for several years when finally his house caught on fire. His brother went down to help him, to see if he needed any help. When this brother went into Earl's house, Earl stabbed him to death. We don't know why. Well, by this time Earl was in pretty bad shape. We let him plead guilty for maybe serving ten years. You had to serve a minimum of ten, but we didn't think Earl would live that long, so we let him plead guilty for ten years. They took him to the penitentiary. Regularly after that, the judge would say, "Well, Earl is on the prison volleyball team now. He's made a miraculous recovery." Or, he'd say, "Earl was playing a little touch football yesterday. He's really doing well." Of course, he was lying, but Earl finally did die in the penitentiary.

Woodson Wood, Maysville, February 20, 2002

84. "Guilty Man Smelled the Blood"

One of the worst homicides I've ever heard of was here in Carrollton. I was in the courtroom with this criminal psychopath. The old saying was that a psychopath would kill someone over a bottle of whiskey and not feel guilty about it. They had no shame or no guilt.

This was one of those cases that had people you hardly ever see, not too many times in your law career. These are just evil people. This guy was charged with cutting another worker's throat. They worked in the redrier, which is right down the street from here where, when these big auction houses sold the tobacco when the auctioneers would come through, they would haul it over to the redrier and they'd stuff it in these wooden barrels and heat it up to dry the moisture out. Then they'd store the tobacco here until the tobacco companies was ready for it.

During the season that they were doing this after the tobacco market, they'd hire one hundred to two hundred workers; thus a lot of people around here supplemented their income by working seasonally in those places. This is where this all started one night. There were workers at the redrier, and one was a drifter from Michigan. They went over to a little dormitory that was located kind of off in an alley. It was a concrete block building. They were hiding from their work, and they had a bottle of whiskey between three of them. For some reason, they argued over this bottle of whiskey. One of them stabbed another one.

I was sitting in the courtroom listening to this. The two were convicted, but the one that did the actual final killing said, "Yeah, I took the knife and cut his throat because I knew he was dying. I knew the other guy had already cut him."

But the testimony was that the dormitory lights were out and it was pitch black. The attorney asked this fellow, "How do you know that he was bleeding?"

The guy just coldly, matter-of-factly, said, "I could smell the blood." And he said that he finished the fellow off by cutting his throat.

That was the most cold-blooded case I think I ever heard. The guilty man was sent to the penitentiary for life, I think. And I think he had another life sentence in Michigan. He was only about thirty-five years old.

Stan Billingsley, Carrollton, March 20, 2001

85. "Killing of College Female"

The legal case in which I was likely the most frightened ever took place back in the 1970s. It was then that I had an awful lot of criminal cases. One case that was really a big one, and was also one in which all of us involved were very tense, was the Clawvern Jacobs case. He was accused of killing a girl here at Alice Lloyd College, and he's on death row right now.

Even before that, maybe ten years, he was out with this gunman and they accused him of killing an older woman. But he never did know whether or not he killed her. And one of the strange things about that case was that he was on the driver's side of the car. We had a witness who claimed that one of her sons and her son-in-law was hunting for her that night—was going to kill her. Somebody came up, and he said that she was drinking mixed beverages. He said that he saw images on the outside of that windshield. Well, someone struck him on the left side and gave him a huge cut.

Well, the woman was sitting on the right side of the vehicle. She had two .38 pistols. Her son-in-law had one of them, and she had the other. Of course, this fellow got hold of it and had it on under his belt. Someone shot straight down and struck her in her right shoulder and cut the artery under her arm. Also, someone struck her in the head on the left side with some kind of blunt instrument. They meant to kill her. Actually, either one of those instruments could be what killed her.

Of all things, after a while this boy apparently realized that something was happening. He took off from there in his car, and he swore up and down that someone was after him, following him in that creek. So he got down on the creek and he dumped her body out into the creek. Her sweater was in the car, too, so he takes her sweater and throws it up into a tree.

He said that someone was still after him, so he drives that car all the way over here to Hindman, then down to the jailhouse. He claims that those people followed him until he turned down toward the jail, then they didn't follow him any farther. He goes into the jail and tells them what happened. But he didn't tell them that he'd killed anybody; but they found her the next morning there in the creek.

They saw blood on this thing, so they accused him of knocking her in the head with one of these old headrest things—has a big iron piece to it, and that big iron piece stuck down into the seat. They claim that thing was in that car and that she was struck in the head with that. Yet, there was no blood on that, there was no skin, nothing. It was as clean as it could be.

Another thing they tried to accuse him of is robbing her. But she had already given him money—so many thousand dollars, I think to go up north to Ohio or Michigan, or somewhere. She had a great big purse, a real huge purse, and they claimed he took her money from that purse. Yet, of all the blood there was in that car on everything else, there was not one speck of blood on the inside of her purse. If he had opened it up with blood on his hands, it would have gotten on her purse. He was sentenced , but later on he was paroled. Actually, he got a new trial, but they wouldn't try him anymore because he had already served his time before parole. He served four years.

Then he was accused of killing this young girl at Alice Lloyd College. He's on death row now at Eddyville. That was the first murder that they had ever tried him for. I was concerned about that, because her people are good people, but they won't take nothing off of anybody. I was threatened there myself a couple of times, as I was this boy's defense lawyer. But in later years, her people have all liked me. I had known most of her family since I was a small kid. We had lived in a coal-mining camp across the mountain in Floyd County. Then, they moved to the Carr Creek community. I had an uncle that lived there, and he just loved those people.

I talked with one of the prosecuting attorneys years later, and he said, "I have my doubts about that case, too." He wasn't sure that the boy who is now on death row was the one who killed the college student.

James Bates, Hindman, December 18, 2000

86. "Erroneous Murder Charge"

One interesting story that really isn't too humorous is about this bad murder case. Two young people had been killed with a shotgun, and we had a suspect but he claimed that he didn't do it. He said that he was there and saw another man do it. The police went and picked that man up, but of course the man denied killing them.

In court, I said, "Well, if you can tell me where you was, and prove where you were, I will not charge you with murder. But I have a witness who said that he was there and saw you do it."

He said, "I can't tell you where I was."

His name was Henry. I said, "Henry, you've got to tell me."

He then said, "Well, at the time of the murder, I was committing a burglary."

I said, "Henry, you just made that up."

He said, "No, I committed a burglary."

I said, "Prove it to me."

He said, "I had two people with me."

He then named another man and another woman. So we went and got this other man, and I said, "He's going to be charged with murder, unless you tell me that at the time of the murder you were with him on a burglary."

So the guy said, "Well, I was."

So we went and got this woman and she said she was with them. I said, "Well, all three of you are making this up to get him out of the murder charge."

They said they stole television sets and all sorts of items. I asked, "Well, what did you do with them?"

"Well, we sold them to this man, and he knew they was stolen."

I said, "Well, if we find the TV that he said you brought to him, then I will say that you have a perfect alibi—that you were committing another crime at another place."

So we went to this guy, and he said, "I didn't buy this stuff."

I said, "Look, we're not really after you. We're trying to determine who killed these two people."

So, he finally said, "Well, the TV and all the other stuff is in the back room."

So we had to arrest three people for burglary, one man for receipt of stolen property, and they all had to confess to get him out of the murder charge. We ended up trying the murder charge, and then in the murder trial, he said this guy did the killing, and we had to prove they were committing a burglary.

The man who was charged with murder got two life sentences. All the others got probated, because they kindly helped us.

Morris Lowe, Bowling Green, March 9, 2001

87. "JUSTIFIABLE KILLINGS"

Back in the '70s in Knott County, Kentucky, a man named Raymond Little was into a family blood feud with his family and the Berrys [pseudonym] from over on Caney Creek. Now, there's some interesting things in isolated places, one of which is the product of people marrying cousins. That works both ways.

The Berrys had married each other for a hundred years, but their IQ is about thirty points higher than the national average. It's like horse breeding. It works both ways. They are really smart people. Well, they had a blood feud going, and one of those Berrys had shot at one of Raymond's sons. They had some kind of court appearance with each other. So Raymond went into the district courtroom in Knott County, and four of those Berrys were sitting on the back row. Raymond walked up to them and kind of got their attention behind them, then opened his coat just enough that they could see that he had guns, which caused them to get up to flee. He pulled his gun out and shot and killed those people right there in that courtroom.

He was tried in court. They tried to give him the death penalty. He spent two years in jail before his trial. He couldn't make bond until he was tried. At his trial, the jury found him guilty and sentenced him to two years. So essentially, he got out of jail for time already served.

What we argued in that case was a more old-fashioned form of self-defense. Our theory was, if you get into a feud with somebody, and somebody has got to die because the feud is that strong, then it is not a bad thing to get the drop on them. You don't have to be too fair in your fight during the first chance you get. If it's going to be him or me, go ahead and let it be him.

Raymond was a tough man, and the jury weren't afraid of him, but he was so powerful in his demeanor that he just really had a great sway over the jury.

That's probably the most serious case that I've had, because here's a man who could have gotten the electric chair but went home after a killing that people beyond the mountains would never be able to understand.

Lawrence Webster, Pikeville, November 9, 2000

88. "OVERLY SCARED DEPUTY SHERIFF"

Victor Tackett was a brilliant man from Pikeville who was a great writer. But he was not a writer. He was just an ordinary kind of country fellow with a lot of intelligence, and he loved words. He was very bright. Looked like Andy Griffith's buddy Goober. Victor loved to fool with politics, and for a long time he was chief deputy sheriff to Sheriff Charles "Fuzzy" Keesee, who was a long-time sheriff of Pike County. In those days, he had as many as eight hundred deputies, and they all wore brown-shirted uniforms. Mr. Tackett said he wouldn't take five hundred dollars and wear one of them shirts through Murphy's, which was a dime store here. He didn't want to be seen in that kind of get-up. He was too proud. He usually wore a suit, but he did carry a .45 automatic pistol.

This story that I'm about to tell converges with another story. Another woman of letters in Pike County was Truda McCoy. She was a published poet and quite well known for her intellect and her poetry. But beneath it all, she was a mountain woman of old-time values. She came to see Jean Auxier, an old-time attorney whose life span was from about 1897 until about 1996, and told him a sad story. Jean Auxier was in the early stages of Alzheimer disease, and he kinda sat around about half-asleep when he talked with his clients, and nodded and agreed with whatever they said. Didn't really pay much attention to them.

So she began to tell him, said, "Jean, I've got a son-in-law that's coming in from California, and he's been threatening to harm me and my family. You wouldn't let him do that, would you Jean?"

Well, Mr. Auxier just kinda mumbles, "No, no," under his breath.

She said, "If he was going to hurt you and your family, you would get him before he got you, wouldn't you Jean?"

Jean just kinda nodded, "Yeah, yeah."

She said, "Thank you," then got up and crossed the street to the courthouse. Now, this brings us back to Victor Tackett.

There was a workers' compensation hearing going on on the first floor of the old Pike County courthouse that was built in 1937. This hearing took place back during the early '70s.

Victor Tackett had been sent as a sort of bailiff for this workers' compensation hearing. Said he just sat there—didn't do anything. So he was there in his suit as the chief deputy sheriff of Pike County.

As Truda McCoy left Jean Auxier's office, she came into the courthouse, and lo and behold, as she was going up the steps to the second floor, down those steps came her wicked son-in-law from California. She pulled out a pistol and shot him five times.

The Pike County courthouse was built of tile and concrete blocks, thus it is very sound and it echoed like a Martin guitar. And those five shots were fired within fifty feet of the workers' compensation hearing room, where Victor Tackett, the chief deputy sheriff, was at. Those five shots sounded like fifty shots bouncing around the walls.

Inside that workers' compensation hearing was Kelsey Friend Sr., the legendary black-lung lawyer of the mountains—also state senator. Gerald Jones, attorney from Prestonsburg, the judge in workers' compensation cases, was also there, along with another attorney perhaps, and the bailiff.

After all that banging noise (and those people got very disturbed), Truda McCoy ran into that room with that pistol smoking. Kelsey Friend dived under the table. The hearing officer jumped into a large trash can, and Chief Deputy Victor Tackett got up and ran out the back door, hollering, "Somebody call the law!"

And he, himself, was the chief deputy sheriff.

Lawrence Webster, Pikeville, November 9, 2000

89. "Local Physician Kills Prominent Person"

The biggest murder case I was involved with—more publicity and more people involved, who they were and everything—was Dr. Frank Bowman [pseudonym] of Monroe County for killing James Kirkland [pseudonym]. He was tried there in Tompkinsville, but the jury was from here in Metcalfe County. My law partner and I were employed to be in the trial, but the lead attorney was Rodes K. Myers from Bowling Green. We were associated with Rodes.

Bowman and Kirkland were both prominent citizens, so that case went on for a long time. Me and my partners were defending Dr. Frank Bowman for killing Kirkland. Paul Carter was the prosecutor. Bowman killed Kirkland back in the 1970s. One of the major issues in the trial was to determine why Bowman killed Kirkland. The Kirkland family was one of the oldest families to settle in Monroe County, and they settled down there at Center Point on the river. Very prominent people—slave owners, big land owners.

Mitchell Kirkland was one of them, and he had a family. At that time, he was one of the biggest landowners in Monroe County. His land was right there where Meshack Creek runs into the Cumberland River. Frank Bowman's brother, Bandy Bowman, married one of the Kirkland girls. So Dr. Frank killed his brother's brother-in-law. At that time all of them lived there in Tompkinsville.

Frank just took a gun and went to Kirkland's house, as I remember it. It might have had something to do with a woman. When Frank got to Kirkland's house, he waited until Kirkland came out, then he shot and killed him. There wasn't too much history to it as far as animosity is concerned. No trouble between them—no animosity or anything like that.

Frank Bowman was a very prominent physician at that time, and was right up until his own death. He was a leading citizen of the county, and was the son of a doctor. I still don't understand why he did that.

There was no evidence whatever, but my personal opinion as to why Frank killed Kirkland had to do with drugs. Now, back then we didn't know about drugs what we know now. You just didn't hear about anybody taking drugs back then, but I think that Frank possibly got on drugs, or something like that. I've always felt that something like that was what was the matter with him. As far as I know, no evidence ever came out that the two of them had any disagreement over a contract, or over a woman, or anything like that. And Frank was found not guilty of killing Kirkland. Kirkland had a store there in Tompkinsville, and it was stated by numerous people that James had said that he was going to kill Frank—that he sent him word that he was going to, and all that. Frank eventually killed Kirkland, but wasn't convicted for doing it.

Cass Walden, Edmonton, June 8, 2000

90. "Death Penalty, Right or Wrong?"

Back when I was commonwealth attorney in the 1960s, if we had a homicide case, I'd qualify the jury for the death penalty. But you couldn't get a jury. They'd just get up and walk out because they don't believe in the death penalty. They said that they couldn't give the death penalty. We went through a terrible ordeal back in the 1960s. People simply lost their way. Honestly, they lost their way.

There was a black man that went into a Convenient Food Store in Muldraugh, robbed the store, then shot the clerk and killed her. I'd had all this experience with juries in death penalty cases. So the defense attorney came to see me and he said, "We'll plead my man guilty, if for a life sentence."

I called the father and mother of the girl that had been shot and told them what the lawyer had said. They said, "We want death."

I said, "The jury won't give him a death sentence. This is what they have offered, and this is as much as I can get."

They said, "We'll not agree to that, so what are you going to do as commonwealth attorney?"

Here's what I did. I said, "It's not your decision; it's mine, and I'm going to take life in prison." Well, those people are still mad at me, and I understand that. But I drew a conclusion from my previous experiences, and from what I knew in some, and that's just the way it is.

Kenneth Goff, Leitchfield, May 8, 2002

91. "Man Plots to Kill His Best Friend"

We've had four major tragic events in Muhlenberg County in my legal career, which started in 1975. The first case I'm talking about occurred back when I was a young lawyer taking criminal cases at the time and getting appointed. I got appointed to one of the principals in this case.

There was a man here in Greenville named Jarvis, and his wife wanted to get a divorce. She was having an affair with a fellow named Ricky Sims. What happened is, this Jarvis fellow's body was found. He had been shot and killed. His body was found out on an old coal-mining road, out in what we call the River Queen Mine area, right outside of Greenville. Immediately, Ricky Sims was interviewed and then charged, and he even made a statement that he had committed the murder. Then he made a statement denying it. I got appointed to him after he had already been interviewed by the police several times. But the police and the prosecutor, who at that time was Dan Cornette, just didn't believe Ricky Sims did it. So the case was further investigated and it ended up that a man by the name of Johnny Marshall Smith got charged with the murder, and Ricky Sims got charged with complicity to the murder—helping in other words.

The case got tried. Ricky Sims entered a guilty plea to his role in the murder and got a twenty-year sentence if memory serves me correctly. But Johnny Marshall Smith said that he himself was not guilty, that he had nothing to do with it, and they had a trial up here in Greenville. Well, Johnny Marshall Smith was convicted by the jury of "murder for hire," which made it death penalty eligible. What was significant about it is that it probably was the first death penalty conviction in the state of Kentucky since the reinstitution of the death penalty. It had been banned from about 1972 until about 1976. So in '76 we became one of the death penalty states again.

This trial occurred in 1977 or 1978, and this man got convicted and got the death penalty. That case ended up getting reversed for various reasons by the appellate court. And instead of retrying, he pled guilty and ended up with a life sentence. I'm told that he's now been paroled out of prison.

What happened is, Ricky Sims was having an affair with this Jarvis woman and she wanted her husband killed. She had her own good reasons why she wanted to get him killed. Well, Ricky was going to do it but he didn't have the nerve, so he found out about this Johnny Marshall Smith, who apparently had nerve. And the two of them got together and arranged with the Jarvis woman to have her husband killed. Johnny Marshall Smith agreed to do it for two or three guns that Jarvis had around the house—a shotgun, a rifle, and maybe even a pistol. I've forgotten how many, but I know there were several weapons involved. So it was agreed that Ricky Sims would lure the Jarvis fellow out at night to this location, and Johnny Marshall Smith would be there and kill him. And that's what happened. Ricky Sims was not only having an affair with this Jarvis woman, but he was also Mr. Jarvis's buddy. I mean, they were friends, but Sims just fell in love with his wife.

So, on a real rainy night, Sims ended up walking to the Jarvis house here in Greenville and told them that his truck had broken down outside of town, and he wanted to know if his buddy, Jarvis, would come out and give him a jump or check under the hood to see if he could help him. So they drove out there together. Sure enough, there was Sims's vehicle on the side of this abandoned road, and they get out and this Jarvis fellow was starting to help Sims by pulling up the hood. Sims gets out of the way, and Johnny Marshall Smith comes up out of the bushes with a gun and kills Jarvis point-blank.

At the trial, Ricky Sims took the witness stand and told the story. And I'll never forget that one question that was asked of him, "Well, wasn't that Jarvis fellow a friend of yours?"

Sims said, "He was the best friend I ever had." That was sort of chilling when he said that.

David Jernigan, Greenville, May 17, 2002

92. "THE DEATHS OF TWO LITTLE BOYS"

On Halloween day, 1982, a fellow by the name of David Whittinghill got visitation permission with his two little boys. I think they were one and two years old, or two and three. He met his soon-to-be ex-wife up at the police station. He didn't have a car, so he was just going to have his visitation by walking around with the boys. He walked them out here to Luzerne Lake, which is our water supply for the city of Greenville. He walked these two little kids out there on a beautiful Halloween day; the temperature was nice and pleasant. The next thing anybody knows, David Whittinghill was running to some house somewhere out there around the Luzerne Lake area and reporting that his children were missing—that he'd laid down to take a nap, and they were supposed to be napping also. When he woke up, they were gone. Well, fire and rescue people all showed up at the lake and it wasn't very long until the two little bodies were found floating in the lake. They had drowned.

The case proceeded into 1983. By that time, Dan Cornette had left the commonwealth attorney's office and was the new circuit judge. And I was the commonwealth attorney, so I inherited that case to prosecute, and I did prosecute it. We brought a judge in from Logan County to try the case—Judge Bill Fuqua. This was a death penalty eligibility case because of multiple deaths. It was a highly circumstantial case, as we had no eyewitnesses; we had no confession, nothing. We tried the case for about a week during the fall, 1983. The jury returned a verdict, finding David Whittinghill guilty of killing both of his sons by drowning them. His punishment was two life sentences in the penitentiary, and he is still there today.

David Jernigan, Greenville, May 17, 2002

93. "GIRL RAPED AND MURDERED"

In January 1997, when I was still commonwealth attorney, a young Greenville girl, who was either sixteen or seventeen years of age and whose name was Sarah Hansen, went to Minit Mart here on Main Street in Greenville about eight o'clock one night to rent a video tape to take back home. Her boyfriend was going to show up some time or another, and they were going to watch a movie. She never returned back to her house and, of course, her parents got concerned. The boyfriend showed up and he went out looking. About 10:30 that night, her body was found in Luzerne Lake in the same location where the two little boys' bodies were found in 1982. It turns out that the autopsy revealed that she had drowned, but that she had been raped and stabbed. Her throat was cut. The actual cause of her death was drowning, but she had bled considerably and probably would have died anyway.

A fellow by the name of Robert Keith Woodall ended up being interviewed, investigated, charged, and indicted for killing her. He was tried for her rape, kidnaping, and murder. What had happened is that apparently when she left the Minit Mart she was driving her parents' van. She got into that van, and he must have been hiding somewhere in that van. More than likely, at knife point he directed her to drive to this secluded area at Luzerne Lake and raped her in the van, then cut her throat in the van, then dragged her some fifty yards or more to the pier and dumped her body into the lake.

I went on the bench during this time period, and I was precluded from being the judge on his trial, so Judge Bill Cunningham from Kuttawa/Eddyville ended up being the judge on the case. My successor as commonwealth attorney was Ralph Vick, who tried the case. The defendant, Woodall, pled guilty to the crime but he wouldn't accept the punishment being recommended by the commonwealth attorney, which was a death penalty, so the trial was solely about what should be the proper punishment. It didn't take the jurors in Caldwell County but about thirty minutes, after listening to about a week of evidence, to decide that the death penalty was appropriate for Robert Keith Woodall.

He is on death row right now at Eddyville.

David Jernigan, Greenville, May 17, 2002

94. "MAN KILLED FOUR VICTIMS"

This tragedy happened either in 1998 or 1999. Four people were killed on or about the same time by this man. His name was Terry Wedding. He killed his mother and father, and then turned around and killed a young man and his wife, who were also family members. They all lived in a little area together out west of Greenville. The young man that was killed was a Greenville police officer. So Terry Wedding ended up being charged and pled guilty. His defense was insanity, and he did have some serious mental problems. His story was that he believed his parents were going to do something to him, or whatever. So he beat one of his parents with a baseball bat, then shot and killed the other, and then went back into the mobile home where they lived and was sitting there when Joey Vincent, who was the Greenville police officer, and his young wife were getting in the car with a child. They had a young child. Terry Wedding came out and shot and killed both parents, then took the child back into the trailer. He didn't do anything to the child. Of course, the police responded and went down there and found Wedding and gathered up the evidence.

He had been institutionalized over at the mental hospital in Hopkinsville. Apparently family members, of course, instituted that type of proceeding to get him hospitalized. The officer, Joey Vincent, may have had something to do with that, so that was sort of the connection on that case.

Joey Vincent's parents are raising the child, I believe. This child's mother, who was also killed, was the one that was related to the Wedding fellow.

That was a case about homicide, but with a defense to it of mental insanity. But that defense plea didn't work. He tried to portray a defense of not guilty by reason of insanity, but before he ever went to trial, they ended up pleading guilty. So that took away that defense, but he still was entitled to put on that kind of evidence to the jury that was going to set the punishment, because jurors might not give a death penalty to someone they believed was mentally incompetent. But he got the death penalty and is presently on death row. He has already run through his state appeals, and he's lost. So now he starts into federal courts on the next round, and there's still some other procedures he can utilize in state court thereafter. But I'd say it will be ten years before we will know the answer.

David Jernigan, Greenville, May 17, 2002

95. "PAYMENT FOR SERVICES RENDERED"

The homicide cases that I tried were all in my early years of practice. I remember one time that I was appointed to defend this blind black man that lived down on what was then called Burks Alley here in Bowling Green. That was one of the really destitute sections of town where a lot of things took place.

This black fellow was alleged to be a bootlegger. What happened is, somebody broke into his house late one night and he thought he was about to be robbed, so he pulled his gun and shot him and killed him. He was indicted for murder, and it was going to trial. I was appointed as his defendant and we tried the case. During the trial, he told a very convincing story. We took a couple of days to try the case and he got an acquittal. I never expected to get any money for my service, but the old fellow sent me one hundred dollars!

Charles English, Bowling Green, May 27, 2002

96. "A TOUCHING SITUATION"

I had this very serious homicide case as a young lawyer. A young black man, whose name was Johnny Starks, along with two other young black men, were out north of town just south of Smiths Grove and Oakland, and robbed an old man one Sunday afternoon. His name was Manning. The testimony was, from the other two accomplices, that Mr. Manning was on his knees begging for mercy, and Johnny says to him, "If you don't tell me where your money is, I'm going to shoot you." Then, he went ahead and shot him right between the eyes. That created a lot of furor and interest, and was a very highly charged case.

Judge John Rhodes was on the bench, and he was one of the finest circuit judges, judges, and lawyers that ever graced the benches of Kentucky courts. Judge Rhodes appointed me to defend Johnny. I was a young lawyer and had two kids—was trying to buy a house, and got appointed to this case. You can imagine the time it took. We couldn't get a jury in Warren County, and had to call a special venire of jurors from Simpson County to try the case. Morris Lowe was the prosecutor. We offered to take a life sentence, but they wouldn't take that. Judge Rhodes was very concerned in that he had never sent anybody to prison for a death sentence. He talked with me about it; we tried it. I used Red Clarence Darrow's argument in one of his death cases. I used that argument to the jury, and the jury gave him life.

Johnny went on and was a good inmate, served as a lot of people like that did in the governor's mansion as a cook or server, and ultimately was paroled. He came back ten or fifteen years or more later. . . . He died only three or four weeks ago [May 2002]. I saw in the paper that he had died, and I went down to the funeral home to see Johnny's body. One of his children was there when I was there. That was a very nice experience.

Charles English, Bowling Green, May 27, 2002

97. "The Ted Bundy Story"

This is something that happened in Florida. We were working for Team Defense in Atlanta and had clients from all over the South. We had a client down in New Orleans and we decided he needed a lot of tender loving care. So, my husband and I were going to drive to New Orleans to visit him. One morning I was in the office by myself and I got a call from someone that wanted to talk with Millard Farmer, who was head of the organization for which we were working. He was upset that Millard wasn't there. I hung up the telephone, and Millard came in a little bit later. I told him about the call, and he said, "Well, I think I know who that is. So before you all leave the state of Georgia, call me, as I may want you all to go talk with this person."

So we called him before we got to the Georgia-Florida line, and he said, "I want you to go talk to this guy over in Pensacola. He was picked up last night by the police, and he's not giving his name until he talks to an attorney, and he wants somebody from Team Defense to go talk to him."

So we go over and we get in there. Since we were volunteers, we didn't dress up. My husband had a corduroy sports jacket in the back of the car that he would put on in some situations. We were dressed for traveling. We got to the police station in Pensacola, and my husband had on this cruddy jacket. We found out that this guy wasn't talking to his lawyer from Atlanta. So we go in, and my husband was introduced to this guy that's been picked up, and he goes back to talk to him.

This really tough police woman was there. She says, "Where's this lawyer?" She was told that he just went back there with the defendant, then she said, "We've been waiting all day for that?!"

The person the defendant turned out to be was Ted Bundy, and he had just been picked up in Florida after killing a little girl in Lakewood, and also after killing those two sorority girls in Tallahassee. So, that's who this person was, and he didn't want to let his name be known because he was on the FBI's Most Wanted list, and he felt like if he said his name, it would be all out. He said, "I'll tell you my name but I want to call my family first to let them know what's coming."

So they worked this deal out, and they asked him, "Well, who are you?"

He said, "I'm Ted Bundy."

Amazed, they said, "Who?" At that time, he was the most notorious, the most wanted criminal in the country. Well, then we get in the car, and almost by the time we got to the end of the parking lot, the police announced that they had caught Ted Bundy, and that was before he had a chance to call his family.

We came back through Tallahassee en route back from New Orleans. My husband wanted to see Ted Bundy. So he met with him again in his cell. He had been moved up to Tallahassee because he had been charged with the deaths of these sorority girls. He was eventually executed in the late-1980s.

That's my Ted Bundy story. It took place in 1978.

Forrest Roberts, Owensboro, June 7, 2002

98. "Son Kills His Mother's Lover"

My husband, Allen Holbrook, represented this young guy who had killed his mother's boyfriend. I think he was in his early twenties when he killed this man. He killed him in cold blood and admitted it, but he was acquitted. This fellow was a very mean man, and he kept beating this boy's mother up. Well, the son just got mad one day—got fed up with it, and killed him.

It went to court, but he was acquitted.

Forrest Roberts, Owensboro, June 7, 2002

99. "In Support of Ignorant Client"

I'll never forget the case about this poor fellow that was ignorant, and he had been charged with a murder for a shooting at a poolroom in Mays Lick. I was very sympathetic toward him. My wife prepared a pie and cake and stuff, and I took it to him at jail. I really got wrapped up in his case more than any other case I ever had. So I attempted to negotiate with Woodson Wood, the commonwealth attorney, to get the charge dropped to voluntary manslaughter. Woody finally agreed that he'd let him off for ten years. I said, "No, that's too much time. This poor fellow can't stand that." So we went to trial, and I think I cried a little and all, and got him off with a three-year sentence.

John H. Clarke, Maysville, February 20, 2002

100. "Was It a Bird or a Bush?"

Daniel Boone Smith, the commonwealth attorney here in Harlan County, was prosecuting a defendant for shooting Ancil Bush, while sitting on his front porch. The constable in charge of the investigation soon found a shotgun leaning up against a tree in the vicinity of Mr. Bush's house. Upon opening and smelling the breech, he found that it had been recently fired. He went on to trace the ownership of the gun, and found that the gun belonged to the defendant, who had personal reasons to want to see Bush dispatched. The defendant was indicted and, in the course of the trial, Daniel Boone approached the defendant and asked him, "Is this your shotgun?"

"Yes, it is," the fellow said.

"Did you own the gun and did you have it with you on the day that Ancil Bush was murdered?"

"Yes, sir," said the defendant.

Daniel Boone asked him, "Did you fire the shotgun that day?"

The fellow responded, "Yes, sir."

Then Daniel Boone asked him, "What did you fire at?"

He said, "I thought I saw a bird and I just shot it into a bush."

Daniel Boone just grinned, tossed his head in the air, and asked, "Are you sure that wasn't Ancil Bush?"

He was finally convicted of the killing.

Eugene Goss, Harlan, May 22, 2002

101. "LAW IN A NUTSHELL"

. . . I went over to a county adjacent to Rowan and had a jury trial in which my client was an elderly man accused of shooting a young fellow. And as the state and the evidence would have it, he professed that he shot this fellow in self-defense. Unfortunately the fellow got shot in the back, which is always troubling for self-defense cases. However, my client articulated during the trial that the fellow had come over to this garage and beat him up and, in fact, was coming back to beat him some more. When he drew this gun, and the very moment he decided to fire, the fellow winced and turned, and that's how he got shot in the back.

This older fellow was a delightful fellow. We put that case on the best we could. He had no prior criminal history—was just a good old boy. I tried that case, and lo and behold the jury found him not guilty. Of course, he was elated; he was in tears. He was jumping up and down—gave me a big hug. I don't know that I was such an egotist that I had something to do with it but I was really feeling good about what we had accomplished. The jurors are an awful bunch because they're so doggone realistic. This juror walked up and said, "Don't get too full of yourself. That boy he shot is a bootlegger and he's been nothing but trouble, and he's just terrorized this entire community, and frankly he just needed shooting. And we weren't going to find your guy guilty, no matter what was said." I was certainly deflated, because I knew that my fine, articulate closing argument had no bearing whatsoever on the verdict. They were logged onto letting this fellow go before I even walked in the door.

So I guess that's law in a nutshell.

Keith McCormick, Morehead, June 22, 2000

8

BLUNDERS

Legal professionals do the same thing day after day, much like persons who work in machine shops; thus, because courtroom proceedings are routine, judges and lawyers rarely commit blunders in court. However, those professionals who have never previously served as a judge, defense lawyer, or prosecutor often make errors, some of which are downright humorous to those witnessing them. As the following stories show, even seasoned courtroom participants occasionally commit laughable mistakes.

102. "OOPS, THE JUDGE BLUNDERS IN COURT"

Judge Winn was a pretty rough acting fellow. He was a pretty good judge, but he could be kind of rough, too. We were over here in court, and there had been a fellow that came two or three days before that from Campton. He was a crippled fellow, named Roberts, in a wheelchair. He had some kind of case and was back the second time.

Judge Winn knew who he was but he couldn't place a name on him. Well, I was up at the bench conducting business with him, and the judge asked me, "Who's the old gentleman in the wheelchair?"

I said, "That's Mr. Roberts from Campton." So the judge kind of nodded his head, and I said, "But don't get him mixed up with Ironsides on television." When I said that, I started back to my seat.

About that time, I heard Judge Winn say, "Mr. Ironsides—er, I mean Mr. Roberts."

Several other lawyers were huddled at the end of the bench and they turned around and looked, and finally they realized or understood what had happened. The court reporter, who was a good friend of mine, and who traveled around with the judge, accused me of setting him up!

Old Judge Winn recovered pretty quickly though, and I don't think the old crippled man ever realized what the judge had said. He just wheeled his chair up there and took care of his business.

Asa R. Little Jr., Frenchburg, November 26, 2001

103. "Lawyers Overcome Judge's Decision"

I have practiced law since 1948, and in my long career, I guess on more than one occasion I should have been sent to jail for contempt of court because of the things that I might say to a judge to try to block his way of thinking or his ruling.

I recall a specific case many years ago when I was county attorney. J. Douglas Graham was the commonwealth attorney. The Lion's Club at Clay City had a drawing. They were giving away a car and a rifle. There was a man from Winchester whose last name was Reed, and he was the announcer down at the racetrack. So what they did, they had this little girl about ten or twelve years old go over and reach her hand in a drum and take out a ticket, and take it across the stage to this track announcer, who then read the name and the number. Well, by George, when he read the name and the number, it was his daughter.

Well, the Lion's Club got to thinking about it, and they said that there's something rotten about this. So, they started looking into it, and refused to give Reed's daughter the car because they said that he had switched the tickets—that he palmed the ticket of his daughter and read it instead of the one that the little girl took to him. So they refused to give the car to her.

The track announcer and his daughter sued the Lion's Club. J. Douglas Graham and I were representing the Lion's Club. And this track announcer [Reed] came in with a bunch of witnesses.

At the close of his testimony, Judge Irvin Turner said, "I've heard all the evidence I want to hear, and I'm going to award this car to the plaintiff."

Well, I hit the floor and said, "Judge, are you not going to hear our side at all?"

He said, "No. I've decided that I'm going to enter a judgment for the plaintiff."

And I said, "Judge, do you realize that you're entering a judgment on false and perjured testimony? Do you realize that that's what you are doing?"

Well, of course, he kind of hit the ceiling, and he told the foreman of the grand jury, who was an old man named John Chaney, a good friend of mine, told him to come up there. The judge wrote out a little verdict giving the car to the Reeds, and said, "Now you sign this."

Well, John said, "I would like to hear the rest of this case, Judge, for I've heard some things that I don't like about signing in favor of the Reeds."

The judge said, "Sign."

Well, Chaney didn't know what his rights were, and he thought if a judge said to sign, you had to sign, so he signed. Then I said, "Judge, I wish you wouldn't do this."

And he said, "I've made up my mind."

Then I said, "No, Judge, I'm not going to let you do this." About that time, Doug, who was sitting there beside me, jumped up and started telling the judge why he shouldn't do it, and I said, "Judge, you have my solemn word that this is perjured testimony—that you are giving this car away, and if you'll just let us put on our side of the case, we'll prove it."

The judge looked at me and said, "You are county attorney aren't you?"

I said, "Yes sir."

He said, "If these people have perjured themselves in this case, why didn't you go before the grand jury and indict them?"

I said, "Judge, they just perjured themselves an hour ago, but I'll tell you one thing, if you leave this open until tomorrow, I'll have a special grand jury in here and I think I can assure you that they'll indict Mr. Reed and every one of his witnesses."

He said, "I'm going to go ahead."

I said, "No, you are not. I don't think you should. I don't think I should let you." And Doug kept digging in there, too.

Doug Graham and I had been on opposite sides in a case that involved a whole community. I was representing the state board that claimed to own this church building, and Doug was representing the community that claimed it should be theirs, I guess by possessory rights. It had been in their community all these years, and they had used it for whatever purpose they wanted to use it.

Anyway, the judge says, "This is the end of this case."

About that time, poor old Mr. Chaney jumped up and said, "Judge, that's really not my verdict, and I would appreciate it if you would let me take my name off of it. That's not the way I see this case."

The judge said, "You signed it and that's the way it's going to be."

Then I said, "Well, Judge, you've got to do something about this. You cannot do this. It's not right. It's not just."

The judge then said, "Well, Sheriff, take John [lawyer]."

And just about that time, Doug Graham got in again digging at the judge. So the judge sent us both to jail.

The next day, we empaneled a special grand jury and sure enough, just as we thought, they indicted Reed and all his witnesses for perjury. We thought we knew what had taken place, because it [the actual winning ticket] was absent from the drum. The name that had actually been drawn out by the little girl was a lady whose name was Steele, who lived down here on the river below town. So the grand jury returned the indictment. And when we went back in the courtroom, the judge . . . to say that his face was red, boy, when he saw all these indictments and realized that I had been telling the truth, and that he had been misled by this other crowd. Well, he was embarrassed—didn't hardly know what to do. And the plaintiffs were represented by a very capable attorney named Rowady, from Winchester. He saw that if his clients went to trial on that charge in this county, they were in real big trouble: big trouble. So he went up before the judge before we could say anything and in lawyer talk said, "Now, Judge, we are not admitting any wrongdoing, but I think a way to amicably settle this case would be to give Mrs. Steele the automobile, or whoever the Lion's Club says owns it, and, in return, let them dismiss their indictments against us."

The judge thought a minute and I guess he thought, "Well, this is a good way out of an embarrassing situation." He looked over at us and said, "Well, what do you fellows say about it?"

We went back to talk to two or three of the Lion's Club members of Clay City, and they said, "Well, all we really wanted was for Mrs. Steele to have the car. We don't especially want to see these people go to jail, so if you all want to do that, do it."

So that's how the case was concluded. The rightful person got the car, and the people who lied about the car got their cases dismissed.

John L. Cox Jr., Stanton, November 26, 2001

104. "Marijuana Found in Purse"

One time I was defending a lady for shoplifting. She supposedly had stolen two packs of Virginia Slim cigarettes by sticking them in her purse. She had bought eighty-five dollars worth of groceries, and she went out. Of course, the security people grabbed her and brought her back in. They charged her with theft. Her purse was rather large, and I had asked her to bring it to court. During the trial, I put her on the witness stand and qualified her by asking, "Is this yours? Has this purse continuously been in your possession? Is this the same purse that you had then? Has anybody else had this purse in the meantime?" Of course, the answer was no.

So I qualified her, then asked the clerk to mark the purse as the defendant's exhibit number 1. And before I had to provide evidence, I took the purse over to the prosecutor and asked him, "Would you like to look at this purse?"

He then opens this rather large purse. The woman who was being charged for theft was in her early twenties. He opens the purse, and the jury is sitting right there in front of him. He reaches way down inside the purse and pulls the zipper to this little pocket there in the purse. He says, "Ken, look here." And he pulls out a marijuana joint rolled up in a piece of cellophane. So, I grabbed the purse and said, "Your Honor, I move this purse be admitted into evidence."

The judge says, "So admitted."

So, then we asked for in-camera [in the judge's chambers] conference and went back there, laughing so hard.

This is a story about where you can pull defeat from the jaws of victory. The jury acquitted her on the charge of shoplifting, but I had to plead her guilty on the possession of marijuana.

As a follow-up to all that, one of the observers in the courtroom had spread a rumor around town that the prosecutor had found a joint in a defendant's purse in the courtroom, and immediately the judge, the defense lawyer, and the prosecutor went back in the judge's chamber and smoked it!

That's a true story. We didn't smoke it, but that was the rumor.

Ken S. Dean, Madisonville, April 15, 2002

105. "Judge Mistakenly Calls Ex-Wife While in Court"

I'll tell you a funny story on myself. I was sitting on the bench when I had a domestic violence case in court. I got them to put a telephone in because you feel isolated up there, and sometimes you need to call to find out why the sheriff hasn't got somebody there, or whatever.

The violence case was about this lady who had come to the clerk and accused her boyfriend or husband of striking her. The sheriff served this fellow, and he was supposed to be in court. I called the case, and he came up but she was not there. She had been given the court date. She started all this procedure and accused him, but she's not in court.

I'm always nervous about cases like that, because maybe she has been intimidated not to be there. And I also get a little upset that somebody would swear out something against somebody and accuse them of something, then not have the backbone to come up there and see the thing through. That's just an easy way to slander somebody. Maybe he didn't do it. I don't know. But he's denied the opportunity of either being cleared or being heard.

I can get a little testy sometimes and have to watch my temper. So I decided to just call her. Where is she? Had to get her phone number out of the file and call and ask her why she wasn't in court.

A lot of times, they'll say, "I just forgot. I'll be right there." Then we'd go ahead with it. And if she was in danger, we'd issue the protective order to protect her as best we could.

Anyway, this lady that was to be in court didn't show up. So I picked up the phone and got this lady's number, then dialed it. She answered the phone, and I said, "This is Judge Billingsley, and I'd like to know why you're not in court today." And this lady yelled at me, "I don't have to put up with your shit anymore," then slammed the phone down.

I was stunned, so I looked at that number and recalled the number I had dialed. I had dialed my ex-wife!! The number was just one digit different, and I had dialed my ex-wife. I thought, "Oh, my God."

I said aloud, "My god, that was my ex-wife," and everybody in court started laughing at me. It was awful. I had to call her and her husband and apologize and explain everything. Of all the numbers in the world to call, I did it! So I've been very reluctant to pick up the telephone in front of a crowd anymore.

Stan Billingsley, Carrollton, March 20, 2001

106. "Sheriff Mistakenly Enters Jury Room"

As an attorney having practiced in Jamestown for thirty years, there are various things that we tell about the courthouse. Courthouse stories I guess you would call them. This particular one that I'm about to tell about, I was present and experienced it. It is a story of "no-no's" that don't go on about court. On this particular occasion, a felony case was being tried in Russell Circuit Court. We had a new sheriff, who had only been in office about a month. As the law requires, and as is the practice, after the summation of all evidence and closing arguments, the court swears the sheriff. He administers an oath to this effect: "You do solemnly swear that you will take this jury; you will keep them; you will suffer no man to speak to them, and you will not do so yourself."

This oath was administered to the young sheriff, and he took the jury to the jury room. Shortly thereafter, we were just sitting around waiting for the verdict. I wandered out into the hall to get me a drink. I went by the jury room door, and there was no one guarding the jury. I slipped back in and told the deputy, who was an older man, that nobody was guarding the jury.

"Oh, yes there is."

I said, "No, there's not. I've just been out there, and there's nobody out there in the hall guarding the jury."

He said, "Oh, the sheriff is in the jury room with the jury."

I said, "Oh, surely he's not."

Well, I go up to the bench and tell the judge that the sheriff is in the room with the jury.

He told me, "Go out there and knock on the door and tell them to come in."

The judge would never embarrass anybody. So he lined the jury up. The jury had been out about fifteen minutes. He said, "Now, you all have been out quite a spell. It appears like you are not going to be able to reach a verdict. So I will just dismiss you."

The minute that the jury turned and left, I said to the sheriff, "What were you doing in that jury room?"

He said, "Well, the judge told me to go with them, and I thought he meant go in the jury room with them." He said, "I didn't bother them. I was just setting in there listening to them, and I kind of enjoyed hearing them arguing in there."

Lige Coffey, Russell Springs, July 11, 1988

107. "Facing the Courtroom Audience"

When I was a young lawyer, I started practicing law with Dave Frances

and Henry Potter, and Dave was very active in state politics at that time
. . . , and was appointed by Governor Combs as chairman of the Public
Service Commission. John Breckenridge had just been elected attorney general.

Back then, people from Edmonson County always got into disputes about the school system. Well, school was about to begin, and
they were concerned that one of the school board members was selling
green beans to the cafeteria. There's a statutory prohibition against any
board member to sell things to the school system, since it may be a
conflict of interest. So, the group that thought that was totally improper
for him to do that came to see Dave Frances and Henry Potter. Well,
Frances and Potter didn't want to handle the case, so they delegated it
to me.

Well, I kind of got the thing fired up, and Tom Duncan, who was
a reporter for the *Courier-Journal,* lived up the street from me here in
Bowling Green. He became interested in the case, so I was invited to
go see John Breckenridge, who was attorney general. He had to file a
suit to oust the school board member, and there's a procedure called
the quo warranto procedure, whereby the attorney general can designate somebody to file the action on his behalf. So Breckenridge desig-
nated me to file this action against the school board member so as to
have him ousted. Well, that was in August, and it was about time for
school to start. So, I filed the action, and it made the front page of the
Courier-Journal. Our purpose was to eliminate all sorts of educational
sins in Edmonson County by reason of this school board member selling green beans to the cafeteria. Well, because of what was taking place,
they delayed the opening of school. We had a big hearing over there. It
was about the first hearing I'd ever been to like that, and there was a
motion before Judge Bratcher. Well, three lawyers, who were Bev
[Vincent], Charlie Whittle, and Bill Logan, were on the other side. I
was over there virtually by myself. The courtroom was just packed.
Most of them had walking canes and were walking around the courtroom with their canes. Judge Bratcher was on the bench, and somebody made some remarks. It came time for me to argue my motion,
and I turned around and argued the motion to the audience rather than
to the court. Well, Judge Bratcher obviously ruled against me and said,
"This is the first time I've ever been on the bench and saw nothing but
the back of a lawyer when he was arguing the motion."

Charles English, Bowling Green, May 27, 2002

108. "Some Good and Bad News"

A somewhat bombastic Hazard lawyer once told his client, a person who was there to obtain workers' compensation, "I've got good news for you. I just read your doctor's report and you are totally disabled."

His client responded, "That might be good news to you, sir, but it isn't very good news to me and my family."

Eugene Goss, Harlan, May 22, 2002

109. "Oops, the Jury Makes a Mistake"

A wonderful storyteller here in Paducah had a wonderful deep bass voice. His name was Adrian Terrell, and his son is practicing here now and is a good friend of mine. Mr. Terrell tells that when he got out of law school, as when I did, much, much later, we did not have the public defender system, so lawyers use to get appointed to defend people who could not afford a lawyer. And so he had defended this man who had allegedly stolen a watch.

Apparently, he defended him successfully, and the jury came back and reported him not guilty. Then, the accused turned to his defense lawyer, Mr. Terrell, and said, "Mr. Terrell, does that mean that I can keep the watch?"

Richard Roberts, Paducah, November 2, 2001

110. "Lawyer Goes Running Back into the Courtroom"

One of the favorite stories lawyers like to tell is about Judge Ed Johnstone, a wonderful judge, back when he was trying cases as a lawyer, not as a judge. They were under the rule of separation of witnesses; that is to say, the witnesses do not hear the testimony so they can't contrive their story to fit with what else is said. And when the witness is under the rule, of course, you're not supposed to tell them what was said.

Well, there was a little break, and Ed had gone out in the hall and was talking with one of the witnesses out there waiting to testify, when court resumed and he hadn't gotten back to the courtroom yet. It was bad enough he was talking to the witness. Waddell was the judge and he ran a tight courtroom. He used to call for order in court by thumping the eraser-end of a pencil. That's how tight the courtroom was under Judge Waddell.

Anyway, Ed had been out talking to this witness when court was resumed, and with a disgusted voice, the judge turned to the bailiff and says, "Go out and get Mr. Johnstone." About that time, Ed came running into court and was zipping up his pants!

Ed is still living in Princeton. He was a great judge because none of the lawyers could ever do anything that he personally had not done. Of course, he is a friend of lawyers, too. He is a good judge to practice in front of. He is most recently a United States district judge. Before that, he was circuit judge for Livingston, Lyon, Caldwell, and Trigg counties.

Richard Roberts, Paducah, November 2, 2001

111. "POPULARITY OF STUMPY THE LAWYER"

Our present United States district judge is a former partner of mine whose name is Tom Russell. He is being a great judge. He made his reputation as a great, great trial lawyer with a wonderful personality. His personality was so good that it disguised the fact that he was also a very fine scholar, but that was downplayed with it. Tom is not a very tall person, and his nickname from his freshman year in college through today is Stumpy. He uses that in a manner so as to make himself popular and liked. So it was ordinary to call him Stumpy.

One day he was trying a case in front of Judge Lassiter over at Murray, and there was a need for the lawyers to come up to the bench and talk to the judge. Judge Lassiter just sort of leaned over and said without intention, just because it became natural, "Stumpy, will you and Mr. Avastock approach the bench?"

That shows how well accepted he was, even in court. That was in front of a jury!

Richard Roberts, Paducah, November 2, 2001

112. "JUDGE SOMETIMES FELL ASLEEP"

I used to hear stories about a judge who was off the bench when I started practicing law. It was always told around town that he would get off the bench and sit at the table occasionally with the attorney and his client during a trial.

He was also always accused of falling asleep during trials. Luckily, he was off the bench before I got here, and luckily we don't have judges who fall asleep anymore.

Sue Brammer, Maysville, February 20, 2002

113. "Jurors Need Weapon Information"

It's customary in cases that we'd have, and it is now required by law, that you ask the judge to give certain instructions to the jury. We had a case in Newport, and Judge Swinford was in this one. He took great pride in instructing the jury off the top of his head. He would just write on a piece of yellow paper and outline his instructions. And he would just talk to the jury. I've never seen a judge do it before or since, but he was very brilliant in doing it. One case that he was involved in was when this person had a sawed-off shotgun. He told the jury, "Now, ladies and gentlemen of the jury, this shotgun in this case is nothing but a gangster weapon, and it's illegal." He hadn't told the jury what kind of length the gun was supposed to be, or anything about the gun. He just said, "It's illegal and gangsters carry those, and they can't be carried."

That was all the information he gave to the jury. I said to myself, "Oh, my goodness, we're going to have to start asking for jury instructions about gun sizes." But it worked out, as we didn't get reversed in that case.

The decision in that case was a hung jury, and the next time we came around to trying that case, I made sure that we had instructions that told the length of the barrel and to keep out of the "gangster weapon" sort of thing.

Eugene Siler Jr., London, June 20, 2002

114. "Man Mistakenly Sits in a Juror's Seat"

One of the most unusual stories I've heard in a jury trial was told to me by a circuit court clerk over in Marshall County, whose name was Toad Brien. Toad had been in the courthouse for many, many years when I talked to him about this story. He was both county court clerk and circuit court clerk. He was kind of an institution. I don't think he was ever beaten in elections. He died about five or six years ago.

He told me that they were trying a case over there in Marshall County one time—a big, high visibility case, probably a murder case. The courtroom was packed full of people. Of course, everybody was maneuvering around for a good seat. They had a recess, and the jury came back. They were sitting in their seats, but Toad looked at one of them but didn't recognize him. He went to the judge and said, "Judge, I think we've got a juror that's not supposed to be sitting there. You'd better call the roll."

So the judge interrupted the proceedings and said, "We're going to call the roll of the jury." Well, when he called the name of one of the jurors, this man answered from way back in the courtroom. The judge says, "Sir, what are you doing sitting back there?"

This fellow said, "Well, when I came back from the break, somebody had my seat."

As it turned out, this guy that came in during the break saw this empty seat there, and he thought, "Well, yeah, I've got a good front-row seat," so he just climbed in the jury box and was sitting there watching the trial.

That story shows just how polite some people are. See, this juror came back, but since somebody had his seat he just went to the back of the courtroom. However, that was indeed an unusual episode.

Bill Cunningham, Eddyville, January 21, 2002

115. "Humorously Mistaken Wording"

I've got two stories that wind up in a way that ties them together, so here goes. There's a black church that was into it, and the members kind of divided, and they had a lawsuit among themselves.

The preacher, who probably weighed three hundred pounds and over six feet tall, was on one side.

Of course, I always read the file. You had to read that. In other words, I knew the case before I went to try it. So when I got over there, I called the lawyer and said, "This case needs settling," and I told him how it ought to be settled. There were four or five lawyers, and one of them objected. So I told him, "You'll have to settle it."

So he told me, "If you tell me to, I'll tell them to settle it."

Well, he went out, talked to them, and they settled it. The lawyers came back and said that it was settled. Of course, the courtroom was full of black people—just a sea of them. So, I walked into the courtroom and had court called to order. They called the jury in and everything. I told the people there in the courtroom, "This case has been settled."

That big black preacher stood up, threw his hands up in the air, and yelled out, "Praise the Lord. The Lord's been here today."

And there I sat, like I was the Lord.

The next part of this story is about a fellow who referred to himself as a Mexican American. But I told him that there were no Mexican Americans, that he was either Mexican or American. And I don't know why people refer to themselves, or tolerate being referred to, as Jewish American, or African American, Italian American. You are either an American, or you're not. If you are American, you are entitled to the same privileges as every other American, no less or no more.

But the rest of the story is about this fellow with the name of Jesus. I learned since then that it is pronounced "Hay-suce," but didn't know it at the time. Anyway, he was charged with something and was sitting out there in the crowd. They handed me the indictment, and I says [using the Biblical pronunciation], "Jesus, approach the bench."

So he got up and came up to the bench and stood there in front of me, and I read the indictment to him, then entered a plea of "not guilty" for him, so that he could get himself a lawyer.

Well, there was some lawyer from Louisville. After that, I recessed court, and this lawyer from Louisville was out there in the hallway. There was another lawyer out there in the hall with him. The lawyer from Louisville says, "I have a new experience every time I come down here. Today, I saw God arraign Jesus!!"

Kenneth Goff, Leitchfield, May 8, 2002

9

MISUNDERSTANDINGS

Although many of the lawyers and judges interviewed are superb story-tellers who can express themselves clearly, they often must use legal terminology that average citizens do not fully understand. Some of the more humorous stories in this book are the result of witnesses, plaintiffs, defendants, jurors, and others who either misunderstood what was being said or tried to speak in what they considered to be proper "legalese."

116. "GRANDMA'S QUILTS"

The funniest story that comes to my mind involves an estate case that I had about fifteen years ago. This lady died and she really had no assets of any value other than Grandma's quilts. She had eight or ten of her grandma's quilts, and I was explaining to my executrix of the estate that she had a duty to preserve and protect the estate. She told me that all the quilts had disappeared and that she couldn't find anybody that would own up to it if they had any of them.

So I said, "The only thing that I know to do is that we'll just issue a subpoena, and I'll have all five children to come in to court. I'll put them under oath and ask them whether or not they have any of Grandma's quilts."

The first lady I put on the stand, I said, "Mrs. Smith, do you have any of Grandma's quilts?"

She says, "I refuse to answer based on the Fifth Commandment."

To this day, I don't remember if I ever went back to see if it was "Honor thy father and mother" or "Thou shalt not steal," or whatever it was.

The judge assured her that the Fifth Commandment didn't prevent her from having to answer the question. Well, sure enough, all the quilts were subsequently delivered to my office. She at least knew where they were and got them under her control.

Joe Evans III, Madisonville, July 28, 2000

117. "GUILTY PERSON MISUNDERSTANDS JURY VERDICT"

This happened over in Cumberland County years ago before my knowings. I don't know the boy's last name, but his name was Billy, and this was told to me by some of the lawyers in Burkesville as absolute truth. And I believe it to be true, even though it's one of these court tales that has been stretched.

Billy lived way out in the country, and neither he nor his family ever came to town. He got charged with a minor theft case out in the county. Maybe he stole some hams of meat, or something like that, at this country storehouse. He was brought to town and they tried him in court.

The prosecuting attorney was a Hurt, who was a great big tall fellow from Columbia. He had a booming voice. As they were trying Billy, he kept referring to him as "Little Billy here." He'd point toward him and in a big voice tell the jury, said, "We've got to get rid of people like Little Billy here. We don't need people out here stealing our stuff." Well, just on and on and on he talked about Little Billy and how they had to get rid of him. As it come to the close of the case, the jury retired. Billy was scared to death. You could see him shaking as he sat there at the table, saying nothing.

When the jury came back, this pretty large fellow that was foreman of the jury likewise had a big voice. The judge asked if the jury reached a verdict, and the foreman stood up and said, "Your Honor, please, this is a hung jury."

Billy was just sure that meant they were going to hang him, so he jumps up from his seat and says, "You'll never hang Old Billy." He ran out of the courthouse and kept running. It took them several weeks to ever find him up in the hills. They explained to him that he wasn't going to be hung, but he was sure that he was.

A lot of these stories are about people out in the country who are just as intelligent as people with big intelligence, but have no education and no experience with the court system.

Robert L. Wilson, Jamestown, April 19, 2002

118. "COMPENSATED, BUT NOT COMPREHENDED"

Before I became an attorney, I was a policeman in Louisville. We worked with this fellow from Frankfort, who was truly from the country. His name was Keeton. And he had an accent that was really hard for everybody to understand. He was a witness in a case, and an attorney had called him up and was talking to him on the phone. We were all standing around the Adam District Station House, which is the east end of Louisville over by the river.

We were at the station house, and of course it's built in a big octagon around the station man's desk. From the phone on that desk is where he received this phone call from the attorney. I tried to arrange to take his deposition about an accident he had worked.

Sgt. Ed Brote was standing there. He was a very nice man—a former state policeman; very trim, very tall. He was standing there listening to all the goings-on. Back then, you were allowed to pay the officer an honorarium to give these depositions, if it was not during his regular work shift. I forget what it was, but maybe it was fifty dollars if you had to come in on an off-day.

I'll never forget how awful his language was. He just came right out on the phone and said, "Now this is my off-day, and I want to know if I come down there to your office, will I be comprehended?"

Of course, we all started to snicker and carry on. The sergeant said, "Keeton, you may be paid for this testimony, but you will never be comprehended."

That's a true account. He thought he was going to be *compensated*.

Keith McCormick, Morehead, June 22, 2000

119. "LADY MISUNDERSTANDS WORD"

I had this lady come in my law office one afternoon. She was an older lady, not really elderly, but probably in her fifties. She told me that she had gone home, and that she and her neighbors shared a driveway there at their houses. Well, when she got to the house, there was a caution tape up across her driveway, and a sign that said *No trespassing. Violators will be prostituted.*

So she had come to see me to find out what she could do about that sign! That really happened.

Melanie A. Rolley, Madisonville, April 15, 2002

120. "Male Juror Needs to Go Home"

I think it was Mac Swinford who told this story but I don't think it is in his book, *Kentucky Lawyers*. He told about jurors being intimidated sometimes—not apt to speak up fully. Sometimes, even when they do, they try to elevate their vocabulary to match the surroundings.

So they were trying this case back years ago when a wife of one of the jurors was about ready to give birth. Back then, they'd say, "She's about ready to be confined." So the judge asked, "Is there any reason why any of you cannot serve on this jury?"

Her husband raised his hand, said, "Judge, my wife is about ready to conceive."

He meant to say confined. I'm sure everybody laughed about that, especially when the judge said, "I'm going to excuse you because if there was ever a time that a man needs to be at home, it's right now."

Bill Cunningham, Eddyville, January 21, 2002

121. "Oops! Misunderstanding"

This is a story about legal vocabulary and everybody trying to understand it. They were trying this case up in the mountains during real cold weather. The doctor that was to testify in the case was called out on an obstetrics call. So, they all recessed and were standing around this pot-bellied stove waiting for the doctor to get back, just having general conversation. One juror said, "Where is the doctor, anyway?"

Someone said, "Well, he had to go out on an obstetrics call."

A juror said, "Yeah, if this weather doesn't clear up, we're all going to catch it."

Bill Cunningham, Eddyville, January 21, 2002

122. "Illiterate Husband Misunderstands the Judge"

One of the early cases in which I was involved here in Powell County was one in which the county attorney was on the other side, although it was a divorce case being tried in the Powell Circuit Court. He was acting outside his official duties as county attorney. The couple in the divorce case was named Dick Randall and Pearl Randall. Many stories are told in and around Stanton about their relationships and the funny things that happened between them in interactions.

In this particular case, I was representing Dick, and Mr. Strange, who was then county attorney, was representing Pearl. Dick was a middle-aged illiterate man who had never gone past the second or third grade in school, and he worked as a farm day-laborer, and this has been many years ago. I guess his average pay per day would be something in the neighborhood of five to seven dollars, and he worked five days a week. So, he would make thirty-five to forty dollars a week.

The problem was that he and Pearl had about ten or twelve children. Well, when the judge got ready to try this divorce case in open court, like they used to do in those days, after hearing the evidence and arguments of counsel on both sides, the judge said, "Dick, I realize that you are a poor man. I realize that you cannot pay this woman much, even though you've got a whole bunch of kids here. So, I'll tell you what I'm going to do. I estimate that you make about $30 a week, so what I'm going to do is give Pearl $15 a week for support of these children."

Dick clapped his hands enthusiastically and said, "Thank you, Judge, thank you, and I'll try to help them a little myself."

John L. Cox Jr., Stanton, November 26, 2001

123. "THE TINY ORGASM"

We worked on a law case for a lady out in a little town called Farmers, Kentucky. She had gotten into it with her husband. Things had broken down between them, and ended up with her shooting him. After that, he was referred to as "Geppy."

We went to interview her. I was working at the time with this wonderful trial attorney whose name is Patricia Van Houk. She is a real character. We went and interviewed this woman, and we were getting a social history—who she was married to and how it all ended up.

As we were taking this history down, she told us that this one man was her first husband. It was the man that she was shot with, though, that she considered to be her first lover. She had had sex with her first husband but she had never had an organism. Well, Patricia and I laughed till we cried!

When we went outside, I said to Patricia, "Patricia, just exactly what is an organism?"

She said, "You know, that's a really tiny orgasm."

Keith McCormick, Morehead, June 22, 2000

124. "Charged for Sodomon"

I got a call from Mrs. B.———, who said, "Larry, you've got to go over to the jail and get my boy, Eugene, out."

I said, "What's he in there for?"

She said, "I believe they got him for sodomon."

I said, "What in the world is sodomon?"

She said, "I believe they said he fumbled a girl."

I said, "Well, I fumbled every one of them I've tried to fool with, so I believe I can help you."

Lawrence Webster, Pikeville, November 9, 2000

125. "Cartridges in the Knee"

I had a client here in Harlan who received a work-related injury to one of his knees. He came by my office one morning, and I asked him how his knee was progressing. He replied, "Lord God, Goss, I was out to see the doctor yisterdy and he told me that them cartridges in my knee was all blowed, and my propeller had a hickey under it."

Now, that's just the way he said it! Actually, the doctor told him it was his patella [kneecap] bone, but he thought the doctor said his propeller was blown.

Eugene Goss, Harlan, May 22, 2002

126. "Court Flea Bargain"

Mark D. Goss, a Harlan lawyer, inquired of his client who was accused of a felony, "What would you consider to be a favorable resolution in your case when it goes to court?"

The client looked at him rather seriously and responded, "I would like for you to flea bargain it down to a demeanary."

Eugene Goss, Harlan, May 22, 2002

127. "Driving with Contacts"

A driver was pulled over to the side of the road by a constable and accused of reckless driving. Noticing that the driver's operating license required him to wear glasses while operating a motor vehicle, the officer asked him, "Why aren't you wearing your glasses?"

The driver responded, "But, sir, I have contacts."

The constable replied, "I don't give a damn who you know, I'm still givin' you a ticket."

Eugene Goss, Harlan, May 22, 2002

128. "Common Jail Food"

A well-known Harlan County prostitute was being incarcerated in the Harlan County jail. In the process of being locked up, she protested and said, "I can't go in there."

The jailer replied, "Susie, there is a warrant out on you, and I've got to put you in. Go on in there."

Susie then protested with these words, "If I am going to go in there, you'll have to get me a box of Kotex."

The jailer replied to her and said, "Hell no, Susie, you'll eat Post Toasties like all the rest."

Eugene Goss, Harlan, May 22, 2002

129. "Juror's Misunderstanding"

After several days of trial, the jury was having difficulty deciding the guilt of the defendant, who was accused of the crime of perjury. One old fellow on the jury had listened intently to the evidence and to the jury deliberation, but had not uttered one word during the deliberation. One distraught juror looked over at him and asked, "Uncle Ed, what do you think we ought to do?"

Ed said, "Well, I think he ought to be made to take the child and keep it!"

Eugene Goss, Harlan, May 22, 2002

130. "Politically Savvy Document"

I had a client one time who was a real character. She told me she knew the paper she had was legal because it was signed by a "notorized republican."

I won't call her by name, but her first name was America. She was a great lady.

Forrest Roberts, Owensboro, June 7, 2002

131. "Judge's Word Misunderstood"

A Harlan man was accused in federal court in the early 1940s of unlawfully charging veterans for services rendered. His brother was called as a witness against him by the government prosecutor. After taking the stand, he turned to Judge Church Ford and said pitifully, "Judge, I ain't got no education and this is my brother they're tryin' to send to jail. I'm an ignorant man, and I'm afraid they'll cross me up."

The judge replied, "Sir, I won't let them take any advantage of you, so just tell the truth as you know it and everything will be all right." The brother nodded, feeling very comforted.

The prosecutor said, after establishing the brother's identity, "It is alleged in the indictment that one . . ."

Upon hearing the word "one," the brother rose slightly from his chair and looked defiantly at the judge and complained, "See, Judge, he's already throwin' that shorthand at me."

Eugene Goss, Harlan, May 22, 2002

132. "Breathtaking Federal Court Appearance"

Especially in days gone by, courts were more informal here than even they are today. And they were extremely more informal than they were in federal court. There used to be a wonderful judge in Bowling Green whose name was Mac Swinford. Judge Mac was one of the most stern-looking fellows I've ever seen. He had a red face, and his eyebrows were real thick and as white as snow. His hair was just snow white. He sat up on a rather high bench. In fact I've argued cases before the Supreme Court of the United States, and their benches were not as high as his was, nor as impressive looking. It was therefore a bit scary and a bit intimidating to go into his courts.

I went over there once, and there was this little fellow standing before Judge Swinford. The way they would arraign someone, they'd ask the clerk to read out the charges. This clerk kept reading and reading and reading, "The United States vs. Ethan Jones." Jones was a black man.

The clerk went on and on and on. It took forever to read the charges. There were fifteen to twenty charges: "The United States vs. Ethan Jones." When the clerk got through, the judge looked down, looked over his glasses, said very slowly, "Mr. Jones, how do you plead to these charges?"

Ethan looked up at him, said, "Well, Judge, I was going to plead not guilty, but if the whole United States of America is agin me, I guess I'd better plead guilty."

Well, that straightened him out.

Robert L. Wilson, Jamestown, April 19, 2002

133. "WOMAN MISUNDERSTANDS COURT CHARGE"

We seemed to have gotten a lot of interesting cases out of Clay and Leslie counties. In this one case from Leslie County, a man and his wife were charged with growing marijuana in a field. They found one of these assault weapons that was made in China out there by the marijuana. Of course, that enhances the sentence if you get a possession of a firearm involved in a drug trafficking offense. So, they were charged.

I was the judge in this case, and the prosecuting attorney had them on the stand. They denied knowing anything about the marijuana patch in the first place and denied knowing anything about the assault weapon in the second place. Come to find out, they had bought it at a store there in Hyden, and so the prosecuting attorney asked this woman on the stand, "Well, now, you and your husband also bought that Chinese assault weapon, and you had it out there in the field?"

The woman said, "No, you've got it all wrong. We never salted no Chinese; we never saw no Chinese out there."

So, she missed the whole point as to what the charge was all about.

Eugene Siler Jr., London, June 20, 2002

10

UNEXPECTED RESPONSES

Skilled trial lawyers are particularly adept at examining witnesses on the stand in an effort to uncover the truth. Unexpected responses to their questions can make the task enormously difficult and occasionally very humorous. As the first story in this category reveals, judges also sometimes receive funny responses to their questions.

134. "SHERIFF'S RESPONSE TO THE JUDGE"

My cousin Wendell Wilson is a great big fellow, about six foot six, good looking, has a big smile, and a wonderful personality. During his first race for political office, he made a door-to-door campaign. He'd never been in the courtroom. He was elected sheriff and won by quite a landslide against a very powerful political family at that time—the Gaskins family.

The first time Wendell was in court, he demonstrated to me his innate intelligence, although he had no experience. We had this young fellow up in court who had been convicted of a minor theft crime and was sentenced to the penitentiary for felony. And the judge, Kenton Cooper, had a habit at that time of asking all the officers of the court what their recommendation was in reference to probation. . . . He'd always ask the arresting officer what he recommended. So he asked the sheriff, who was the officer that arrested the young fellow, what he recommended.

The sheriff said, "Well, sir, I'm new at this job, so my position is I think it's my job to fetch them in here to you, and you do as you please with them." The courtroom was full of people, and they all laughed.

Robert L. Wilson, Jamestown, April 19, 2002

135. "Humorous Response to Judge's Question"

I had this inmate down here at the Kentucky State Penitentiary in Eddyville and was arraigning him. He was entering a guilty plea. When a person enters a guilty plea, I advise them of their rights; ask them if they are under the influence of any alcohol; if they have ever suffered from any mental disease or defect; or do they now suffer from any mental disease or defect. Is anything impairing their judgment this morning because of consumption of alcoholic beverage, homemade brew, or anything like that? That always brings a smile to their face.

I had one inmate down at the penitentiary one day, I asked him, "Sir, did you ever suffer from mental disease or defect?"

He said, "Well, I was in the mental institution once, but I didn't suffer."

I sure got a kick out of that, and do at other times, depending on the way they respond—the way they say things.

Bill Cunningham, Eddyville, January 21, 2002

136. "Really, Who Is a Judge?"

We had an elderly judge in district court here several years ago, and this woman went to court and took her five-year-old kid into court with her. The judge was sitting up on the bench, and he had on his robe. The little kid walked in and looked way up there at the judge sitting on the bench, and he asked his mother, "Mama, is that God?"

She said, "No, but he thinks he is."

Ken S. Dean, Madisonville, April 15, 2002

137. "Passing Drug Test"

I represented the mother in a custody case I had. This mom and dad were fighting over the custody of a seventeen-year-old. The other attorney is questioning my client, and he tells her he has requested drug testing from the commissioner. He said, "Now, if the commissioner recommends that all the parties be drug tested, do you have a problem with that?"

My client looks at him and says, "Well, I can't pass a drug test."

I just about fell out of my chair! I thought she was getting ready to tell something I hadn't heard about. But she went on, telling that she was on some medication that made her think that she wouldn't pass a drug test.

Melanie A. Rolley, Madisonville, April 15, 2002

138. "Humorous Courtroom Responses"

When I first started law practice, I was in a divorce hearing involving a case for maintenance. I was representing the husband. The other attorney was seeking maintenance for his client. After their separation, my client had moved in with another woman, so the other attorney was trying to show that they were living together as husband and wife and that my client was supporting this other woman. The other attorney went on to ask questions such as, "What does this woman do for you? Does she cook? Does she clean?" He went on through all these questions, and my client kept saying no to everything: "No, she doesn't cook for me; she doesn't clean for me; she doesn't buy groceries; she doesn't do anything."

The other attorney says, "Well, what exactly does she do?"

My client looked at him and says, "She just sits."

The attorney got really tickled about this. He had to get up and leave the courtroom, and the commissioner was laughing, and I was laughing, but our clients were just sitting there like they were thinking, "What just happened? What's so funny?" They didn't see any humor in what he had said.

The other attorney that had walked out laughing came back in. He thought he had composed himself. He sat down, then took one look at my client, and he burst out laughing again. He had to get up and leave the courtroom again. It took him several tries before he could actually sit down and finish his questioning.

Melanie A. Rolley, Madisonville, April 15, 2002

139. "Judge Buttin' In"

My friend, Judge Bill Fuqua in Russellville, told me this. Said when you stop being a trial lawyer and go on the bench as a judge, you have to learn to be an arbitrator rather than a participant. We all have to go through that learning process, and one of the things that we have to learn is to not butt in, but just let the lawyers try their case and don't fall err to thinking that we can do it better than they can do it.

Judge Fuqua points that out by saying that he hadn't been on the bench very long until he was trying a case where a fight had ensued and the defendant was accused of taking a rock and bashing in the other fellow's head with it. Of course, according to the victim, that rock was half the size of Gibraltar, but to the defendant it wasn't any bigger than a BB shell. So the issue got to be how big was the rock. A bystander was called as a witness mainly to describe the size of the rock. But he wasn't a very articulate witness, and the lawyer was having a hard time getting him to say how big the rock was. So Judge Fuqua said that he watched it for a little while, then thought, "Well, I can do that better than he's doing it. I'm going to help him out."

Finally, he leans over and held up a paperweight, then says, "Now, Mr. Witness, I want you to tell the jury if that rock was bigger than this paperweight."

"Yes, sir, it was bigger than that."

Then the judge held up a tape dispenser and said, "Well, was that rock bigger than this tape dispenser?"

"Yes, sir, it was bigger than that."

Then the judge asked, "Well, was that rock bigger than my head?"

The witness looked back at him, eyeballed him pretty good, and said, "Judge, it was about that long, but it wasn't that thick."

Fuqua said that was the last time he ever interfered.

William R. Harris, Franklin, August 22, 2001

140. "The Judge Who Looked Important"

I had a recent experience in court in which the issue arose as to whether or not this defendant in a criminal case was competent to stand trial. Court rules put some obligation on the trial judge to make that decision, so they go through kind of an inquiry process. One of the things that we are required to inquire about is whether or not they understand the legal process, whether or not they understand the role of the prosecutor, and the jury, and the judge.

I asked this fellow, who wasn't the sharpest knife in the drawer, and it looked like a borderline case as to whether he was competent, if he understood the role of the commonwealth attorney, who was the prosecutor.

He said that he understood that the prosecutor was going to try to prove that he was guilty and have him sent to prison. Then I asked him if he understood the role of his attorney, and he said that he understood it, how that his lawyer was supposed to try to keep him out of prison and to make liars out of everybody that testified.

Well, that was a pretty good grasp of it. Then I asked him if he understood what the jury does. He said, "Well, yeah, the jury sits here and they listen to it, then they decide whether I go to prison or not."

I thought, "Well, this guy's got the essence of it." And I would have been okay if I had stopped there, but I asked him, "Well, do you understand what my role as the judge is?" Of course, I was thinking he would say, "Well, you decide on the evidence, and the law," and something like that.

He looked at me and said, "You know, I've been studying on that, and I think what you do is sit up there and look important."

Everybody else in the courtroom laughed, so I did, too! Then I said to him, "Well, I believe you are competent. I think you understand."

William R. Harris, Franklin, August 22, 2001

141. "Lawyer's Death Favored by a Friend"

I can't remember exactly how this was told. I didn't know either one of them. Many years ago, two lawyers here, Judge Lightfoot and Pap Berry, did not get along. One of them died first. I forget which one. Shortly after that, the other one was walking down the street and met someone who knew him, and said, "Are you going to so-and-so's funeral?"

He said, "No, but I'm in favor of it."

That supposedly really happened. Stories like this were passed down to me by older lawyers.

Richard Roberts, Paducah, November 2, 2001

142. "Mountain Man Charged with Rape"

Frank Hadad, who died a few years ago, was perhaps the best-known lawyer in Kentucky because of the high profile criminal work he did. He was not so much colorful, but because of the people he represented and the results he got, when somebody is that active things always happen around them. In a sense, Bill Johnson in Frankfort is filling that role now by doing a lot of the high-profile criminal cases. I do not know the mountain lawyers. Chances are you will find some great characters over in the mountains. But I do remember a number of years ago talking to a lawyer named Cawood. I forget his first name. Anyway, he told me this story that I've always enjoyed.

Cawood was about to leave his office one day. This fellow was sitting out in his waiting room. Mr. Cawood said, "Can I help you?"

He said, "Yeah, I've got this here piece of paper and they told me I needed to see a lawyer."

Cawood looked at it, and it was an indictment for statutory rape. He said, "I think you do need to see a lawyer." So he undertook to learn what it was about and learned that this fellow had been dating this girl who was underage. Her parents had been wanting to break up this relationship, so they thought the best way to break it up was to have a statutory rape charge brought against him, and they did.

Mr. Cawood went on to ask the fellow what happened on this day mentioned in the complaint. The fellow said they went to a motion picture show, and another place to get a hamburger and coke, and another place where they went out and parked. That was where three counties come together. Mr. Cawood was thinking that maybe they indicted him in the wrong county, thus they may have had a venue defense. So he turned to this guy and said, "Tell me, where did you have intercourse?"

The guy says, "Huh?"

Cawood says, "Well, where did you screw her?"

He says, "The usual place: between the legs."

Mr. Cawood was looking for the geographic location, and that was the answer he got!

Richard Roberts, Paducah, November 2, 2001

143. "OLD LADY NOT ALLOWED TO TELL IT ALL"

Many years ago I was in court here in Powell County. I had graduated from law school in 1948, and I had just come up here. I believe that it was the first term of court. They had just made a new court district consisting of Powell, Wolfe, and Breathitt counties. They appointed Irvin Turner of Jackson as the judge. And the commonwealth attorney was J. Douglas Graham. At Campton, there was a defendant that was being tried in a murder case. The commonwealth attorney a lot of times would kind of try to get in hearsay—kind of fudge a little bit. But he was a dear man and a friend of my family for many years. But the judge refused to let him fudge very much. The defense attorney would object and the court would ask Mr. Graham what he thought about it.

Then, he would rule on it in this particular case, usually against the commonwealth.

Anyway, an old lady came up to the stand—got on the stand and was sworn. And then the commonwealth attorney started asking her questions. Well, about every other question, the defense attorney would object. Many times the court would affirm the objection. Finally, it was very obvious that the old lady wanted to tell everything that she knew, and some she didn't. And she would add on things, then the judge would stop her. She finally got aggravated and the commonwealth attorney said, "Now Aunt So-and-so, what about this angle of the case? You knew this man real well. What do you think about him?"

The old lady glared over at the commonwealth attorney and looked up at the judge, then says, "I've been trying for the last thirty minutes to tell you all about this case, and this old fellow [the judge] sitting up here won't let me talk!"

John L. Cox Jr., Stanton, November 26, 2001

144. "Weirdly Intoxicated"

We had in court this young girl who was on probation. She had drug and alcohol problems, so one of the conditions of probation was that she abstain from alcohol. When she'd report to the probation officer, they would test her and found that she had alcohol in her system. So they wrote her up and moved to have her probation revoked and send her off to prison.

She showed up for court that day, and the probation officer testified that she reported to him on a certain date, and that he did the test and found her positive. So he wrote her up as "positive" and recommended that she be revoked.

When it came her turn there in court to give her side of it, she said, "Yes, Judge, I admit that I was intoxicated." Then she said, "But I had not been drinking." I knew her pretty well, so I called her by name and said, "Now, you've heard what the officer just said."

She said, "Well, yes, I admit that I was intoxicated, and the reason I was is that my boyfriend got out of prison the day before, and I'd spent the night with him. I'd just left there to go down to the probation office. I was intoxicated on *love*."

When she said that, the whole courtroom just erupted in laughter. That was one of those instances where no one in court made an effort to hold back their laughter. That was so funny that I just laughed out loud. Then I just acted like I didn't hear it and sent her off up the river.

William R. Harris, Franklin, August 22, 2001

145. "OLD MAN RECOGNIZES THE JURORS"

An old country fellow was testifying on the witness stand, and the lawyer asked him, said, "Sir, would you look at those people setting there on the jury?"

The old fellow leaned out of his witness chair and looked. The lawyer then asked, "Do you know more than one-half those people setting on the jury?"

The old fellow then looked at them again, and said, "From the looks of them, I probably know more of them than all of them put together."

Ken S. Dean, Madisonville, April 15, 2002

146. "THE NON-THINKING LAWYER"

Alvie Hollon of Hazard told me about a case. Some years back, they had a system of appointing a defense lawyer for someone who was poverty stricken. The court had appointed this legal assistant to be the lawyer for a woman in a severe case.

Well, they went to court, and the commonwealth attorney appeared that day. He had brought his assistant with him. So they got started in the trial, and this woman said to the judge, "Judge, I want to say something."

The judge said, "Well, stand up and say what you have to say."

She said, "I want me another lawyer."

The judge said to her, "Well, Mr. Doe is a fine lawyer. He has a good reputation. So I've appointed you with one of the best."

She said, "Nope, I want two lawyers."

He asked, "Why do you want two?"

She said, "They got two on the other side, so I want two. Because when one of them is up talking, the other is thinking. But when my lawyer is up talking, they ain't *nobody* thinking."

Edward Jackson, Beattyville, July 20, 2001

147. "Sex with a Hippie"

A woman was setting on the witness stand, and the lawyer asked her, "Did you, or did you not, on the night of June 23 have sex with a hippie on the back of a motorcycle in a peach orchard?"

She thought for a few minutes, then said, "What was that date again?"

Ken S. Dean, Madisonville, April 15, 2002

148. "Fellow Who Doesn't Talk Well"

There's a fellow from up the river here in Pike County named Chuck Moore [pseudonym]. He is a good ol' boy who, when he gets into trouble, he likes to hang around the law office. He's a pretty simple-minded fellow who doesn't talk plain. He talks about the time he learned to "skrim-m-m," when he first went "skrim-m-m-ing" in the "riber." He said, "I jumped into the riber, head first, at the mouth of Red Creek, and busted my head on a damned Frigidaire in the riber."

See, people used to put their garbage in the creeks and rivers around here. That "Frigidaire" was garbage in the river.

One time, he was telling me about that, and I said something back to him real smart-alec-like. My wife, Cheryl, said, "Aw, Chuck, don't pay any attention to Larry. He's just a smart alec."

Chuck said, "He 'posed to be a smart alec. He a damned 'turney."

Lawrence Webster, Pikeville, November 9, 2000

149. "Lawyers Are Not Thinkers"

A lawyer was asking this lady some questions. He asked her a rather long question, and she thought and thought and thought. Finally, the lawyer said to her, "I notice it is taking you a long time to answer."

She said, "Yes, sir, I'm not a lawyer, I have to *think* before I speak."

Ken S. Dean, Madisonville, April 15, 2002

150. "In Need of Dictionary"

There's was a state police detective here in Pikeville who's a very funny, bright, delightful fellow. His name was Richard Ray. I was defending a fellow for doing something and Richard was trying to get me to plead him guilty. We were outside the courtroom and Richard said to me, "Larry, I've got five or six people that saw him do that."

Well, we didn't plead guilty, so we were having a preliminary court hearing. This fellow was under oath. He had one or two people that saw him do that. He got up and testified, and when it came time to cross-examine him there on the witness stand, I said, "Richard, what happened to those other four or five that you talked about outside?"And he just kinda grinned.

I said, "Was that rhetorical *hy*perbole?"

He looked at me, and said, "I'm a gonna get me a dictionary and look up what you just called me." Then he asked, "Is there a *low*perbole?"

Lawrence Webster, Pikeville, November 9, 2000

151. "Jury Trial over Ear That Was Bitten Off"

In law school, the professor was teaching us the danger of doing too much cross-examination of a hostile witness. The rule to be learned was that you never ask a question to which you don't already know the answer.

The defendant in the case that really occurred in east Kentucky involved a maiming. The defendant was charged with biting the victim's ear off in a barroom fight.

The defense attorney asked the witness, "Did you actually see him bite off the victim's ear?"

The prosecution witness had to admit that he hadn't actually seen the ear bitten off.

At that point, the professor said that the attorney should have rested and stopped any further examination of the prosecution witness. But being full of self-confidence and pride in his success with the first question, he turned to the jury and in a very sarcastic voice with arms raised up to the heavens, shouted, "Well, if you didn't see him bite the ear off, just what did you see?"

The prosecution witness in a low voice responded, "I saw him spit it out."

Stan Billingsley, Carrollton, March 20, 2001

152. "The Nice Feller"

A person was put on the witness stand to attest to the character of the defendant. This person got up and testified, "Well, I'm a neighbor of the defendant and I believe that he is a person of good reputation."

The prosecutor got up and said, "Well, did you know that he has been convicted of several crimes?"

The witness said, "Yes I did."

Said, "Did you know that he beats his wife?"

The witness said, "Yes, I did know that."

"Did you know that he gets drunk fairly regularly and won't work?"

The witness said, "I knew all that."

The prosecutor said, "Do you still think he has a good reputation?"

The witness said, "Yes, it takes a lot more than that to give a feller a bad name up where we come from."

Lawrence Webster, Pikeville, November 9, 2000

153. "Lost Driver's License"

I had a guy one time fairly recently. I was trying to show that this guy had been convicted of many things and that his testimony wasn't really believable. When asked if he had had recent marijuana convictions, he said, "Yeah." He owned up to those.

He was not a really bright person. I also had evidence that he had had his license revoked. But he had multiple licenses. He had Illinois and Missouri licenses, and he had a Kentucky license. So I said, "Isn't it true that you've lost your Illinois license?"

He said real quick, "No, no, I haven't lost it. I've got it right here."

Byron Hobgood, Madisonville, July 2, 2000

154. "Like a Dog in Court"

Paul Huddleston was an excellent trial lawyer. I recall when he filed a suit against the New Holland Company. That was a tractor manufacturer that manufactured farm equipment. There was an accident that happened in southwest Warren County. The New Holland salesman was coming over the hill out near Hadley, and Paul Huddleston's client pulled out of a side road right in front of him. The New Holland fellow hit him, and they had a pretty big bang-up there. Paul filed the suit for personal injury against the New Holland Company. He was representing the plaintiff, and I was representing the defendant. Judge Robert Coleman was on the bench. Paul's client was claiming severe back injury—back pain.

Back then, Dr. L.O. Toomey was a well-known Bowling Green physician and was very conservative. He was the one you always got for the defendant to make an independent medical evaluation. Well, Dr. Toomey had examined Paul's client and found no injury and no cause for him having any pain. He was right explicit in saying that the only thing this fellow had was arthritis from the aging process. Well, I put Dr. Toomey on the stand, and he testified extensively about that if this fellow had any pain, it was due purely to arthritic pains that were natural, not traumatically caused.

It became Paul's turn to cross-examine Dr. Toomey, and the doctor was right articulate. He had been cross-examined many times. Paul says, "Now, Dr. Toomey, isn't it true that arthritis has been described that it's like a sleeping dog, and that trauma will awaken that dog and bring it into suffering reality?"

Dr. Toomey looked at Paul and says, "Paul, let me tell you this. I've seen that old dog kicked and awakened more in this courtroom than any place in the world!"

Charles English, Bowling Green, May 27, 2002

155. "A Fast Driver"

I've heard about this state trooper that pulled a young man over for doing 80 mph in a 60 mph zone. Delighted with his catch, the officer grinned broadly and said to this fellow, "Son, I've been sitting here waiting for you a long time."

The young man looked him square in the eye and said, "Sir, I got here as quickly as I could."

Eugene Goss, Harlan, May 22, 2002

156. "Nigger Head on the Lower Mississippi"

This account was told to me by the port captain of one of the towing companies. Most every stretch in almost every river has some place in it where there is a little piece of bare land that juts out into the river, and historically such a point has been called a "nigger head."

On the front of a towboat there is a capstan, which is used to wind and pull in the ropes when making barges or pulling an anchor on a sea vessel. The official term for this is "capstan," but it has also been called a "nigger head." Well, this port captain told me that they were trying a case involving an engine on a boat in the United States District Court in Mississippi. So, he put on this deckhand to testify and asked him if he remembered the incident. The deckhand said yes. Then he was asked, "Where were you?"

The deckhand says, "On the Lower Mississippi coming down on Nigger Head Point."

Not wanting to embarrass him, the judge very kindly asked his lawyers to come back to the chambers in the judge's office and explained that he didn't mean anything by it, but that they just couldn't use that expression in court. Was there something else that they could call it? So, he pulled out a map of the river and decided, "Yeah, this is mile whatever on the Lower Mississippi." So, the judge goes back on the stand and asks this fellow where he was.

The fellow says, "Well, we were coming down by the bend at mile whatever on the Lower Mississippi."

Then the judge asked, "Well, where on the boat were you?"

He said, "I was walking over by the nigger head."

Richard Roberts, Paducah, November 2, 2001

157. "Bad Hair Hoskins"

We had a case from Clay County in which two fellows were charged with the possession of marijuana. They had grown it, and they had big sacks full of it when the federal agents came over there and seized it up. The last names of these two fellows was Hoskins. One of them was named William Hoskins, and he was known around the county as Bad Hair Hoskins. The U.S. attorney had returned an indictment through the grand jury against William, or Bad Hair, Hoskins. I was the judge in this case, and his attorney stood up before me and said, "Now, Judge, I object to this indictment. It's very prejudicial to my client. There is no basis for him to be called Bad Hair Hoskins. It's not a nice name, and it's just going to hurt my client."

I said, "Okay. If it's that big of a deal, we'll just ask that that name be stricken from the indictment." Then, I told the prosecutor, "Now, don't you have any witnesses to talk about Bad Hair Hoskins."

He agreed to that, then the case went on pretty well. When William Hoskins's side put his case on, his lawyer called his first witness. However, he had forgotten to tell his client about this. He said to the witness, "Do you know my client, Mr. William Hoskins?"

This fellow said, "Oh, do you mean old Bad Hair there? Yeah, I know Bad Hair! Nobody calls him William. We all call him nothing but Bad Hair."

His lawyer said, "Well, I give up."

I never did know why he didn't want to be called Bad Hair, but to me that's a humorous story.

Eugene Siler Jr., London, June 20, 2002

158. "BLACK CHURCH IN LEITCHFIELD"

The black people here in Leitchfield built a church down here, and the man that put the heating system in was a city councilman—a very influential man here in this town. Well, after they got the church built, they had an all-day meeting with dinner on the ground. It was cool, so they had the furnace on. They ate and went back in church. Within an hour after they went back, they started passing out. The were asphyxiated from that gas that was escaping from the furnace. Well, one of them, Katy, came up to my county attorney office. Of course, I had a rule that I sued anybody; I didn't care who it was unless it was my mother, my father, and my brother, and my wife if I was in a good humor with her. I sued everybody else!

Anyway, she'd been to every lawyer in town. One was Mr. Otto, whom I beat in an election, and the other was Mr. Cubbage, a real prominent lawyer. Neither of them would take her case, so she came to me. And I said, "Yeah, I'll represent you. We'll sue them." I was going to sue the heating man, who was a city councilman. Back then, that class of people—people have a tendency to be subjective, and they judge you by what they would do if they were in the same circumstance. I knew that some time or another, she would accuse me of "selling her out," and that happened. One day she came to see me and said that she'd heard that I was selling her out. So I said, "I'll tell you what to do. You can go to Louisville and get this lawyer, Jim Crumblin," who at that time was head of the NAACP in the state of Kentucky. I said, "Go up and see him and see if he'll help me in this case." She did, and of course he wanted a small fee for his services—four to five hundred dollars. When she came back and said that he wanted a fee, I just gave her the money to give him. After all, I needed some insurance, you know.

Well, we tried that case, and the judge gave a directed verdict against us, and we filed a motion for reconsideration. So, he set his judgment aside and gave us a trial. After we had tried that case, and the judge had heard the evidence, the judge gave a directed verdict against us. Well, we appealed the verdict on the basis that up until then the law was that the standard of conduct, or the standard of workmanship, was that of the community, i.e., the standards of the other people in that community. And we appealed it, and the basis of our appeal was that every person in Kentucky had a right to the same standards as every other person regardless of where they lived, and that the standards were those of the fire marshall.

So we got a new trial, and we won it, although we didn't get much. But during that trial is what I am getting to. They got Katy on the witness stand, and the defense lawyer asked her this question, says, "In what way did this asphyxiation affect you?"

She answered by stating, "Every time I passes gas, I get sick." Naturally, we thought of her bowels when she said that!

Kenneth Goff, Leitchfield, May 8, 2002

11

MOONSHINING

Of the various folk heroes who have captured the imagination of Americans, few occupy such a prominent position as the moonshiner. With the ability to rig up stills in remote mountain hollows and outsmart revenue agents, these brewers of illicit alcohol were nonetheless no strangers to the Kentucky court system over the years. The following stories illustrate the cleverness—and occasional fierceness—of those practicing a traditional craft that has increasingly been displaced by the manufacture and sale of other illegal drugs.

159. "FEMALE MOONSHINE WHISKEY MAKER"

There was a woman in Pikeville named Emma Morton [pseudonym], and she stayed in court a lot, probably because she was firm and tough in her principles. She and her husband did two things for a living. She made moonshine whiskey, and he collected sales tax. Back in the first days of the sales tax, they sent people around to each merchant on a regular basis to collect the sales tax.

Emma's husband traveled all over east Kentucky in an old Buick car, and she made moonshine. Well, he would load that car up with moonshine, and he had a perfect excuse to be going to every store—sell it! He could go to every store to collect sales tax and leave moonshine.

Well, after he died, his Emma had a new neighbor named Jones Sartin [pseudonym]. She called him "That Old Sartin," and they couldn't get along. And Sartin claimed that she went out to feed her chickens one day and reached in the bucket where the corn was and pulled out a pistol and started shooting at his feet. But she denied firmly that it happened like he said.

Here's the way the questioning went in court. The other lawyer said, "Mrs. Morton, did you take a bucket out to feed your chickens?"

She said, "Yes, I did."

He said, "Did you take a gun out of that bucket and start shooting at Mr. Sartin?"

She said, "No, I didn't."

The lawyer said, "If you didn't, how come all these neighbors have testified that from a short distance they saw him suddenly start dancing about?"

She said, "Well, I reckon the Lord just set his feet on fire."

The lawyer said, "Well, there was another time before that that you admitted shooting one of *his* chickens, didn't you?"

She said, "That ain't got nothing to do with this."

The lawyer said, "But you did do this, didn't you Mrs. Morton?"

She said, "I told you that ain't got nary a thing to do with this."

The lawyer said, "Judge, I move that you direct Mrs. Morton to answer this question."

Judge Ventress said, "Yes, it's a proper question. You must answer it."

She looked up at the judge and said, "Judge, I ain't answering no more questions about Sartin's fowls."

The fact is, it intimidated the judge and the other lawyer. She never did answer any more and they didn't ask them.

Lawrence Webster, Pikeville, November 9, 2000

160. "Moonshine Whiskey Maker"

My good friend, Attorney Sid Easley, over at Murray shared this story with me. We were talking about Lawrence Griffith, who was one of the three inmates who, along with Harry Ferling and Tex Walters, tried to shoot their way out of the penitentiary in 1923. Lawrence Griffith was some type of murderer out of Mayfield, Graves County, but his folks were really from Tennessee.

Sid's story goes like this:

My dad in his early adult years was a WPA foreman, building many roads in the hills south of Lynnville, Graves County. That area was settled soon after the Jackson Purchase was opened, but the once fertile hills were quickly eroded by continuous tobacco cultivation. It was poor, like much of Marshall County before TVA. Dad enjoyed telling Wiggings stories, and as you know, Lawrence Griffith was convicted of killing the Wiggings. I recall him telling me the story about Joshua Wiggings, the grandpa of them all. Josh was well known for his ability to make moonshine. When he was being tried in Paris, Tennessee, for stealing, he took the stand in his own defense. On cross-examination, the prosecutor said to him, "Joshua, are you the Joshua that made the sun stand still?"

Joshua proudly responded, "No, I'm the Joshua who made the *moon* shine."

Bill Cunningham, Eddyville, January 21, 2001

161. "JUDGE TAKES A DRINK OF MOONSHINE"

This story was told to me by an older lawyer who is now deceased. It happened in federal court in Bowling Green. It was an alcohol case. The revenuers went out and made raids, and they wound up from this area in court there in Bowling Green. There was a man from an adjoining county here, whose name was Joshua. He made moonshine whiskey. Well, he got raided and wound up in federal court. His trial was set. Of course, it was quite a long trip to ride a horse and go from this area to Bowling Green.

On the morning that the case was called up in court, he had not shown up. After awhile, they finally made it in. He, along with the witnesses, were riding their horses to get there. They went up to the courtroom. The marshall went up and told the judge that this fellow by the name of Joshua had arrived. So the court was put into session. When the judge called him up to the bench, in a joking type of way, the judge said to him, "Are you the Joshua that made the sun stand still?"

Joshua responded, "No, Your Honor, I'm the Joshua that made the *moon* shine."

And, of course, he comes back and tells his friends about that and that the judge had dismissed his case. He says, "It's all because as we went through Smiths Grove on the way there riding our horses the train was coming through there. And the judge was on the train. They had to stop at the crossing. The judge walked out onto the platform, and I gave him a drink of my new moonshine."

Lige Coffey, Russell Springs, July 11, 1988

162. "LAW ISN'T ALWAYS OBSERVED PROPERLY"

I had a study partner in law school whose father ran a general store up in Knott County. His son got caught transporting whiskey across the state line from up in West Virginia. They stopped this kid and searched his car without a warrant. Then they went to his house and searched it without a warrant. They found all the whiskey. The boy's dad went in to talk to the judge, whom he knew personally. He said to the judge, "Judge, how can they just come in there and search his house and car and everything without a warrant?"

The circuit judge responded, "Now, you know we don't always do things according to the law around here." And he was the highest judge in that county.

Ken S. Dean, Madisonville, April 15, 2002

163. "KILLER TOSSES WEAPON INTO THE RIVER"

One of the most interesting trials that I recall had to do with Kim Bradford [pseudonym]. I was born right across the river from Coe Ridge, the black community there in Cumberland County. We lived on the farm that Cass Ross owned, and my daddy was the tenant on the Ross place. And right across the road was the Richardson farm, where Kim's daddy was born. It was right there on the river. Bob Kirk had a store and post office there at Meshack. The Coe Ridge blacks worked a lot for people around there. And there was a store at Center Point. So there were two to three stores within two miles of each other.

The Coe Ridge blacks would bring their moonshine whiskey over there to these stores on Saturday, where a lot of white people were gathered, grinding their corn at the grist mills. Church-goers were against the blacks bringing whiskey over there. That was a community concern.

There was a white man over there on Kettle Creek whose name was Kim Bradford. He was the ringleader that organized and marketed Coe Ridgers' moonshine liquor. He was a white, mean outlaw. I don't know how many people he had killed. There was one white man who was a magistrate, and he was trying to break up that moonshining business. Of course, the revenue men were in there all the time trying to break them up, too. Trying to break up moonshining was a big thing because Prohibition had come on. That Coe Ridge liquor was really a big thing, for they were really making it. Well, somebody hid in a cave and shot and killed this magistrate. He was just going down the road and they shot him with an old-fashioned muzzle-loading rifle.

Nobody knew who killed him, but they had all the evidence and indicted Kim Bradford—the Monroe County Grand Jury did. Jimmy Carter and Heb Lawrence defended Bradford. They were his lawyers. I was in high school at that time, and I'd got interested in law and everything. I got to be a pretty good friend of Jimmy, and I was kind of the runner.

The people from the Meshack, Center Point, Elbow, Turkey Neck Bend, Coe Ridge, Mud Camp, and Salt Lick Bend communities were there at the trial. Bradford's role in liquor traffic was talked about a lot, but the point that I've always thought about that didn't come out in the trial, a thing that I found out later, was that Bradford knew about this new thing back then—testing a gun to tell what gun had been fired. That was a new science. They didn't think a man could look down a gun barrel and tell who shot it, you know! I didn't believe it either. Nobody believed it. I remember at the trial, they brought an expert from Frankfort or Louisville or Nashville. Well, he qualified as an expert, so he testified that he could look down a rifle barrel of a gun that had been shot and tell if this was the gun that the bullet had come out of. They had found the bullet in the magistrate's body. So this expert testified that the bullet they had found in the body had come out of a gun that they got out of Kim Bradford's house. They searched his house and found this rifle, and this man stated that that was the gun that had fired this bullet.

I can remember Heb Lawrence and Carter saying, "You know that no man can look down the barrel of a gun and tell if it had fired the shot." And it didn't make any sense to the average man in that day. Anyway, they turned Kim loose.

Well, actually, I found out many years later what had happened. Bradford knew that they might check his gun, so he put the gun that actually killed the magistrate in the Cumberland River, and put another gun up there in his house. They searched the wrong gun. Bradford was afraid they'd examine it and come out and say that wasn't the gun. But this expert didn't say that! So they based this case on false evidence. Bradford wasn't convicted; he come clear. The jury turned him loose.

He had thrown into the river the real gun that was used. I don't know who actually found the real gun, but I got my information years later.

Alan Huddleston of Cumberland County is the one who served as prosecuting attorney in the Bradford case. He was a well-known, well-respected prosecutor for about forty years. Paul Carter was a well-known prosecutor in Monroe County. They had great ability to influence the jurors by their oratory.

Cass Walden, Edmonton, June 8, 2000

164. "Judge Shields Whiskey in a Coffee Cup"

When I think back about my state court days, the constitutional amendment in 1975 changed the makeup of the judiciary system dramatically. In other words, in the old days, legal matters in court were still politically driven. The Republicans had their candidates, and the Democrats had their candidates, and they went all the way from the police court to the court of appeals.

And some of the judges would show up drunk at court. I remember going down the old Congress Alley over where the courthouses are here in Louisville, and one judge just staggered in to work. Another judge whom I knew in the criminal division kept a coffee cup on the bench. One day I had gone over to the bench to help a client stay out of trouble. Well, I was leaning over the bench looking at the judge's coffee cup. It was coffee-looking, but it was not coffee-smelling. So, I breathed it through my nose, and this judge there in the criminal branch of circuit court said, "Get your nose out of my bourbon."

Boyce Martin Jr., Louisville, December 7, 2001

165. "Blind Deputy Sees Moonshine Whiskey Maker"

This is a story that took place under Federal Judge H. Church Ford. He was one of the finest federal judges that I ever knew, along with Mac Swinford, who was also a storyteller. I was prosecuting under them. They were the two federal judges in the eastern half of Kentucky. Both were fine, fine men.

Anyway, in Breathitt County I was prosecuting a case. I put on the stand my witness, Hollis Gibson, who was a federal agent. He testified that he was with a deputy sheriff from Breathitt County, that they were on one ridge and that they saw this moonshine still over there on another ridge. Gibson recognized who it was, and he told the deputy sheriff, "You stay here and watch and I'll go down the hill and then go up the other hill and I'll catch him up there."

Well, that moonshiner heard Hollis coming, and he wasn't about to get caught so he ran off. But Hollis testified that there was an illegal moonshine still up there. Then I put the deputy sheriff on the stand and he said, "Yes, I was with Hollis Gibson, and we were on this ridge and looked over on the other one, and there was this man running this moonshine still."

I said, "Did you recognize him?"

He said, "Yes, I did. I could tell who he was from one ridge to another over there." And he went on to tell who this fellow was.

Well, that was good enough. I turned him over to the defense lawyer, Ollie James Cockrell, and he asked him one question, "Aren't you drawing a pension from the state of Kentucky for being blind?"

He said in a low, low whisper, "Yeah-h-h."

Well, I like to have died when he said that. Judge Ford came up out of his seat and he hit the desk and, man, did he start gnawing on me! And everybody there in the courtroom was laughing about it. The deputy sheriff was trying to convict that fellow by saying he saw him from one mountain to the other, and him blind! He swore that he saw him—recognized him.

Judge Ford threw that case out of the court right quick, but he gnawed on me something terrible for bringing such a case as that to court. Well, I asked him for a recess. He granted it, and I took that federal agent, Hollis Gibson, back there. I called him every foul name you can imagine for bringing a damned case like that in court. And he knew that that fellow couldn't see from one ridge to another. Well, that ended that case!

Later on, the judge and I had a discussion and I told him, said, "Judge, I didn't know that this fellow was drawing a pension for being blind."

B. Robert Stivers, Manchester, July 19, 2001

166. "Use of Whiskey to Heal Snakebite"

This happened to me and another lawyer here in Paducah named Bill Westberry. That was the only time either one of us has seen on record and under oath that whiskey is good for a snakebite. We had a lawsuit back in the mid- to late-1960s involving a little country cemetery and had to get into the history of it, so Bill and I were taking a deposition from a fellow up in Crittenden County. This was a little cemetery at a

Presbyterian church, and our witness's name was Abadean Clements, and I couldn't think of a more appropriate name for a Presbyterian. Anyway, we were getting into the history of the cemetery, how long it had been there, how it had been maintained, etc.

Mr. Clements, who was testifying, was in his sixties or seventies at that time, said that the cemetery had been there as long as he had ever known. And he remembered once when he was a boy that he and another bunch of boys were cutting through the cemetery and jumping over the log. Well, two or three of them got over the log okay, but about the time the next one came along, a copperhead snake reared up and bit one of them.

Well, they looked up and old Mr. So-and-so was going down the road in his wagon, and they yelled and waved at him and he ran over there to them. He saw what had happened, went across the road to the barnyard and grabbed a white chicken, pulled out his pocketknife, cut the chicken open, put it on that snakebite and it turned the chicken plumb green. And he said that he always had a jug of whiskey under his wagon seat. So he came back with it, made that boy drink that whiskey, and [Mr. Clements] said that it made that boy awful sick, but said it saved his life.

So Bill and I got sworn testimony about the use of whiskey in snakebites. And Bill and I are willing to believe that it did indeed help to save the boy's life.

Richard Roberts, Paducah, November 2, 2001

167. "WHISKEY SELLERS"

When I started practicing law back in 1968, there wasn't hardly any moonshining going on. There was one moonshiner here in Russell County, and my dad used to defend him. He was a sly old fellow. He was accused of selling moonshine whiskey and accused of selling legal whiskey in a dry county. His name was Bill Maynard. At that time, Dad was prosecuting in this case, as county attorney.

Bill came up to the courthouse on court day. They started court at 9:00 A.M. and started trying cases at that time. But usually the mornings were filled with little cases, pleas, and whatnot, but the trial cases were usually in the afternoon. Mr. Maynard noticed how court matters were handled, as he had observed the way they did court. Back then, a few hours were always picked by the sheriff. Then, during the trial, they'd just tell the sheriff to go out and summons in some men for jury service. Mr. Maynard had also noticed that. Anyway, he'd asked Dad if he didn't care to put his case off until one o'clock. Dad agreed to it. So, Bill had all his friends notified and to be available standing outside the courtroom at one o'clock. Well, sure enough, it worked just as Mr. Maynard thought it would.

They called the case at one o'clock and sent the sheriff out to pick the jurors. All of Maynard's big buddies were out there unbeknownst to the sheriff. He brought them all into the courtroom, and Dad said he looked over at the jury and recognized every one of them as Maynard's neighbors and best friends. He said, "I could have give up, but he beat me."

Usually, the bootleggers that I knew would also sell legal whiskey. They were always well-thought-of people. And they had to be. First of all, they had to have customers like any other merchant. You know, you don't deal with somebody if you don't like them. And secondly, they had to be good enough fellows so that their neighbors wouldn't turn them in all the time. One of the whiskey sellers I represented would give money to the churches all around his community. You couldn't find anybody in the community that would say bad things about him.

Robert L. Wilson, Jamestown, April 19, 2001

168. "Medicinal Use of Moonshine Whiskey"

I used to get appointed to defend moonshine whiskey cases all the time down here under Judge Swinford. The best moonshine whiskey cases was back when Big Six Henderson was the revenue agent. But this story is about my partner, Wayne Priest, who got appointed to defend a fellow. It's a story about an old black fellow down in Todd County. They got him for moonshining and keeping his moonshine whiskey in a little smokehouse behind the house.

The TVA had taken the Land Between the Lakes down there, and they had to move a bunch of cemeteries. This black man had been hired to remove a lot of those remains. In the case that ultimately resulted in his being charged for making moonshine whiskey, he was claiming that what whiskey he had in the smokehouse was to help make some sort of peach combination that he used for medicinal purposes, because in moving all those bones from the graves, it got into his respiratory system, and that he was using the whiskey just to keep his respiratory system in order. Anyway, Wayne tried that case and the jury acquitted this black man.

Charles English, Bowling Green, May 27, 2002

169. "Elderly Whiskey Maker"

Back in the 1930's, Judge Church Ford sentenced a seventy-year-old man to jail the third time for moonshining. He imposed a stern ten-year sentence, whereupon the defendant complained, "Judge, I'm seventy years old. I can't pull a sentence like that."

Judge Ford, who was known for his total lack of humor, replied, "Well, do all of it you can."

Eugene Goss, Harlan, May 22, 2002

170. "Whiskey, or Something Else?"

A deputy sheriff from Edmonson County stopped a well-known moonshiner on suspicion of violating laws regulating production of spiritous liquors. He asked the suspect for permission to examine the contents of the trunk of the car, but the fellow refused to let him do it. The deputy sheriff, noticing a liquid leaking from the bottom of the trunk, raked his finger across the wet spot and put it to his lips. To his great delight, the suspect then opened the trunk. Trouble is, in the trunk of the vehicle were two rather mangy, incontinent coondogs—two dogs that simply couldn't hold back on what they had done.

Eugene Goss, Harlan, May 22, 2002

12

COAL MINING

⚖

Coal mining was at one time the most important economic enterprise both in the eastern Kentucky mountains and in some of the state's western counties. Mines constituted the major source of employment for numerous men and a few local women from the early to middle years of the twentieth century. Mining is still an important operation in a few mountain communities, but its significance is rapidly diminishing.

Coal-mining stories were at one time told and retold on a daily basis at the mines during breaks and at home by the miners and family members. Lawyers and judges became especially important in the lives of the miners and their families during and after periods such as the Great Depression, when mine owners and operators sought to cut wages.

Some of the following stories may strike a bit of humor, but the realistic nature of mining activities alluded to is nevertheless easily discernable.

171. "NATURAL COAL WITH NO BRITISH THERMAL UNITS"

Back in the early 1970s—'71 or '72—there was a coal boom in this part of the country. An old fellow owned this block of coal, and some people went in to mine his coal. Well, he tried to sue them to recover royalties on what coal they had taken out.

They had him in court out there and upon the witness stand. He was trying to build his coal up to make it as high priced as he could. He was trying to get the top dollar out of these people that took his coal. So, he was telling them there in court what fine coal it was.

They asked him, "Did the coal have sulfur in it?"

He said, "No, it was fine coal."

They asked, "Well, what about dirt?"

"No, no dirt in it. It was fine coal."

"Well, what about rocks? Was there any rock in it?"

"No, no rock in it. It's the finest coal ever was."

Then they said, "Well, what was the Btu's in it?"

He said, "There wasn't none of those doggone things in it either."

See, "Btu" stands for British thermal units. The higher it is, the better quality the coal. If coal doesn't have any Btu's, it's not worth anything!

The old fellow is dead now, but he still has living relatives around here.

James Bates, Hindman, December 18, 2000

172. "It Wasn't Coal in the Water"

As county attorney, you always have to play politics a little bit. You deal with big families, and you certainly don't want to make them mad at you.

One day this fellow came in back in the mid-1980s, and he had another fellow with him. Both of them were from pretty good-sized families, but I knew the other fellow had a real *big* family, so I sure didn't want to do him wrong and cause them to be irritated. Well, he'd already been to the county judge's office, and the county judge had done exactly what this fellow said.

So the first thing he said to me when he came in was, "I want you to call Frankfort for me." Said, "This coal company over there has ruined my water."

I thought that maybe I'd better do that, because here I've got two guys from big families. I'd better just pick up that phone and call Frankfort about the water. He said, "The county judge has already called them."

So I started to pick up the telephone, and was about ready to call. Then I asked, "Have you had your water tested, or anything?"

He said, "Yes, I have. I've had it tested."

I asked him, "Who tested it?"

He said, "The health department tested it."

Then when I asked him if he had the report with him, he said, "Yeah, I've got it right here."

He pulled out the report and showed it to me. And I looked it over, then looked down at the bottom. Right down at the bottom, it had the words "colonic matter." It stated down there that there was colonic matter in his water, and that it had destroyed his water—that it was not safe to use. He was warned not to use that water, that it was contaminated.

He told me in the meantime, said, "We pulled the foot valve out—the thing that goes from the end of the pipe down into the well. We pulled the foot valve out, and it was covered with coal."

Well, I looked at that report, and thought, "Just what am I going to do?" I was ready to call Frankfort, and a lot of people always said that the people in Frankfort thought we were crazy anyway!

I was about ready to call, but I asked him, "Do you know what this word colonic means?"

"Why, sure," he said. "I know what that word means. Do you mean to tell me that you are a lawyer and don't know what that word means? That means that there is coal in my water and it destroyed the water." He thought the coal had really done the job.

So I went to get a dictionary, found that word "colonic," and brought it back in to let him look at it. Well, after he looked it over for awhile, he sort of changed his mind and walked out.

See, he was trying to declare that coal had got into his water and had destroyed it. He saw this word "colonic," that it was in his water, thus making it unsafe to use. He thought that coal had done it.

And the judge had already called Frankfort. I often wondered what he told him, because he didn't look at that report. And I was about ready to call them, too!

James Bates, Hindman, December 18, 2000

173. "UNWILLING TO ENTER THE MINE"

We do a lot of coal-related work. We represent coal companies, and sometimes we represent utility companies against coal companies. I had a case one time in which I was representing Orange and Rockland Utilities, a large utility company based in New York, but right in the corner where New York and New Jersey come together. . . .

This case occurred on the day that the Oklahoma City Federal Building was bombed. We had a long-term supply contract involving the coal quality issue, in which the coal company had produced coal where my utility company said that it didn't meet certain specifications. The grindability was not adequate. Grindability deals with how soft or how hard the coal is. So we were to inspect the mining conditions in these two mines. One of the things we wanted to see was the roof conditions, because it was important to show that there was bad top, or bad roof conditions, in this mine, which had impact on certain mining aspects which affected the litigation.

I had an assistant general counsel from New York, who was a woman. And I had an outside female lawyer, who was my co-counsel, from a New York City law firm. And these two women were all charged up about having to go into a deep mine. When you go into a deep mine, you generally have to go in flat on your back on one of these tracks. I've gone into deep mines all my life. My family was in the coal business in western Pennsylvania, so I am very familiar with coal mining, deep or strip, or whatever, but especially deep mining.

So in this case, we had to go back seven and one-half miles into this coal mine to look at these mining conditions. I got some overalls, steel-toed boots, self-rescuers (which is a device you have to have in a deep mine), safety glasses, and hats, all of which represented the whole, complete gear works.

The female counsel from New York was a very aggressive trial lawyer, a hard-charging woman. Well, I got them all outfitted, and we got to the first mine site. I had an engineer with me, and he and I got ready to go down under in the mine and look at the mining conditions. The two women are there and they're really happy to be there outfitted in their overalls, their safety helmets and everything else. The mine manager gives us the mine safety talk, which is an essential thing that has to be done for the strangers going into the mine. Then we leave the mining office and walk down this path. As we get closer to the mine opening, the two women see that the mine opening is only so high, and that there's this little track that we're going to have to lie down on to get into the mine. These women said, "Well, we'll just wait here."

So they opted not to go into the mine even though I had them completely equipped, completely ready to go in. Well, I and the one with me went under and went back seven and one-half miles and spent probably four to four and one-half hours back there in the mine. When I came out, we were told that there had been a bombing in Oklahoma City. No one knew at that point how bad it was. All we knew was that there had been some bombing. But later on, while driving back in the car that early evening, we found out how bad it was.

I did have the fellow who took us in to at least take the two women lawyers into the mine about fifty feet. So, he talked them into lying down on this track, or flatcar, and took them in. Then he turned the flatcar around and came back out. I had him to take them into the mine so they could say that they'd been in a deep mine. But I never told anyone else, including the general counsel for the company, who had authorized both of these woman coming down to the mine, that they just stood around and waited for me to go back into two mines that they didn't go in.

I don't think the women had claustrophobia. I think they just didn't want to go into a deep mine. Anybody in their right mind probably wouldn't want to do that, but I'm used to it because I represent a lot of coal companies and I go underground fairly frequently, and doing this doesn't bother me. But they didn't want any part of it, even thought I went through all these elaborate steps to get them the necessary equipment.

Richard Getty, Lexington, April 30, 2002

174. "MINING IN GRAYSON COUNTY"

In the late 1950s, and early '60s, the coal companies were absolutely tearing up Ohio and Muhlenberg counties by strip mining. I was going home one day and Mr. Benchman said, "Let me sell you my farm." I knew Mr. Benchman and where he lived, but I didn't know anything about his farm. I said, "How many acres do you have Mr. Benchman?" He told me that it was over one hundred acres. I asked him, "What do you want for it?"

He said, "Two thousand dollars."

I said, "I'll buy it."

He said, "You haven't seen it."

I said, "I'll buy it."

He says, "I'll bring the deed up to you."

I said, "That's not necessary. We can go in the clerk's office and we can get a copy of the deed there."

So that's what we did, and I gave him his two thousand dollars. But I didn't go to look at the place till probably six months later. I went down there, and it had a little tobacco base to it, but there wasn't any land on the farm level enough to raise tobacco. It was just gullies. You wouldn't believe the gullies that were there—just one big gullied-out place. It did have a little timber on it, though, so I sold that for about eight hundred dollars

Maybe a year later, a fellow by the name of Amos Johnson came to see me, and he said, "I want to buy that place."

So I said, "Amos, I'll sell it to you, but I'm going to keep half the mineral rights on it." Somebody had told me that there might be some coal on it and that some outcroppings had been in those ditches or gullies.

He said, "All right." Then he gave me two thousand dollars for that place. I'd made eight hundred dollars on it thus far, and I kept half the minerals. And I wrote in the deed that he could use all the coal for his own use that he could dig with pick and shovel.

A year or two later, he came to see me, said, "Kenneth, I want the mineral rights." See, somebody had been talking to him about the coal.

I said, "Amos, I'm not going to give it to you."

He said, "I need it."

I said, "I need to get some coal to burn for the winter. I told you that you could have all you can dig with pick and shovel. It's down there in the branches, so go down there and get it."

Well, he got mad at me, but he sold the farm. Finally, it changed hands four or five times. Then in the middle '70s, they started stripping coal down there in the Millwood section of Grayson County. So the fellow who owned the surface, and half the mineral rights, called me and asked, "Would you sign a lease to strip?"

I said, "Yeah." Of course, by that time they'd make them reclaim it. So, we signed that lease, and would you believe that my half of those minerals brought me thirty-six thousand dollars? They had the strip mining done in about eighteen months.

The fellow who sold me the land for two thousand dollars never knew about all this, because he had already died before that happened.

Kenneth Goff, Leitchfield, May 8, 2002

175. "Heckle and Jeckle as Coal-Mining Entrepreneurs"

When I got out of law school in 1971, I went back to Hazard, where they had an established bar that had most of the profitable work in their hands. When the first Arab oil embargo happened, and the price of natural gas was deregulated, thanks to those two things the price of coal appreciated very dramatically and in a very short period of time.

That resulted in what we still call the "coal boom" in 1974, and prices went literally from seven to eight dollars a ton to fifty, and sixty, and seventy dollars a ton. And when that sort of thing happens, you get all sorts of people coming in—some very sophisticated people that run big oil companies, and some that make up to $150,000 in the paving business in Akron, Ohio, for example. These people think they can get in on the action with a relatively small amount of money. We had more time than money, so we got more of the action than we might have if we were more established.

One of the anecdotes that comes to my mind is as follows: At that time, back around 1974–75 during the coal boom, there were a couple of brothers who were locally called Heckle and Jeckle because they were dark haired and looked a great deal alike and both had very little in the form of formal education. But they were smart, if not to say sly. They had gone up into the upper end of Perry County, where the maps showed coal and where the higher seams of coal up on the hill had been stripped. But to the local people, the deep or underground mine seams were known to pinch out and be small and spotty, so it wasn't a profitable area in which to put in a deep mine. These two men had nonetheless punched back into the hill a few hundred feet and purchased a fairly large coal pile from a producing company, and had stacked it up next to the mouth of the mine. They had also bought a few old pieces of equipment and, to my knowledge, they sold that so-called mining operation to three successive investors, on the premise of what was a good deal of money to them—maybe $50,000 or so, with the promise of more to come out of production; but if production didn't reach a certain level, they could retake the premises.

When I was approached by my client, who was a businessman from off somewhere, they had already run one fellow off. So, my client was the second one they had worked this deal on, and assuming that they were far too stupid to cheat him, he had bought the operation as a "pig in the poke." He had taken it on faith that the coal was laying there and had been pulled out from under that same hill. He hadn't checked the title on the property, although they had good leases; there just wasn't any coal under them [the hill]. So, he had engaged to mine a specific amount of coal and was to pay them so many dollars per month. But he wasn't able to do it, so I advised him that he might as well cut his losses and get out, which he did.

The funniest part of the story though was that during the third time around, Heckle and Jeckle met their match. What happened was, they were on their way up there to tell the third guy that he needed to vacate the premises and let them have it back, and they ran into one of the fellows who was well known to them. He had masqueraded as a miner, and thinking that he was, they had left him behind them and he was coming out of there, and they were on their way in. Well, he waved to them and got them over on the side of the road. He told them that he thought they'd better leave this third fellow alone and to consider that they had done all they could with that job. He went on to say that he had seen the third fellow that had bought mining rights around back on the other side of the hill putting some bags of quicklime in an auger hole in the side of the hill. So, he thought maybe that this third man was planning on getting even in a very specific and unpleasant way. In other words, he was going to shoot and kill them and put their bodies back in this auger hole in a pile of quicklime and let nature take its course. In other words, this third man saw himself vested insofar as getting any of his money back from them, and he wasn't going to give them anything back except a hard time. The guy that told them that may have been exaggerating, but they didn't choose to go find out.

Asa "Pete" Gullett, Shelbyville, June 3, 2002

176. "Mineral Rights Lawsuit Many Decades Later"

Something that I thought was real funny has to do with the broad form deed. Prior to the end of the 1900s, the investors came up with the idea that, in order to hold minerals in eastern Kentucky, without having to take possession of the land, they would sever the mineral estate from the surface. Thus, they came up with what was called the broad form deed. In effect, it allowed the land owner, who, as one case says, had previously owned the land "sky high and hell deep," . . . to sell his coal, in place, to a person, whoever it might be, that wanted to buy it, at so much an acre. And he continued to hold the ownership of the surface, just as he always had—could farm it, build a house, or whatever. However, it was subject to the right of the mineral holder to come in at such a time as they might choose and mine the coal, and use such of the surface as they needed in any way they pleased in order to mine the coal. In effect, that is what the broad form deed was. Of course, that deed fell out of favor as time went on and the people became more sophisticated and the price that had been paid per acre became in modern money a pittance, although it was by no means a pittance when it was paid. Of course, the state legislature finally put a broad form deed amendment in front of the voters, and they passed a constitutional amendment that limited the effect of the broad form deed

Most broad form deeds that you'll encounter in running titles and checking titles to minerals, or to land, are preprinted. Even if they were loose, and had been copied into the deed book by hand, each one would have exactly the same language in it, which would let you know that the entrepreneur, or speculator, that was buying up the coal had used a pre-prepared form.

We were running some titles over in Morgan County, and we found a whole series of instruments. Each of them was somewhat different from the others. They had all been to the same person, who was from Canada, and had all been taken between 1910–1920. Those deeds really gave us a lot of trouble because we were looking at this from the viewpoint of developing the coal. See, our client was thinking about buying this property, and he was thinking that he would be buying it from the surface owners. We were worried that these things would be held to be broad form deeds, and the language in them was really hard to interpret, even for a lawyer, i.e., whether it was a lease, which would have run out over time from not being developed, or whether it was a deed, which of course never runs out. And possession doesn't help you at all in a broad form deed because, by case law, a broad form deed presumes that surface owners can hold this surface as a trustee for the mineral holder. So by merely staying on the surface, he cannot adversely possess the mineral back.

Well, we really puzzled over those things, and finally concluded after a lot of work that some of them were leases and some of them were deeds. It turned out to be a moot point as far as we were concerned, because our guy walked away from the deal. He didn't buy the package of land. But we'd sit around in the courthouse running those titles and talk to the local lawyers. They had seen them too, and speculated about them. Well, we'd laugh and think, "Well, so what?" My daddy was raised in Morgan County, and I have other family members there, but nobody had ever heard of this fellow from 1917 or 1918, whatever the date of the last deed was, down to the present day. So, the story I'm telling happened in 1975 or '76, when one day I ran into one of my friends over there, and he said, "You'll never guess what happened. Somebody bought that spread of mineral and put a mine in it, and he was up there mining coal one day, and right up on that job comes a jeep, and this little ol' lady gets out of it. She's eighty years old—had on a pair of high top boots, and blue jeans tucked into the top of the boots, and she had on a heavy sweater. She was the daughter of this guy from Canada that had taken those deeds back in 1917, and she wanted to know what in the devil they thought they were doing in mining her coal."

I know that they ended up having a lawsuit over the ownership of that mineral, but since I wasn't engaged in it, I never did hear how it turned out. But I thought it was odd that she would just come out of thin air. Of course, we always said that if you couldn't puzzle out who owned a piece of property, the best way in the world to find out is put a bulldozer blade on it and turn a little of the dirt over. By doing that, the lost heirs will come out of the woodwork in a hurry.

Asa "Pete" Gullett, Shelbyville, June 3, 2002

177. "Coal-Mining Court Case"

I saw a pretty piece of lawyering done over some coal one time—a nice piece of courtroom work—litigation skill. My client was a coal company that had leased a large tract of coal to put in a really big, deep mine in the upper end of Perry County. My client was a very reputable coal company, and they had plans to make this mine a really large mine. If you're developing a large underground mine, the style of doing it eastern Kentucky is that you drive all the way through from wherever your entry point is to be located, to as far back as you're going. Then, you go off to the sides on the retreat as you come back out. . . . What you do in mining coal is to leave pillars of coal to support the top of the mine, so you therefore end up with a checkerboard pattern of coal pillars there inside the mine.

The property of these people that ended up suing my client was at a specific location, and we took just a little edge of the coal in the first set of headings that drove to the back of the mine. Then they started driving headings off to the side, and the plan was to take the rest of their coal when they got back out on the retreat from the deepest point. What happened was that they could never hold the top in that mine. The roof kept falling down on the inside of the mine, thus the property turned out not to be feasible because the cost of mining was driven up quite a bit. Of course, the lease had a clause in it that said if the coal was not mineable you could turn the lease back over to the people. So, that's what the mining company tried to do. As you might expect, the people didn't want it that way, so the dispute came down to whether my folks could mine the coal or not.

The landowners had to go all the way to Lexington to get their lawyer, and he was a Puerto Rican gentleman—a real good lawyer. But my star witness was a local fellow, who was the mine foreman. He was going to come into the courtroom and tell how that roof kept falling in the mine, and he was going to describe it in a very moving way because, as a matter of fact, he had lost a miner in one of those roof falls. He was killed. One of the things we pictured to ourselves very gleefully is just how is this obviously foreign person, who was their lawyer, going to question this man's veracity in front of a jury that looks, talks, and acts just like my witness. His [the landowner's] lawyer told me later that he worried about that very thing most of the night, and he came up with the answer and it worked. He got a judgment against us. He said, "You know Bob (which was the young man's name) is a fine person—a good hard-working Christian man. And his boss and this company is a good company. They do right as best they see it. They pay their bills and they pay their wages, and they treat people fairly. And when you're a good person and you work for good people, you start thinking they are always right, and that's what we're looking at here today."

So, he didn't say he [the foreman] was telling a lie—didn't attack him in any way. He just very subtly said, "You know, you get to thinking you're always right."

I was sitting there when he said all of that, and I said, "Well, he's got us now. That was a good lick."

I'll tell you right now, that was a tough case. The judge deferred to the jury the question as to whether the coal was mineable, and everybody hired experts to testify as to whether or not it was. Of course, we had engineers that said it wasn't, and they had engineers that said it was.

Asa "Pete" Gullett, Shelbyville, June 3, 2002

13

MENTALLY DISABLED

In the words of Beattyville judge Edward Jackson, "Mentally retarded persons fall into two categories. One category consists of those that have always been mentally retarded, and, two, those who get retarded when they get a little old. When these matters come to court, they get a twelve-person jury and usually they are uncontested. The jury decides whether they are mentally retarded or incompetent, then the court appoints someone to handle their affairs."

Although humor is not intended, some of the stories in this category conclude with what rings forth as humorous commentary and actions, primarily on the part of the chief actor, who is the mentally disabled person.

178. "THE FELLOW WHO WOULDN'T WORK"

I was county attorney here in Knott County at the time this happened back in the 1980s. Back then, if a person had mental problems, they would get mental wards for them. It wasn't much of getting petitions, such as they do today, to send them to the hospital. They would actually put them in jail back then and hold them a little while. But you had to give them a hearing back then within seventy-two hours. And another thing they came up with was that you had to have an attorney—had to be represented. And if they weren't represented by an attorney of their choice, then the court would appoint an attorney for them.

So they had this old fellow out there in court, trying him on mental weakness. So, the commonwealth put its side on, as to his condition.

Finally, his lawyer called this mentally retarded fellow to the stand. About the first question that the lawyer asked him was, "What do you do for a living?"

The client said, "Nothing."

The lawyer said, "Don't you work?"

This fellow said, "Why, no, I don't work." Said, "I draw a check. Do you think I'm crazy? Certainly, I don't work."

He really said that! I witnessed it.

James Bates, Hindman, December 18, 2000

179. "Thief Removes Ski Mask from Face during Robbery"

I've been thinking about the dumb crooks that I run into when I was a prosecutor. But the dumbest crook of all was a man whose last name was Wimpee. Well, on one cold, wintery night it was snowing. It was bitter cold. Down here on Main Street in Bowling Green, there was a liquor store called Park City Liquors. There was one man working there that night, and Mr. Wimpee went down there in the snowstorm with a gun and robbed the liquor store. He wore a ski mask. When he came in the door with his gun, he had his ski mask on, and during the robbery he took his ski mask off. He then proceeded to rob the man of the money. Of course, the man saw him and could identify him because he had his ski mask off. Then, before he left and went back out in the snow, he put his ski mask back on as he went out the door.

Later on when we caught him, I said, "You know, Wimpee, you're supposed to wear the ski mask inside when you pull a robbery."

He said, "Well, it was cold that night but it was hot inside the store!" He only got a light mitigation sentence because he was so dumb.

Morris Lowe, Bowling Green, March 9, 2001

180. "Juror Unwilling to Pay"

When I was a lawyer, in Covington we had a case that I'd heard about, but I was not in the case itself. It was a civil case involving a car wreck and one party suing the other one. And I heard from the judge, he said, "You know, we've got a message from the jury that they want to talk to me. I'd asked them for a note, and they sent a note up that said, 'Can we excuse a juror?'"

The judge finally had a hearing in the case, and they said, "Well, there's one juror here whom we can't handle."

The judge said, "What was it?"

They said, "Well, when we got to the point of finding that one party owed the other who was involved in the car wreck some money, the question was raised, 'What are we going to give this man?'"

This one juror kept saying, "Well, I can't give him anything. I don't have any money."

They responded, "No, you don't understand. We're supposed to make an award."

He kept saying, "I can't give him a thing. I don't have any money."

So, they had a hung jury based on the fact that this man didn't understand what was going on. Later on, I told the judge, "I know exactly who that juror is because we questioned him in another case, and he didn't seem to know anything about anything."

To me, that's a humorous story about a jury member.

Eugene Siler Jr., London, June 20, 2002

181. "MENTALLY INCOMPETENT CLIENT"

One of the first court cases in which I was ever involved took place when we were taking this fellow to Hopkinsville. Back then, when you took someone to Hopkinsville, you took them there to put them in an institution called the Insane Asylum. That was a place where people were known as crazy. Hopkinsville is looked upon in this area as the place where you take somebody that is mentally incompetent.

When we started back, we saw that we had the wrong person there in the car with us. So we had to take him back and swap him for the right person—my client whom we had taken over there.

Sam Boyd Neely Sr., Mayfield, June 7, 2001

182. "MORON OFFSPRING OF PERSONS GENETICALLY RELATED"

I had a case one time in which I was presiding, and the evidence was such that I had some reservations as to whether or not the man was actually guilty. But I was giving it some thought, and we got some reports and looked at them. This man got a five-year prison sentence for raping his daughter. Of course, she was a grown woman when they were in court. But she was fourteen or fifteen when she had a baby. I looked through the reports and found that the child of the two parties was a moron. Every time a parent has a child by an offspring—a son or daughter—there is a 90 percent chance that they will be moronic. It has to do with genetics.

So I didn't probate the father, for after looking in the files I knew there was no need to do it since the child was moronic.

Edward Jackson, Beattyville, July 20, 2001

183. "Uneducated Client"

Judge Phillip Morgan, who was a district judge back then, tells about one fellow coming to court over in Wayne County. Morgan always had a pretty formal court. As a defendant would appear before him, he would always go through a set ritual with him. He would first ask him his name, his address, and his birthday so that he would have some identifying proof that it was the proper man that appeared before the court. That was a good habit to have. But sometimes, those questions were a little too difficult. Some of the folks that lived way back in the hills, and some of their older people, never went to school. There's a lot of them that have never been inside a schoolhouse. That was true until just a very few years ago, even within my own legal practice time. I used to represent a bootlegger over in Adair County, and he told me that he had never been inside a schoolhouse, nor did any of his brothers and sisters.

Anyway, Judge Morgan had this one fellow come before him. He asked him to state his name, and the defendant told him. Then the judge said, "Tell me your address."

The fellow looked quite puzzled, and then the judge knew that he didn't know his address. So to try to keep from embarrassing him, the judge says, "What I mean is, how do you get your mail?"

He said, "They just bring it to me."

The judge looked at him, said, "Well, okay, now tell me what's your birthday?"

Well, he looked at the judge again, puzzled. So to make it a little easier for this fellow, the judge says, "Well, how old are you?"

He said, "Now, Judge, if you're going to ask all these questions, I'm going to have to get my sister up here. She keeps up on all the family records."

That shows that this fellow had no idea how old he was; no idea.

Robert L. Wilson, Jamestown, April 19, 2002

184. "Keeping a Family Story Alive for Generations"

There's a family in Perry County that has within two successive generations had a son that killed a father. Of course, they are ignorant people in the extreme, and they live on the side of a hill out in the county and breed back with one another. They are really pretty tough people, although some of them in every generation of the family have broke out of that crossing of bloodlines and made their own way in another place. But a lot of them are still right there on that hillside, and it still goes on.

When I was a very young lawyer, two of the people in that family came to see me in my office. They told me a story about what I took to be how their father had been tricked into selling his coal and had been cheated, but didn't realize what he was doing. It wasn't hard to believe that their father could have done something and not understood what he was doing. They told what happened in great detail right down to relating how there had been a lawsuit about it, and what different witnesses had said. So they thought something could still be done about it.

You have to understand that I was a young lawyer and that these fellows weren't talking in technical terms. They were ill-educated in the extreme. But that was the gist of what they said; I told them I had plenty of time and that I was perfectly willing to investigate anything in the hopes that I could find something to make a little money. So, I went over to the courthouse and pored through the deeds and found that the story they were telling, even though what they were talking about happened years ago, in 1911 or 1912, to have really happened, but not to their father. It was their great-grandfather. I found that out when I read the old lawsuit there in the courthouse. It just amazed me that their oral traditional account three or four generations removed, and who said what, was in agreement with the court records.

Their remote ancestor had made a deed to his coal to a speculator and had subsequently brought a lawsuit against the speculator that said he had not understood that he was selling his coal, and demanding that the bargain be struck by the court. And as a result, it was litigated out. It went against the family. They held that it was a good bargain and that the man had known what he was doing, that he had signed the deed. There was a good deal of evidence in the case that was quite interesting as far as the background of owning coal and being a mineral company as opposed to mining coal. It described in great detail how the company's agents had advertised and let it be known that they would be in Hazard and buying coal on a certain day. And they had set a table on the front steps of the Perry County courthouse and they had their money in gold in a big box there. And they had a lawyer with them, and any person who wished to sell brought whatever title documents that he or she had, and they would review them and the lawyer would carry them back into the courthouse and look to see if they had been recorded, if it indeed agreed that they held title to this amount of land—twenty acres, or fifty acres, or five hundred acres, or whatever it might be. At that point they would sign a contract for sale and pay them a percentage of the purchase price on the spot in hard money—the remainder to be paid within ninety days upon the completion of a survey.

At that time there was among the anti-mining people a near hysteria, and words like "steal" and "cheat" that were widely used. But those words were not accurate. At the times those bargains were made, it was a good deal because it was the surface of the land that had a value, and these people got hundreds of dollars in hard money at a time when a dollar would buy the labor of the best man in the county for one dollar a week. Most of them lived their lives out on their farms without ever seeing a miner. It seemed a terrible bargain to their grandchildren and their great-grandchildren when coal could be leased for $2.50 a ton and they knew that their great-grandfather had sold it for fifty cents an acre.

What was remarkable to me was that while those family members could not read or write, they all knew they had been cheated by that coal speculator and that they could keep that story really accurate over that long length of time. But I guess if "Barbara Allen" can stay alive for five hundred years and the words stay the same, then their family can, too.

Asa "Pete" Gullett, Shelbyville, June 3, 2002

185. "CHRIST WAS MAN'S LOCAL COUNSEL"

Judge Mac Swinford had a fellow to come before him for arraignment on a federal criminal case, and one of the things that it was the judge's duty to do was to make sure the man had legal representation. And this man was probably somewhat mentally deranged. Judge Swinford said to him, "Do you have legal counsel?"

The man just looked right at him and said, "Jesus Christ is my representative."

Judge Swinford never batted an eye—never missed a lick. He said, "Well, you need local counsel," then proceeded to call up the public defender. He never took issue with this fellow. He simply said, "Well, you need local counsel," and proceeded right along. I guess he'd heard that before, for it didn't faze him at all.

William R. Harris, Franklin, August 22, 2001

186. "He, the Guilty One"

Back in the late '70s there was a man that was being tried for armed robbery at a Convenient Store near Central City. This man and two others had gone in, and they were charged with not only robbing the store at gunpoint, but one of the three had shot the clerk in the head. She lived, although she had some brain damage. The one that supposedly did the shooting was the one that ended up being tried. The other two pled guilty and testified. But at the trial, the prosecutor at that time, who was Dan Cornette, had called the clerk, who had been shot, on the witness stand. He asked her if she could identify anyone in the courtroom who shot her.

The man that was being tried sat there between his two lawyers— a father-son lawyer team. The lady who had been shot was having difficulty in making an identification. She was looking at the older lawyer; she was looking at the defendant; she was looking at the younger lawyer who was sitting between them. She was pausing, and continued to do so. Well, the commonwealth attorney asked her again if she could identify who did the shooting.

She kept looking and looking at all of them. The story goes by courtroom observers that the bailiff, who was seated behind the defendant for security reasons, pointed to the defendant so that the witness would know which one to choose as the person who did the shooting. So when he pointed, she was able to identify the defendant.

It worked, as he was convicted for the shooting.

David Jernigan, Greenville, May 17, 2002

14

Domestic Mistreatment and Divorce

⚖

Stories in this category are diverse, ranging from verbal abuse to cruel, sometimes violent, mistreatment of spouses, and sometimes even of children. Many domestic violent petitions are filed in contemporary times, especially by mothers who go to the courthouse to get a divorce and to win custody of the children; on occasion, fathers file for custody as well. Whatever the reason for court action, these are not pleasant stories.

Lawyers shared few divorce case stories for inclusion in this book. Perhaps they feel that these stories would be of no interest to the readers because so many divorce cases go to court these days, or perhaps they find the cases to be too personal or controversial to describe.

187. "The Silent Lawyer"

In law practice, lots of times people want you to listen to their story. That's the main part of it. They want you to sit down and hear their story. As a county attorney, you could still have civil cases as a private practitioner. I remember when I was county attorney, this couple came into my law office, probably with the intention of getting a divorce. I was there behind my desk. They never spoke to me at all. They walked right up to my desk and sat on it. They started quarreling, so I sat there and listened. They quarreled for one hour, straight. And when the hour was up, they walked out friends! Never spoke to me at all.

They never went to court. More than likely, they are together today. They never ever spoke to me, but they knew I was listening to them talk and quarrel.

James Bates, Hindman, December 18, 2000

188. "Judge Rules in Favor of Accused"

I represented a young fellow, who was a nice enough young man. He had gotten into some trouble during a divorce and sort of fell behind on some payments and had turned over some property. They brought this fellow in in chains. He was a regular worker. He wasn't a criminal, but this divorce had really turned ugly and the judge brought him in and gave him sort of a stern lecture and decided that maybe it would be best if he just kept him in jail until the final divorce hearings could be held.

We argued for bond in that case. That took place in Louisville where they knew that I was once a police officer and not without a reputation for having just limited tolerance. So this fellow was standing there and the judge said, "Well now, Mr. McCormick, if we put him out on bond and he fails to appear again, what will we do?"

I said, "Well, I can assure you that the court won't have to do anything because I will track him down like the hounds from hell and I will curse the name of the family from whence he hails."

Well, the court burst into laughter and this judge who knew me wasn't kidding when he looked down at this fellow and said, "I'm going to put you out on bond because this guy can be a lot tougher on you than I can," and sent him out.

As a police officer I had gone to court a number of times.

Keith McCormick, Morehead, June 22, 2000

189. "Continuous Court Case"

I have a case that's been going on since I first started practicing law. It started in 1995 and is still going. It started out as a typical divorce case. This couple had a small child that was probably about eighteen months old at the time. The case was about to be resolved. The parties had reached an agreement, but they were going to have to have a hearing on the custody and visitation. I represent the husband.

When the wife found out that the court was going to give him visitation, she started making allegations of sexual abuse against the child. We've been fighting this until now, and there is no physical evidence to support her allegations, but the court has just repeatedly been working on the conservative side. They want to protect the child just in case anything had happened. So, for many years, my client has been living under supervised visitation for no reason, because now the psychological reports have come out that there was probably never any abuse now that the child is old enough to verbalize any abuse. But she has never said anything.

We've just about got the case resolved. We are still arguing over the child, but we have agreed as far as custody and visitation. He is no longer under a supervised visitation order. But I admire that man, because since 1995 he has been fighting to be a part of his child's life, and he has undergone psychological testing, lie detector tests—everything, and willingly so. There were never any physical charges, because there was no evidence. It was just because of what the mom was saying, and so often in the legal business we have problems with people coaching their children into what to say. Then when they go to be evaluated, they tell the counselors, psychologists, doctors, or whomever, what they have been told to say.

The parents have joint custody of the little girl now. The mother provides the primary residence for the child, and the father does have unsupervised visitation. He has the child every other weekend, and every other holiday, at his home. This case is still in court because I think the mom is still trying to make some allegations, but I think by this time that the court is not believing it.

Melanie A. Rolley, Madisonville, April 15, 2002

190. "WOMAN'S LEGAL BILLS"

We were approached and hired by this very sweet gal. She was a very special lady who had struggled with some mental health in her lifetime. She was going through a divorce and she was getting ready to lose custody of her children to her husband. Her husband wasn't a bad man. That wasn't an issue. But it was pretty obvious to us, and at the time I think it was starting to become obvious to her, that he was the proper placement for these three kids.

She had struggled with alcohol. She had struggled with men. She had struggled with many things, but mental was the big stumbling block for her. Well, we were beginning to really respect her as we worked on this case, as hopeless as this case was. And she had no real understanding of clothing, or how to appear in a public place. As my partner one time said, "She might appear in a tutu and welder's goggles and a swim fin." That's just the way she was.

My wife is an attorney, so what my wife did, she was a real good helper in this case, because she sat down with this gal and we made her pack up all the shoes that she owned, all the blouses and skirts and dresses that she owned. My wife stapled a color-coded card so that she knew that on day one of the hearing if we said "blue," this woman could pick the blue stuff out. She was bright enough that she could do that. She was not walking around impaired, but beyond that process it was really tough for her.

So my wife's plan turned out to be a great solution. That worked out real well. As I told Bev, "If she never takes the stand, we can pass her off as our client."

We knew that we were going to take a hit in this case, but we went on and did our best. The husband was awarded custody. I guess in the back of my mind there was a certain relief, because my client was not ready to be a parent. Well, I'll never forget that when we got done, I sat down and said we need to talk about what this means and what we do next and whether we need to appeal and that sort of thing. This woman thanked me for all my hard work even though we had lost her case. And she thanked me for the opportunity to show up in court with some dignity and with some opportunity to say what she wanted to say.

But the fascinating thing she had to tell me was that no matter how clouded her perception of the world was she was very tuned in, and she said, "I knew that we were going to lose this the very first day. But I'm glad we tried and I can tell you that I had to do this for my kids because I would not want my kids five years from now, or ten years from now, to know that I agreed that they could go with their father. I want them to know that I was willing to fight for them."

Of course, it was an expensive case. It was a tough case, for when we took it we knew that she did not have anything to pay us. Well, we'd run up about fifteen hundred dollars in legal bills, and we sent out a bill to her, and sure enough the first month this Convenient Foodstore money order arrives for five dollars. She had calculated it out. This was "Payment One of . . ." whatever that was. Then the next month, sure enough without even a bill going out, one of these five dollar money orders arrived. And every time one came, we just virtually shook our heads and thought, "Well, she doesn't have two nickels to rub together, and this is certainly a serious effort on her part." Finally, after a year we had garnered about sixty dollars worth of checks from her. So finally, I got one of the invoices and stamped on it, "Paid in Full." That seemed to satisfy her.

That was in Louisville.

Keith McCormick, Morehead, June 22, 2000

191. "Wife's Initial Financial Assistance"

One of the most interesting cases I've tried, and I've had a lot of interesting ones, was a divorce case in Meade County. There was a dentist over there, and he and his wife were getting a divorce. The wife was a school teacher. I guess they went to college together, and when they finished undergraduate work, she taught school and put him through dental school. I guess they'd lived together ten, twelve years when they sued for divorce.

They'd made money, but they didn't have any money saved up. I felt like she ought to have some money, so I gave her one hundred thousand dollars or something like that. And he didn't have it, but I ordered him to pay it, basing it on the fact that since she'd been responsible for his dental license, she had a part of his license. That was the first time that decision had ever been done anywhere.

The court of appeals sustained me in the case, but since then they say that you can consider what she was paid. However, California, New York, Minnesota, and so on have formed this into a law now in those states relative to any professional license.

Kenneth Goff, Leitchfield, May 8, 2002

192. "Husband Wants to Cut House In Two"

A lot of interesting things happen in district court; far more so than in circuit court. My predecessor, Dan Cornette, went on the bench in January 1983. I remember that very well, because I succeeded him as commonwealth attorney. The very first day on the bench for Judge Cornette was one of the wildest days we've ever had here. There was a fellow by the name of Virgil Everhart, who was going through a divorce. His wife had filed for divorce, and she had a motion asking for temporary possession, exclusive use and possession, of the house pending this divorce case, which is a routine type of motion.

Apparently, Virgil was one of these persons that took a lot of pride in the fact that he had established a home, and he didn't want to give it up. But, I think the previous judge had already ruled that Virgil had to get out of the house and let her have temporary possession. But by the time that Judge Cornette got on the bench in January 1983, Virgil had taken a chainsaw to that house and was going to cut it in two, thus divide it. The newspapers had heard about this, and so her motion was to stop him and get him out of the house. The Owensboro newspaper, particularly the *Messenger-Inquirer*, had reporters here. I think the *Courier-Journal* in Louisville had reporters here as well. The courtroom was packed. Of course, it was a fantastic story, as here was a man that was cutting his house in two. And he had actually already made some progress.

So that was what Judge Cornette had to deal with his first day in circuit court. I'll never forget that when the lady left the courtroom, there were reporters running down the street trying to catch her for interviews.

Virgil kept making a lot of noises through the newspapers. He was great for interviews. But like most cases, that house was eventually sold. The couple divorced and moved on.

Cases like that are just like a day in the life of a circuit judge.

David Jernigan, Greenville, May 17, 2002

193. "The Sexual Finger"

In Edmonson County in the old courthouse they had a rule day, and they'd always have it, particularly in the winter, in the clerk's office. That was quite an event in town because all the lawyers would come to town, and old Judge Bratcher from down in Morgantown, the father of Rhodes Bratcher, who was former U.S. district judge, and two other sons; all three were lawyers.

Anyway, there in Brownsville, they would gather around the stove in the clerk's office, and everybody in town would come. It would be totally crowded. Bev Vincent was the lawyer in this case, and there was another lawyer there whose name was Bill Logan. He is the father of a Logan who is a lawyer in Madisonville.

Bev Vincent had filed a motion against a fellow, compelling him to pay child support. And Bill and Bev just crossed swords on everything. Anytime that they got into something, it was just a real battle royal. So, Bev had filed a motion for the woman—for child support—against Bill's client. So Bev was making his argument against the fellow as to why he was not paying child support.

This fellow says, "Why, Judge, she's been seeing the Honey Crust Bread man out in the cemetery when he comes over here to deliver bread."

Cap Martin, who was then commonwealth attorney and later circuit judge, was there, and he was kind of an outspoken person.

Bev said, "Judge, she told her husband that she loved the little finger of the Honey Crust Bread man more than she loved him."

Cap Martin hops up and says, "Hey, Bev, did she say anything about his middle one?"

That was just a usual episode of the kind of things that you could see or hear over there.

Charles English, Bowling Green, May 27, 2002

194. "HUSBAND SHOOTS AT WIFE"

This happened while I was practicing law in Hazard, back about 1977 or '78. These people were in a divorce case, and they gave their testimony in front of the judge. Of course, you don't have a jury. It was done in the judge's chambers, which are on the third floor in the courthouse. The courthouse sits in a square, with one-way streets all the way around it. And the land is steep. You walk in the second floor in the back, but walk upstairs to walk into the first floor in front.

Well, these people left the judge's chambers and walked through the hallways and came out the front door of the courthouse onto Main Street. And they were arguing every step of the way. The husband reached into his pocket and pulled out a pistol. Well, she knew that he meant trouble, so she ran for her life. Well, he shot her. She ran across the front of the courthouse with him behind her just banging away. She ran up the side of the courthouse, him behind her banging away until he ran out of ammunition. He barked [hit] her one time, just a flesh wound, but it didn't bring her down. That was lucky for her, because he would certainly have walked right up to her and killed her if he'd ever stopped her from running.

Amazingly enough, he went back to his car, opened his trunk, and was in the process of putting his pistol away and getting out a shotgun. He was going to go after her with that. But an off-duty city policeman, who was not armed, just walked up to him and said, "Now, buddy, you can't do that. I'm arresting you and putting you in jail." He then took him on to the jail, just like that.

So that's a family dispute that was heard as a divorce case.

Asa "Pete" Gullett, Shelbyville, June 3, 2002

195. "Woman Shoots and Kills Husband"

This is a divorce case that happened to my partner. He talked to a lady who wanted to employ him in some matter about a piece of land or a dispute over a car. I'm not sure which it was, but that's immaterial. Well, he declined the representation, and some months after that she was in the process of divorcing her husband. They were taking depositions in the case in one of the lawyer's offices there in Hazard. She and her lawyer were sitting on one side of the table, and her husband and the other lawyer were sitting on the other side. The court reporter was sitting at the end of the table taking it all down.

She became angry with something her husband had said, so she reached in her purse, pulled out a pistol, and shot him dead right on the spot. Of course, both lawyers went diving under the table, as you might expect! I, too, would certainly have done that, assuming I couldn't get to the door. Well, she walked to the lawyer's desk, called my partner and said, "I need to talk with you worse than I ever did. I think I'm in a little trouble *now*."

Asa "Pete" Gullett, Shelbyville, June 3, 2002

196. "Married at Age Thirteen"

I remember doing a divorce case one time for a client in Rowan County, and she was twenty-one years old. She'd gotten married at age thirteen, and she had five kids, and at twenty-one she was getting a divorce. I thought, "Oh, my goodness." And she looked a lot older than twenty-one. I wondered what in the world is ahead for her. I have no idea now what her name is, but I can still see her sitting there on the other side of my desk telling me her life story.

I think she got a divorce, but I don't know what she did with the rest of her life. I don't think he had any money to support her, and her kids certainly weren't grown. So, I don't know what finally happened in her life. She likely ended up marrying somebody else.

Forrest Roberts, Owensboro, June 7, 2002

197. "THE UNDISPUTED AND UNBELIEVABLE CASE"

A case that did not happen in Hopkins County but makes some fascinating reading . . . took place in Henderson County. It is a case within the last ten years. The decision starts out, "The facts of this case are both undisputed and unbelievable."

This couple was at a party, and apparently there had been a lot of drinking going on. The wife wanted to go home but the husband didn't. In any event, he decided that he needed to go and use the restroom facilities outside, as the ones inside were already full. Well, he dropped his pants and was squatted down doing his business. His wife got tired of waiting on him, so she got in the car and backed up and she backed over him. She backed over him not only the first time; she backed over him the second time while she was pulling out. I just remember the words "undisputed and unbelievable." She had to pay the damages in that case.

Joe Evans III, Madisonville, July 28, 2000

198. "THE OTHER WOMAN"

I had a divorce case in which my client stood up without being asked. She stood up and told the judge, said, "Judge, the reason that he left me is because I wouldn't do that old oral sex with him." Then she went on to say, "But he's got him one that will do it." Then she turned around and pointed back in the courtroom and said, "And there she is right now."

This woman back there jumped up and yelled, "Yeah, and I'm *good* at it."

Stories like this may not sound real, but here in the mountains you can hear about all kinds of stuff.

Lawrence Webster, Pikeville, November 9, 2000

15

FAMILY DISAGREEMENTS

⚖

Stories in this category are about family feuds and other forms of family disagreements, misunderstandings, and lack of love and respect. In most story categories, humor is an ever-present reality, but such is not the case in family disagreement stories. These are about serious matters.

199. "MEMBERS OF THE FAMILY CLAN, NOT KLAN"

We had one case where we tried it over in Webster County, and it was a very interesting [family] will contest. This man had been declared incompetent, and that was sort of back in the days when maybe incompetency proceedings were not as foolproof as they are now. We have some safeguards now to try to keep somebody who just had a bad day from being declared incompetent.

Anyway, they tried to get this fellow restored to competency, but that didn't work so they sent him down to Western Hospital for evaluation and apparently shot him up with a bunch of drugs.

As it turned out, he left a will in which he disinherited all his natural children and gave it to these small children who were like grandchildren to him, although he had grandchildren and these were not his grandchildren.

In that particular case, we tried that case. And my law partner, a very distinguished lawyer with years of experience used the expression that "these people were warriors within the clan." He was trying to let the jury know that they did not get along well with each other, not just their father who was the person who left the will.

My clients heard the words, and they came up to me afterwards and said, "My goodness, we had no idea that they were in the Klan."

See, they were thinking that it was the Ku Klux Klan. He said, "They were warriors within the clan," and he meant they were warriors within the family.

That was a funny story because they came up just wide-eyed and said, "How did he know that they were in the Klan?" See, he was just using that term generically, which meant that they fought among themselves. And, you know, I sort of wondered at that point if some of the jury might have had that understanding of what was said. That just goes to show how words can sometimes be misinterpreted.

One of the other things I remember from that case that was interesting was that one of the witnesses said, "Dad didn't have any more sense than a rabbit." Well, when he said it, he said it in a low-tone voice, and the jury was half asleep, so most of them missed what he said. My law partner wasn't sure what he said either, so he said, "I'm sorry, I didn't hear that."

Well, this son realized he had made a mistake and he wasn't going to say it again. At that point, my law partner said, "Did you say something about an animal?" because he heard the word "rabbit."

Well, boy, by that time the whole jury was wide awake and wanted to hear what he said, and the son turned and said, "You heard what I said. I said that dad didn't have any more sense than a rabbit." And the jury just cracked up.

That might have well been a turning point. It's hard to know what a turning point is. Anyway, we won the case. They got nothing. We offered a substantial sum to settle that case as a matter of feeling that they were right. And there were indeed two sides to that story. The old man had become difficult and the children had had to go up to get him out of trouble with a girl who was much younger than he was, but who apparently tried to take his money and left him confused at a bus station. So there were certainly two sides to that story. And I think the children did what they thought was right by having him declared incompetent.

All of the foregoing is a matter of public record.

Randy Teague, Madisonville, July 28, 2000

200. "Judge Sentences His Own Son to Jail"

During World War II, my daddy, who was circuit judge, got some wind about my brother Atwood, who is dead now. Atwood, who was still in high school, was going with some fellows to get some whiskey. Well, Daddy sent the sheriff to the house to get him. He brought my brother in—took him up there in front of the bench in the courtroom. Daddy said, "Son, were you out last night?"

"Yes, I was." Well, he just lived in the house with Daddy.

Daddy asked him, "Did you go with a bunch of fellows up to some-place to get some liquor?"

He said, "Well, Daddy, I don't remember."

He said, "Son, did you go to get whiskey with these fellows?" And he named the people.

He said, "I don't remember, Daddy."

Daddy said, "Mr. Jailer, take him to jail over there, and Son, you're going to stay in jail until your memory improves."

Well, Mama hit the ceiling that night, and my aunt was foreman of the grand jury. She raised hell, too, with Daddy. But Daddy said, "He's no better than anybody else, and he's going to stay in there until his memory improves."

And his memory did improve! That's just the way my daddy was. He was an army man and very honorable. When my brother Atwood got out of high school, he went into World War II. There were three of us older brothers already in the service at that time. We had a younger brother who went into the army during the Korean War.

B. Robert Stivers, Manchester, July 19, 2001

201. "Clay County Family Feuding"

The Benges and the Philpotts here in Clay County had a bad family feud. I don't know how many were killed in this feud out in this Fogertown and Little Goose country, Kinkaid country. Houses were burned; people were waylaid. Some of their family members are still living. Killings that took place during these feuding activities didn't go to court. People were afraid to testify in court for one thing, and that was basically the reason why they didn't go to court. I could fill your ear full of information, but I'd better not. Two or three people know that I've put all of this information on tape, and they are wanting to get hold of the typed copy, as well as the tape. But there's no way that they're going to get it until ten years after I've died.

B. Robert Stivers, Manchester, July 19, 2001

202. "LITTLE BOY TESTIFIES AGAINST FATHER"

Of all the criminal cases I've tried, I've lost only one in my career: in a low, district DUI case I was trying just fresh out of school. This happened in district court here in Floyd County. The facts of the case were, my client, who was divorced, had taken his son home from visitation after the boy had been with him for the weekend. He took him home to a different part of the county, and on his way back he was involved in an automobile accident—a one-car accident. He was close to home at that point, so he got out and walked home. He came back to the car, and the police came along and arrested him for DUI.

The defense, quite frankly, was that there was no proof that he had had anything to drink prior to wrecking that car. The only alcohol that he had had was after the wreck, when he was not operating a motor vehicle. The defense thought that there was no way that you could prove that he had had any alcohol before he wrecked that car. The police officer testified, "No, we don't have any witnesses. We don't have any evidence to prove that this guy had anything to drink before he wrecked that car."

It was an absolute winner—no way to lose.

My client probably made a mistake in that he wanted to overkill the case, so he wanted to put on his new wife as a witness and put on his son as a witness. Well, they put on his wife, but she didn't do too good a job; but still, she testified he hadn't had anything to drink before leaving to take the boy home from his visitation.

At that point, we should have probably called it quits, but he persisted, "Put on the boy to testify." The boy was probably nine or ten— a small boy.

At this point, the judge had told me that if we'd just stop and shut up, he's ready to make the verdict. He was going to dismiss the case and not even let the jury hear it. There was no evidence that the guy was drunk while driving the car.

But he pushes, he pushes. He wants to overkill. So they put the boy on the stand. And this nine- or ten-year-old boy looked like a pretty good boy. A pretty good speaker for his age—very honest. He takes the stand and says that his daddy was definitely drinking, that his daddy was lying.

We questioned about the possibilities. I was just trying to save the case at this point. His natural mother was sitting in the courtroom. She had gone through a really nasty divorce with my client. So I thought that there might be some possibility that she had tainted his testimony and not to believe anything he said. So I persisted in trying to do something with him, for at this point he was just hammering, persisting that his dad was drunk when he took him home. So I'm trying to blame the natural mother. I asked him if anybody had talked with him about his testimony, and he said, "Yeah."

Then I asked him if anybody had told him to lie. And he said, "Yeah, my daddy! My daddy told me to lie, and tell the judge that he wasn't drinking, but he really was."

He told the truth, and it was so obviously the truth that there was no question in my mind but that my client was going to get convicted, and I had just lost. But when that boy said, "Yeah, somebody did tell me to lie. My daddy," I wanted to slide under the table. If I could have found a trapdoor in that floor, I would have disappeared right there, for there was nothing you could do with that. The case was over. . . . So I lost and lost big. That's the one trial I lost in my career.

The lesson we learned there is that you have to be really careful with a child witness, because children typically are so blatantly honest. If they're not for you, you've got a problem. If they are for you, you definitely want them on the stand.

The judge laughs about that case to this day. He'd already told us if we hadn't called any witnesses, he was going to dismiss the case.

Keith Bartley, Prestonsburg, November 10, 2000

203. "Some Family Members Worth Only One Dollar"

A lot of times I will have clients come in to me when they are making their will and they have heard that you have to leave one dollar to their children that they want to disinherit. They ask about that, and say, "Well, I have to leave them a dollar, don't I?"

I said, "No, the reason for that is so they couldn't come later and say, 'Well, Dad just forgot about me. He's not mentally in real good shape, and he forgot to name me with the other children.'" And I said, "In order to keep that from being challenged, this shows that they did remember that this one was also a child." But I said, "You don't have to leave a dollar, you can say to them, 'I am leaving nothing to my son, Leroy, under this will for reasons well known unto him.'"

I've had clients that just delighted in that. They'll say, "Boy, that's wonderful! When he reads that, he'll know!" They just love that, but that's a sad commentary on family relationships. But sometimes they don't want to give them that dollar.

Randy Teague, Madisonville, July 28, 2000

204. "Siblings Dispute Ownership of Father's Property"

Lawyers have a lot of dull time, like when the jury is out and we are waiting on a witness and this kind of thing. Tom Waller, with whom I practiced until he died in 1975, was a master storyteller . He was a well-educated, literate man. His stories had a lot of organization and elements of classic literature, but he would deny that they were intentionally constructed that way, and they may not have been.

One of his stories that I've always enjoyed, and he developed it by talking about this man who regularly came to his office to get a deed. During the Depression, Waller's law firm pretty much survived by foreclosing loans for a metropolitan insurance company and would end up selling the foreclosed property. Anyway, a man who was his client had bought some property and he lived in a small town near here. Anytime somebody was driving into Paducah, he would catch a ride and come down to ask if his deed was here. This was just sort of entertainment for him, so he and Mr. Waller got to be good friends. One time he was in Paducah and told Mr. Waller that he was just really tired of all the lawsuits and courts he was in. When asked about that, he explained that his father had taught school in Texas back when land was cheap. He had lived all over the state and bought cheap land in various places in Texas.

When his father died, this man had a falling-out with his siblings, so he left all this land to this one man but none to his siblings. He went ahead to explain to Mr. Waller that in Texas when there is a will contest, it has to be filed in the county where the land is, and that he had been in files in four counties and had been to the court of appeals in Austin twice. He paused a minute and then said, "You know, sometimes I wish that Daddy hadn't even died."

Now, that's the kind of story that lawyers back then would develop and tell.

Richard Roberts, Paducah, November 2, 2001

205. "Getting Ready to Eat Molasses"

Several years ago, this kid went to school one day and had a big mark across the back of his hand that had turned blue. The teacher asked, "What is that?"

The boy said, "That's where Mama hit me with the back of a knife."

Said, "Your mama hit you with a knife?"

He said, "Yes, Ma'am, she did."

She said, "Well, what happened?"

He said, "Well, we were sitting there eating breakfast. We had sorghum molasses, biscuits and butter, and I poured that sorghum molasses out on my biscuit and then cut it off with my knife. When I looked to stick my knife in the butter, my mother hit me across the hand with her knife and said, "How many times have I got to tell you to lick that knife before you stick it in that butter?"

Ken S. Dean, Madisonville, April 15, 2002

206. "Doctor's Maltreatment"

One of the funniest depositions I ever took was when I was defending the Adair County Hospital. Jeff Herbert was defending a doctor. All the action involved in that case had gotten started when the Adair County Hospital filed a suit to collect on unpaid hospital bills against a country woman and her husband, both of whom were likely in their early seventies.

This woman filed a counterclaim against the doctor and hospital for abusive malpractice. Her husband also filed a claim for the loss of consortium—companionship and sexual companionship, and so forth.

Well, this woman was courtly and not too well educated. I started out by asking her to describe what kind of physical ailment she had at the onset that caused her to have to go consult the doctor. She stated that she was having vaginal bleeding, although she didn't describe it. She was bleeding, and she went to see the doctor to see why it was that she was bleeding. So the doctor examined her and performed a minor procedure on her, which I believe was the D & C [dilation and curettage]. At first, he had given her a shot, and she went home. She went on to describe how in a day or two she just started bleeding like a young woman. And she was having pain also, so she went back to the doctor. At that time, he did the D & C, and she said that he just stuffed her full of cotton and must have put two or three boxes of cotton in there. When he did that, she could just barely get around. The doctor had told her not to take the cotton out.

She went back to him and told him that it had been in there three or four days and that she was having trouble going to the bathroom, and she was sitting up with a woman down at the funeral home one night and just had this awful episode. She told him that she came home and that this thing of cotton came out and that she'd never seen anything like it before.

"Well, what did you do with it?" I asked.

Her husband's name was Herbert, or Hub, and she said, "So I called Hub, and he come and took this stuff that I took out of me, and he put it in a coffee can and took it out in the back yard *and buried it!*"

I said, "Well, you got along all right after that didn't you?"

"Well, no, I's just having trouble."

She was sitting there, and in a big chair, all sprawled out waiting for court.

I asked her, "Now, tell me, what is it that you are complaining about? What is your lingering problem?"

She says, "Well, you know, it's kind of hard to explain. Here, let me show you."

She just sprawled, and started to pull up her dress and was going to show us right there!

Well, then it came Herbert's deposition, and I was taking his deposition. "Now, Herbert, what is it that you are complaining about?"

"Well, we just don't live together like man and wife did anymore."

"Well, now, Herbert, what happened?"

He says, "Well, since she went to the doctor and came home and had all this, it's not like it was."

I said, "What do you mean when you say you don't live together as husband and wife?"

He said, "No, sir, we just don't live together any more like husband and wife and do those things like we used to."

I said, "Do you mean that you all don't have sexual relations anymore?"

"That's right," he said.

I said, "Well, now, Herbert, how often did you all have it before that?"

He said, "Well, New Year's, Fourth of July, and Thanksgiving."

So I asked, "Well, Herbert, why is it? Is the reason why you don't have relations is because you don't want to, or she can't?"

He said, "I won't do it no more. She come home after she'd been to the doctor, and she took all of that out of her, and I put it in that coffee can and took it back there in the backyard and buried it, and I wouldn't touch her with a fishing pole now."

Charles English, Bowling Green, May 27, 2002

16

ELECTIONS AND POLITICS

Stories in this category demonstrate both that a rigid political division persists between Democrats and Republicans across the years and that some persons run for office several times but are never elected. Physical encounters between contestants, such as the one described below, have occurred in all portions of the state, as has ballot theft on election days, especially in times past. Some people still feel that honest political campaigns and elections, something to which all Kentuckians should aspire, are yet to come.

207. "MISSING ELECTION BALLOTS"

One of Dad's favorite stories occurred when he filed suit to contest an election in Pike County back in the 1950s for a magistrate race. The procedure at that time, with paper ballots, was that the election officers secured the ballot box after the ballots were first counted. The box was then passed to the high sheriff of the county for protection until the election was declared official.

In the lawsuit, which called for a recount of the ballots, the order of proof was to put on the witness stand all the people who had custody of the ballot box between the date of the election and the time of the trial. So Dad proceeded to put on the various election officials that had control and custody of the box. This included various deputy sheriffs, the sheriff, and finally the county clerk, who had control of the box during litigation.

Sworn testimony of each official was that the box had been secure while under their control. Dad then asked the judge for an order that the box was secured throughout the chain of custody and that it was now fair and appropriate to open the box and recount the ballots. The Court so ordered and the box was opened. To everyone's surprise, they discovered that the box was completely empty with no ballots anywhere to be found. There being no ballots to recount, the litigation was dismissed and the election upheld as originally announced.

Daniel P. Stratton, Pikeville, November 8, 2000, as told by his father, Henry D. Stratton, two-time president of the Kentucky Bar Association

208. "Elections during Early Times"

Back in the old days when they held elections and they had paper ballots, they had what they called a chain ballot. There were certain voters that could be bought, but the people buying them wanted to be sure that they voted the right way. So they would not pay them until they were showed that they voted the right way. So the chain ballot was instituted, which meant that a fellow would go in and vote, but he would bring his ballot back with him. The next fellow would go in, take that ballot, and bring his back so that they could be sure how these people voted. And if they didn't vote for the guy that was buying their vote, they didn't get paid. However, if the ballot showed that they had voted the way they were supposed to, then they were paid whatever they were promised for voting that way.

Sometimes that was protested and taken to court, but it was very difficult to prove. Most people think that there never was a strictly honest election held in Kentucky. When I was county attorney, I was a Republican in a Democrat county. The head of our party was a dentist. (He later moved to Maysville and has been mayor there for the past fifteen to twenty years.) He decided that he was going to stop the practice of buying votes, so he hired a photographer from Winchester to come up here with a hidden camera and take pictures. And as it was related to me by this dentist, they had several pictures of a Democrat precinct worker handing money over. Well, that word got around to the county judge, who was a real strong Democrat, and it being a Democrat county, the sheriff went and arrested this man. All he had done was hang around the polls and take some pictures. They charged him with some law violation.

The chairman of the party came to me and I went to the judge. I said, "Now, look Judge, we have the goods as you well know, and this man hasn't committed any violation of any law that I know of."

The judge said, "He's going to stay over there until he agrees to give up them pictures."

I said, "Well, what about bond?" I thought I could get him out on bond.

The judge informed me that right now there wasn't any bond. It was at most a misdemeanor, if it was any kind of violation. I said that the man hadn't done anything wrong. But the only way I could get him out of jail, I finally went to the [Republican] party chairman and said, "I think in a Democrat county like this, even with the pictures we've got, we might not get any indictments, and if we got any indictments, we probably wouldn't get any convictions. They would come up with some story that claimed to tell what was going on. So tell the man to give the pictures up and go on home. That's the only way they're going to let him out."

He finally agreed to do that.

I still think that most Kentuckians think that there never was a real, honest-to-goodness election in the state of Kentucky.

John L. Cox Jr., Stanton, November 26, 2001

209. "POLITICAL FAITH"

As a young attorney in the late 1970s, I had the opportunity to draft a will for an elderly Pike County gentleman with whom I had the privilege of talking to several times in planning his estate. After everything was completed, he closed the conversation by stating what a nice young man I was and that if I ever ran for public office be sure to call on him for his support and vote.

I thanked him for the expression of confidence, and stated that as a Republican in a county where the Democrats outnumber Republicans three and a half to one, I would probably need every vote I could get.

He responded with the words, "You are a Republican?"

I answered back, "Yes, but you wouldn't hold it against me would you?" To which he responded, "No, I wouldn't, but I'm getting on in years, and I wouldn't want it held against me in the great hereafter."

Daniel P. Stratton, Pikeville, November 30, 2000

210. "THE POLITICIAN WHO NEVER WON A POLITICAL RACE"

A lot of these stories that I have heard, I gathered at the office. I pride myself in having the best loafing office in town. One story that I recall was told by the nephew of a local politician, who was our most famous and most noted one. He was Attorney Silas A. Sullivan, and he ran for many offices but was never elected. He traveled about over the area, and he had one famous speech that he made. It was called "This is God's Country." I never heard the speech, but I understand that is has been documented that he made it before the state legislature one time. His idea in politics seemed to be not necessarily to win, but just to run.

Silas had run for office on one particular occasion, and he had come over to visit with some of his relatives. He told them that he thought that he had done pretty good in the election because he had sold his cow and paid his travel expenses. He sold his sheep and bought a few votes, so it looked like he had done pretty good. His nephew Al said, "Well, Uncle Silas, I don't think that you've done too good."

Silas said, "Well, why?"

Al said, "Your cow is gone, your sheep's gone, but you wasn't elected."

He said, "You know, I never thought about it like that!"

Lige Coffey, Russell Springs, July 11, 1988

211. "CANDIDATE PAID TO END CAMPAIGN"

One time Silas Sullivan was running for an office. He ran for everything, from United States circuit judge, county attorney, and various things. On one occasion he was running, and apparently his opponent didn't know too much about him. His opponent sent somebody with some money to see how much Silas would take just to pull off and not run for this office.

He lived out in the country. Said when they got to his home, he was under the porch floor. He came crawling out and told them that he was under there to get away from the flies. They told him that someone had sent them to pay him his travel and advertising expenses and so forth if he would consider pulling out of the race.

He told them that he would consider it. And he took a nail and scratched around on a wooden board to figure up how much money he had been out. He told them that it would take $7.50, and not one penny less!

Lige Coffey, Russell Springs, July 11, 1988

212. "Lawyer Breaks Lawmaker's Arm"

One of the things I remember is about this commonwealth attorney that I was in the office with, and county attorney, the latter got into a fight with some politicians there at the courthouse and they had him down on the ground in the courtyard. I ran up and pulled this fellow, who occupied some position in the state legislature, off of him. He wasn't a lawyer, but at that time he was a representative in the state legislature.

When I pulled him off, I swung him around and broke his arm. He used some curse words against me. Fortunately, I broke his arm because he really had it in for me, and then he couldn't do anything to get even with me. I had to walk by him each day, but I wasn't scared very much. He had it in for me because I was in the office with several individuals that he didn't like. But that arm-breaking was the last rough thing that happened between us.

Sam Boyd Neely Sr., Mayfield, June 7, 2001

213. "Interviewing Three Absentee Voters"

This story arose from an election contest, but I'll not identify the chief character in this story. My task on the day in question was to interview three people who were named as potential witnesses in this case against my clients. My clients were people who had run for office and were accused of buying votes.

So, I was supposed to interview these three people who had all voted absentee and were alleged by the authorities to be potential witnesses against my clients. What I was looking for in plain and simple language was to nullify as many witnesses as I could. So, I would go to the homes of these people with a tape recorder and interview with the hopes they would deny having been paid and that I could subsequently use that to impeach them if they turned up as witnesses. And we had some luck.

The folks that are accused of selling their votes generally don't live in nice houses in the middle of town. They live somewhere out in the end of a hollow and not in a very nice house. So I spent one whole summer traipsing up and down this particular county talking to all these folks and found it very interesting. But that one particular day was probably the capper because it was blazingly hot, and I always wore a white shirt and a tie, although I generally didn't wear a coat to these things.

I took a local fellow with me to identify and to let these people know that they could afford to talk to me, or that they should talk to me. So we parked on the edge of the road on one side of the creek, but it was quite a little distance down to the creek, and then you had to go up the other side of the creek about halfway up the hill. The people I was going to see were living in a very typical Appalachian home, in which the back of it sat on a hill and the front of the house was set upon stilts. There was a long porch across the front, narrow and lengthy. The yard was just swept dirt. There wasn't a blade of grass in the yard, and they had a ramshackle fence around the place. The other fellow was also big like me, but down that hill we went, then crossed the creek the best way we could, then went up the other side of the hill to the house. I was pretty well winded by the time we got up to the gate.

We hollered into the house, and they told us to come on in. They knew the guy that I was with and knew that he was morbidly afraid of dogs. So they let us get about halfway across the front yard, then hollered, "Look out for that dog." We began looking, as I didn't want to get bit either. Well, out from under the house wandered the mangiest, sorriest-looking little pup that was plumb full of worms—more than you ever saw in your life. That was the dog that we were supposed to be afraid of. Of course, he couldn't have bit a pork chop if he had had one. Well, we ran up the steps up onto the porch.

And the way we worked it out, the matriarch of this particular clan was really running the show. Her name was Stella. In this particular area, there were not many family names, so each little branch of the family had a nickname. So this particular branch of this family were known as the Cat branch. So, she was Stella Cat. So, I undertook to interview her. I introduced myself and pulled out my little tape recorder, and she acknowledged that I was recording her, and I identified myself. I was actually standing at that point. She was sitting in an overstuffed broken-down old chair that they had carried out on the porch. She was at the end of the porch with her back to the side yard, looking down the length of the porch. The right angles to it had a couch just the same. She invited me to sit down, and in doing so I committed a grave error when I accepted her hospitality, because there wasn't a spring in the couch. When I sat down, my knees came right up to my chin and my butt very nearly hit the floor. Well, I was about as big then as I am now, and I was about to smother down in there. Oh, it was hot! I had my sleeves rolled up about halfway, and I had no more than sat down in that old couch until the gnats just about ate me up. So, she took her lighter out, and she had an old tomato can full of old socks and rags, and she set it on fire. I'd seen that done before. It was called a smudge, and it would run the gnats off. Of course, it chokes you just like it chokes the gnats. So, all things being equal, I guess if I had to put up with one or the other forever, I guess I'd rather have the gnats. I was about as perfectly miserable as you could be and still be in this world, sitting there hot and with my knees up around my chin, and putting up with the smoke and the gnats.

I proceeded to ask her about the election and who she had voted for. Well, she was a little disconcerting to talk to because she was as walleyed as anybody I ever saw in my life. One of her eyes looked right straight over to the left, and the other one kind of looked up a little and to the right. I mean she could not possibly look *at* you. I mean, I'm sure she was looking at me, but I couldn't tell it. When I asked her if she had voted in that election, she proceeded to let me know that indeed she had voted in that election, and that she was an old country woman and certainly couldn't be expected to go to town to vote; that she had to vote absentee; that them g——d—— liars in the county seat town had told that she sold her votes, but she had never sold her vote; that she would vote for the candidate that I was representing, no matter what because he was the only one that had ever done anything for them on that creek branch; and that before he come, they had to wade the mud up to their ass every time it rained in order to get out of there.

I asked her if she had been paid anything, and she told me no, that she had voted because that was her right as an American citizen, and she was proud to vote. So, I thanked her for her time and then asked her if I might interview her husband, whose name was Taylor, and who thus went by Taylor Cat. So, she hollered, "Taylor, come out here. This feller wants to talk to you."

Well, I took advantage of that opportunity to get up on my feet to interview Taylor while standing. Well, he came out of that house and was about the most unlikely looking prospect for an interview that I'd ever seen. I think that I'd been told before I went there that he drank some, which of course is the eastern Kentucky euphemism for being an alcoholic. Indeed, he had drunk some. He was absolutely loathsome. He had a beard and had some little chunks of something in it. He had a big amber stain right down the middle of the beard, where he chewed tobacco, and he had peed more than one time in the pants that he was standing there in, because some of the stains were different colors. He got up there, and you could see them. But I had my job to do. I had to interview the guy. . . . He had just the same story. He had voted absentee because he was an old crippled man and couldn't get to town—had no other way to vote. He had voted of his own free will. Nobody had paid him anything. He answered all my questions, and when I got to the end of the questions, I thanked him and told him that the interview was concluded, at which point before I could click off the tape recorder, he leered at me and said in his most ingratiating tone, "Did I tell it right?"

I didn't have the heart to go back and start over, so I just took that. Then I said to both of them, "I need to interview Sid also." He was their grandson. Well, in unison, just as in a Greek chorus, they said, "Aw, honey, you can't talk to Sid. He's in too bad a shape."

Well, I'm thinking, "Oh, good God almighty, he must be dead because he couldn't be in worse shape than you two."

Anyway, I hollered at the fellow who was with me. He came out of the house and we went back down the hill, across the creek, went back up the hill, and got back in the car. When we recovered our breath, I said, "They said Sid was in too bad a shape."

He said, "Well, you should have seen Sid. You would have concurred. When I went in the house, Sid was sitting in the middle of the first room I walked into with nothing on but a pair of blue jeans—no shirt—drinking white [moonshine] whiskey out of a jar, just like in a movie, and chasing it with a Budweiser. I set down there and talked to him and his sister come through the house and said, 'Sid, what in the world is the matter with you that you'd have company in the house and not even put on a shirt?' At that point, Sid set his drinks down on each side of him, got up; his britches fell down around his ankles and tripped him, and he never even put his hands out. He was so far gone that he just went face down on the floor and never moved again."

When we got together for a strategy meeting, we had several accused persons and several attorneys there that evening. I said, "Well, if anybody thinks that the government can make enough of a witness out of those three to be worth the effort, I'll go back and interview them again, because I can't bring this tape into court in the shape it's in." Indeed, we agreed we could just cross them off, and indeed we did not see them in a subsequent trial.

That's always been one of my favorite stories.

Asa "Pete" Gullett, Shelbyville, June 3, 2002

214. "Interviewing Mountain Family about Voting Practices"

There are two pieces to this story. At the mouth of one of the creeks out there in the county, there was an old couple who lived there. They had raised their family, and most of their family members had left home. Of course, they still mostly lived around there—had gone into coal mining, or whatever. This old man and his wife, they'd had one mentally retarded child. It got an amount of play in the *Courier-Journal*. Twenty years ago, the social workers all started raising a bunch of hell about this guy. His parents kept him there in the house, and they liked to sit on the porch, and he also liked to sit on the porch. He was a grown man and a big stout fellow. And since he had the mind of a child, he could be dangerous to a bypasser if they said something to him. His parents were too old to control him physically. So they put a cage on half of their front porch, so when he came out of his side of the house, he walked into this cage. He would sit there and watch the world go by. People could speak to him and he could speak to them. And most of the time, he was perfectly docile. But that cage kept him from wandering off, and kept him from taking up a quarrel with anybody if he saw somebody that he could quarrel with, or want to.

This old man and his wife both voted absentee. Well, we would go by places like that and interview people, and the postal inspectors would, too. We would ask everybody what they were asking, and they would ask them what we were asking. . . . Anyway, the postal inspectors were talking to this old man and his wife, saying, "You voted absentee, you don't have a car, you can't get to town—so who brought this ballot to you?"

Well, this couple knew perfectly well who had brought it to them, but they were both playing dumb. They'd say, "Why, I don't remember if I voted in that election or not. That was four years. I ain't got no idea. I don't know even who was running then."

The fellow kept questioning them. Well, the particular person who had brought the ballot to them was known to Harvey by who his father was. His father's nickname was Bald Jack Horton. Well, Harvey starts jumping up and down and shaking his cage, saying, "Why, it was Bald Jack's boy, Mommy, don't you remember? It was Bald Jack's boy."

I said to the particular fellow that questioned the defendant, "Now, if they bring that simpleton into the courtroom, and he starts pointing a finger at you, and saying 'You carried that in,' no cross-examination will shake that! There is no way to impeach that infant. He'd be like an infant child that rose out of its swaddling clothes and pointed an accusing finger at you. There's just nothing to do."

Anyway, we were up there interviewing witnesses one day. This is the same case, but it is a different story that involves the same people. This witness lived in a house about one hundred yards down the creek from where Harvey lived. We needed to talk to the old gentleman who owned the house, and we also needed to talk to his son, Bill. He told us that his son was about two hundred yards up the road at a garage, where they also had a little poolroom. Said he was up there shooting pool.

So, I was finishing up the election interview with the father, when my partner went walking up the road to find the boy at the poolroom. I finished my interview and was going to follow my partner up there in the car. Well, when I got ready to start my car, there my partner stood looking just as white as a sheet of paper. He was obviously scared to death. I asked him, "What has happened to you?"

He said, "I got up there in front of Harvey's house, and I'll be damned if he didn't have a pistol and he pointed it right at me and said, 'Look at my gun. I've got me a gun.'" Then my partner went on to say, "I don't know what to do: whether to run, or to stand there, or throw up my hands." He went on to say that Harvey laid the pistol down and picked up this handle, said, "I got me a hammer handle, too." He said, "When he picked up that hammer handle, I lit out. I got away from there as hard as I could go."

So, we went into town for a strategy meeting that night. This will show you about people's attitudes. We got laughed at beyond anything, because the local fellows there said, "Everybody knows Harvey's gun ain't got no firing pin in it!"

Asa "Pete" Gullett, Shelbyville, June 3, 2002

215. "LAWYER WITHHOLDS IDENTITY FROM THE JUDGE"

We had a case one time that dealt with an election. You read in the newspapers a lot of times where the press will talk about a source close to the court who said so-and-so, but they never would reveal who said it. Well, years ago, I was the county attorney in Whitley County, and we had a hearing involving the city commission election in Corbin. One of the candidates for the city commission had filed his papers with the county court clerk in order to be on the ballot. For some reason, there was some fault with the papers, as he didn't have enough signatures, or something of that nature, and it was getting close to election time. So, this fellow wanted to have a quick hearing, and I represented the county clerk in this case.

We had a fast hearing in the Whitley Circuit Court. Judge Pleas Jones, who later was on the Kentucky Supreme Court, was the presiding circuit judge. So he had a nighttime hearing, and he went through it all, and it looked as if this man, who was trying to get on the ballot, didn't have the proper signatures, so the county clerk said, "I just can't put him on the ballot."

Judge Pleas Jones showed his frustration and then said, "Well, I'm just going to let the people of Corbin decide it. It looks faulty to me, but I'm going to put his name on the ballot, and that's my ruling."

There weren't many people in the courtroom, and it was all taken down. So, one of the members of the press called me later, said, "What happened in this case?"

I said, "Well, I'll tell you what happened. Judge Jones said it looked faulty as a petition, but he was going to let it be put on the ballot anyway, and just let the people of Corbin decide the issue."

The reporter, Lauren Hooker, said, "Well, I'll report that in the morning news. But I won't give your name, I'll just say, 'A source close to the court said this.'"

So the next morning, he gave his morning report that a lot of people in the county listened to. Well, the next day, I saw Judge Jones and he asked me, "Did you hear that news report?"

I said, "Yes, I sure did, Judge."

Then he said, "The very idea. That Lauren Hooker said that I said that we are just going to let the people of Corbin decide this question. I don't know where he got that idea, but he said it came from a source close to the court. What do you think about that?"

I said, "Well, I don't know, Judge; they just throw these things out all the time." Of course it was accurate, but he didn't want it put in there that the source was close to the court. So, I never did tell him that it was me. If he'd asked me, I would have told him that I was the person, but he didn't ask and I never told him.

Eugene Siler Jr., London, June 20, 2002

17

JUDGES' SUPPORT OF THE ACCUSED

⚖

Judges are typically highly respected, both by lawyers and others appearing before them during court sessions. However, on occasion, judges do make judicial mistakes, thus causing lawyers to appeal the decision for reversal. At other times, the judge may dismiss all charges against the accused, only to find out later that the accused was indeed guilty and continued to commit illegal acts.

Stories in this section portray judges engaged both in various courtroom proceedings and, sometimes, in questionable activity outside the courtroom.

216. "SOME JUDGES NOT WILLING TO BE CHALLENGED"

I represented a widow whose husband was killed in a truck accident. And before he was killed, his employer, without notice to his employees, canceled their life insurance benefits. So we sued the former employer essentially for what is called estoppel law, or promissory estoppel. When you promise a benefit to me, and then I rely on that promise to my detriment, and you fail to follow through, then you can be liable to me for your failure to follow through. That was the case in which I was proud to be able to get a benefit for this woman. We had to try the case twice, but I was able to win it for the woman. When I tried it the first time, the judge didn't think the employer owed that responsibility to this employee, so he dismissed the case.

I appealed the case, and the decision is recorded as McCarthy vs. Louisville Cartage Company, 796 S.W. 2d 10 (1990). The case was tried a second time, and I won it. It was under a different judge, but only because the initial judge had retired. Appeals are kind of tricky in that way. When you're appealing a case, 99 percent of the time the reason you have an appealable issue is because of an error the judge has made. If you succeed in the appeal in reversing the judge's decision because of an error the judge has made, you go straight back to that same judge. Most judges are able to take all that in stride and understand that that is simply the process. We're humans and we're fallible. But some don't like to be challenged, so that can make it difficult.

Peter Ervin, Louisville, April 26, 2001

217. "Little Boy Keeps Running Away"

I was in district court in front of the famous Judge Clay here in Morehead years ago. Judge Clay and I were eventually to become good friends. I was involved in two juvenile cases. After I tell you about this, I don't know why I had any credibility in that court whatsoever. My law firm had been called upon to represent a young juvenile who was famous for running away from home, away from whatever facility he was put in. He was a nice enough kid, as he wasn't like someone who stole cars. But he was a chronic runner—runaway. That was his thing; run away from home, or run away from the juvenile center. Didn't matter where he was, he'd run away from it.

I was talking to the judge about him and mentioned the fact that this boy was not what is called a public offender. He'd never committed any crime other than just running away from home and running away from the authority. That's what he does. He'd never stay where they'd put him. Just run away.

He was a young, young man, maybe ten or twelve years old, so the judge was concerned about what might happen to him *while* he was on the run. I'll never forget my young client telling me and the judge that he had learned his lesson and that he would stop running. Well, since the judge had been around for some time, he was rather skeptical. At any rate, we were making this argument, and the judge was giving some consideration to give him a try back at the house one more time rather than at one of the detention facilities. Well, just about the time I got the sentence out—"Judge, he will not run again"—my client turned and bolted out of the courtroom. Well, you can imagine the impact that had. I turned around and took out after him, and the deputy sheriff and I eventually caught him and brought him back in.

I apologized to the judge, and sure enough my client said that he was scared and that he just felt compelled to run and he did, but he was sorry. He went on to tell the judge that if he would give him a second chance he would not disappoint the judge.

The judge did order that he be released from the detention center, that he be sent back home. And, sure enough, on the trip back to the detention center with the deputy sheriff to pick up his clothes and stuff so he could be released to his folks, he bolted and ran and we haven't seen him since.

Keith McCormick, Morehead, June 22, 2000

218. "The Truck Muffler That Wasn't"

We had been here approximately a year when I was attending court in front of Judge Clay. Judge Clay has since passed away. He was quite a rogue. He was a character. He liked to go out and live in the woods and shoot those long powder rifles. He frequently wore the garb of the era. He would preside over weddings in the woods among these long riflemen and out-in-the-country hunter types. On occasion he would come to court in bib overalls. Frequently he would come to court in bib overalls and not even have a T-shirt underneath. He was just an absolute rogue. He was a veteran of World War II. He was a short, stocky man, a former prosecutor, highly countrified, yet highly educated. But he really understood people and connected with them very nicely. People did love him, although frequently he could be tough.

One hot summer July day he was on the bench and the traffic docket was backed up just as always. The courtroom was full of people, which probably added to the heat as we sat there. I guess we were all looking for that one levity of humanity that might otherwise break the misery. At that point, this young country boy was called up from the back of the courtroom. Judge Clay, who considered everybody under fifty-five to be his own child, called him up. Well, this great big six-foot-four country boy went and stood before the judge. Judge Clay asked him, "Now, honey, what kind of trouble have you gotten into?"

The young fellow said, "Judge, this is an absolute travesty of justice."

The judge said, "Well, what happened?"

"Well, I was driving down Main Street and a city policeman pulled me over." Said, "I've got the ticket right here. I've got the proof right here. They charged me with having a defective muffler."

The judge said, "Well now, honey, why is that so upsetting?"

The boy said, "Well, everybody who knows me knows that I've had that truck for years and it's *never* had a muffler on it. It couldn't possibly be defective."

Well, the court burst into absolute pandemonium. The judge said, "Well, that's as good an argument as any." He slammed the gavel down and said, "Not guilty," and sent him out of the courtroom.

Keith McCormick, Morehead, June 22, 2000

219. "Fishermen Not Guilty"

This is a story about a case I had when I was county attorney. The game wardens were a little more active then, and they caught twelve to fifteen people that were having a fish seining party out here on the North Fork Creek. They brought all of them to court and to this same county judge that I helped educate and get appointed. Incidentally, he had been a truck driver hauling livestock to the local livestock market as his only occupation other than being the county commissioner when he was selected as county judge.

So these wardens arrested all these fellows for seining the fish, and I went to court with the commissioner to prove the case. But the judge just turned his head and said, "Not guilty." In the district court, there are very few juries, so this case didn't call for jurors. And in a case like that, the jurors would likely have kinfolks in that seining party, so they would have turned them loose, too, so I would just go through the motion and get it over with.

John H. Clarke, Maysville, February 20, 2002

220. "Country Judges"

This happened the other day. This old alcoholic came to my office. He is not an ax murderer, but he is constantly on the fringes because of non-support, drunkenness, and things like that. I like him. You can't help but like him. He came in the other day and sat down right here in the office and talked to me about his case.

This is all about rural justice. People don't think any more about calling me to talk on the telephone about their case than they'd think about calling a country judge to talk about a road. But different judges handle it in different ways. Of course, urban judges in big cities don't have that problem. They don't even know the people. They don't get phone calls, but I get phone calls at home all the time. People will call and say, "Hi, Judge, how are you doing? You know that Lindsey case you've got tomorrow—Henrietta's? Do you know that's my daughter? I just wanted you to know."

I'll say to them, "Well, Mr. So-and-so, I don't know what kind of case it is, but I promise you that I'll be fair and impartial."

"That's all I wanted—all I want you to do."

Of course, what they really want you to know is that that's their case and they want you to treat them really special. . . .

I can't talk in depth with them, but I can say, "I'll be fair and impartial." Then I quickly change the subject and ask something like, "How are those dogs doing?"

That's the way a country judge handles things like that. Anyway, this fellow I was telling about that came by to see me in the office, called me the other night and said, "Ya Honor, I'm supposed to be in your court tomorrow. What I want to know is do I need to bring my toothbrush and cigarettes?" Then he went on to say, "Those cigarettes are expensive over there in jail. I just wanted to know if I needed to bring them."

And I said, "[Name withheld], tomorrow is not your day, so you don't have to bring them tomorrow."

And he was serious, just as serious as a heart attack. He simply wanted to know if I was going to send him to jail the next day so he could bring his cigarettes.

Bill Cunningham, Eddyville, January 21, 2002

221. "Judge Supports the Accused"

One time many years ago I was county attorney here in Powell County for about thirty-two years. I was prosecuting a man for carrying a concealed deadly weapon. For some reason, our usual judge could not be there, so we got a judge from Estill County. He is still living. He called me up to the bench and said, "I see that you have a man charged here with carrying a concealed deadly weapon."

I said, "Yes, Your Honor."

He said, "Do you intend to prosecute him?"

And I said, "Yes, Your Honor, that's my intention."

The judge said, "Well, I'm telling you right now, the Constitution of the United States gives a person the right to carry a firearm, *and I am dismissing this case before we hear any of it.*"

I would say the judge pretty well sided with the accused in that case, even though we had a statutory law that said you could not carry a concealed deadly weapon. I could have appealed that case, but I was so flabbergasted that I didn't.

John L. Cox Jr., Stanton, November 26, 2001

18

PHYSICAL ABUSE

⚖

The narratives in this category discuss abuse—occurring at home and in public places—which sometimes results in homicidal activities. The general public and members of the legal profession typically view physical and verbal abuse as something that should never take place.

222. "WOMAN INSISTS SHE WAS CONSTANTLY ABUSED"

There was one case we had in which this lady lived with a fellow. Whenever she'd get mad at him, she'd come in and swear out a warrant that he'd beat her: jumped on her, threatened her, or something. The judge would give her a restraining order against him for coming around her. Then she'd be back with this man within a week, and two weeks later she'd be back with another warrant. Then, she'd dismiss the charges when it came to trial.

The county attorney at that time was Bernard Hargett. They got tired of her coming in so much. He said to her, "If you come one more time, we're going to try it. We'll put you on the stand for you to tell what happened. If you don't, I'm going to get you for contempt of court."

Again, she got another warrant out. Hargett said, "You got the warrant out, so we'll have to try it."

She said, "Okay."

So they arrested the man and it came to trial. She wanted to dismiss the charges again. The county attorney said no. So they put her on the stand, then asked her what happened. She responded, "Your Honor, I just don't remember a thing."

The district judge looked at her and said, "Elizabeth, you've done this too many times to this court. I'm going to dismiss this charge, but if you ever need relief in the future, you'd better go to the aspirin bottle, because you're not going to get it in this court."

Well, it wasn't more than two weeks until they were back together. One afternoon she got mad at him. He was lying in bed asleep, so she got a gun and shot and killed him. We had to try her for murder. She said that he gave her a gun and told her, "Here, if you want to kill me, kill me." She went on to say that the gun went off accidentally and shot him. That opened the door I thought to the conversation he had with a whiskey store dealer. When he went in to see him that morning, he told the dealer, "I've got to get out of there. That damn bitch is going to kill me." So we thought that indicated that he would not have handed her a gun with this feeling. She was convicted for murder and got about twelve years for it.

That's something that they all have trouble with. Some judges will not let the abused spouse drop the charges. They do that all over the state. They'll get charges against their husband or boyfriend and then want to drop the charges. Then they'll bring the charges back up next week, but they'll want to drop them again. That's just a waste of the court's time. It's still going on. They're trying to set it up so if they don't get a warrant out, they don't proceed with it.

Woodson Wood, Maysville, February 20, 2002

223. "Asking One Question Too Many"

About twelve years ago, I was representing a minister in Elliott County who, in fact, had committed the crime he was charged with. He professed, however, that he had not. Well, I took great pride in representing the U.S. Constitution; everybody has got a right to be tried before they go to prison. So, by golly if we wanted to try the case, we would try it.

Everybody told us that he was such an eccentric man—that he was sort of adrift. I didn't pay much attention to that, as he obviously knew what he had to do to defend himself. So, we called and we corresponded, but we never could get together to really get his defense put together for some reason. He was always busy, like his schedule required that he go visit some ailing person in the hospital.

Well, I got directions to his place. Directions are always hard to understand here in this part of Kentucky. This fellow told me, "You go out Highway 7, then go to the first mile marker, then turn on the first paved road to the left. Then stay on that road until you come to the first gravel drive to the left, then take that until the gravel stops. And you know how when a car or tractor is driven over grass, how you'll see two stripes in the grass. Well, follow that about a mile. Then you'll come to two old trailers that are surrounded by trash. They live in one of those two trailers, but I don't know which one."

Well, this minister had told me that his wife would testify on his behalf and that his son would also testify in his behalf. And they would both play a role in my perception of his case. The wife I was to meet first. On the Saturday before the trial I was pretty panicky because I didn't have any details from my client about his defense. So I drove out there, and sure enough there he was out in the yard working or doing something. The funny thing is, their trailer was in a donut of trash. You could tell that it got that way because of the way they disposed of trash. They went to the nearest window and pitched it. So there was about a ten-foot space that was clear because everything they tossed out got at least that far away from the trailer. But from ten feet on out, depending on the how heavy the objects were you could tell how far they had traveled. And believe it or not, in some places the trash was two- or three-feet deep.

So there was the self-appointed reverend standing in the yard. I went up to him and introduced myself and we started to talk. Things were going fairly well when I said, "I need to interview your wife." And he said, "Well, go ahead."

"Well, okay, but to interview her, I need to meet her," I told him.

And he said, "Well, okay, this is my wife." Again there was silence as the two of us stood there looking at each other. He gestured with his hand toward the field of trash and said, "My wife's right here."

About that time I was thinking that this is a really bad science fiction story. Then, all of a sudden, one big pile of cans started to rustle, and up from under this pile of cans appears his wife who promptly introduces herself and says that she'd be proud to help her husband. She was just hiding because she saw a car that she didn't know. She assumed that my car was the Department of Social Services coming to take another kid. That gave me a real lasting impression of them when she arose from under the pile of trash. She told me what her story was and that she was confident that her husband was not involved in this crime and provided sort of an alibi to the crime.

Well, this crime involved a whipping the minister had administered to another person, and a pretty good whipping at that. One of the things we had was his adult son, who was about eighteen, that was living in their trailer home at the time the whipping was supposed to have happened. Actually, the trailer had doors but no windows. It was kind of a free-floating thing.

So we went to court, and his son did show up. His wife didn't make too good of a witness, but his son did show up. In the process of waiting for the jury to get in and get started, I went over to this young boy about fifty times. I asked him if he had been there when the whipping supposedly took place. He said that yes he was. . . . I asked him, "Did you ever see him whip this guy, or anybody else for that matter?"

He said, "Absolutely not."

Well, we get the trial underway and my client takes the stand, and he did all right. His wife leaves the courthouse and can't be found, and so we get to the son. The son takes the stand and does an excellent job. At this point, even I am wondering if the reverend actually wore this guy out—whipped him. We are doing real well, so we put him on the stand. The prosecutor can't believe how well things are going. But he puts his client on the stand to testify and that went okay. And ours went real well, too. So when they got to the end of their case the judge, as he always does, gives the defendant an opportunity to come back. And he asked, "Do you have any rebuttal evidence?"

I said, "Oh, yes, Judge; absolutely. I want to call the reverend's son, please."

The deputy goes out into the hall and brings the boy in, and we set him down on the stand, and I said to him, "Now the person who just testified came in here and swore that this happened. I just want to make sure for the jury's sake that we have this clear. Did you ever see your dad beat this fellow up?"

"Absolutely not—not one time. However, I was in the next room and *I did hear it.*"

Well, things kind of melted down after that. What had looked like a pretty good case. . . . We were over. The first juror into the jury room was coming out when the last one was going in. They voted while they walked around the table, and in under a minute returned a guilty verdict with a maximum sentence for this whipping. Possibly, they were right. So that's the story about asking one question too many.

Keith McCormick, Morehead, June 22, 2000

224. "The Rattlesnake Case"

We had this case where a woman was accused. This young female lawyer with me asked, "How are you going to get her acquitted? The accused woman just got the other girl down and beat her and beat her, and then kicked her while she was down on the floor. There's no way that the jury is going to acquit her."

I said, "Well, just watch."

So we go into the courtroom and show that the person who got hurt was the aggressor. And in the closing argument, I said, "She [the defendant] knocked her [the aggressor] down, knocked her out. That's kind of like my grandpa always told me, when you kill a rattlesnake, be sure you kill them because if you don't, they can still hurt you—still poison you." So that's why she kicked her in the head: just to make sure that she wasn't going to fight her anymore.

So the jury acquitted my client, and as we were leaving the young lawyer said, "Oh, so that was the old rattlesnake defense that you used this time!"

Ken S. Dean, Madisonville, April 15, 2002

225. "Serious but Humorous"

As a young lawyer in Whitley County, I would go to court sometimes just to see what was going on. And we had a very colorful lawyer there, whose name was Garrett Teague Jr. He's retired now. He was representing a sort of weasely fellow who was accused of assaulting his wife.

As usual, Teague was quite colorful. And this woman who was assaulted was a pretty hefty woman—much bigger than her husband. So Teague was questioning this woman on the witness stand about this assault. Teague asked, "Do you want this jury to believe that this little ol' weasely husband of yours beat up on a great big strong woman like you, thus causing you to be assaulted and hurt?"

She said, "Now, Junior Teague, I want you to know that I'm not nearly as strong as I look. I'm under the care of a doctor: I'm bloated and I've got a ruptured navel. He hurt me bad."

So Teague didn't have much to say after she said that about her navel! And I always thought that was a great comeback she came up with.

Eugene Siler Jr., London, June 20, 2002

19

THE BENCH AND THE BAR

⚖️

Lawyer and judge stories are about incidents both in and out of the courtroom that typically do not fit other story categories in this book. These accounts describe judges in life-threatening situations; judges who are not in favor of prosecuting the person(s) charged, perhaps due to personal relationships; judges who support the accused; judges who respond to humorous situations; and so on.

Additional stories in this section are about lawyers, in and out of court, who deal with personal confrontations with other lawyers and judges on occasion; homicidal behavior; possession of and/or consumption of whiskey; lawyers' awesome legal fees; and lawyers' fears of each other. The stories in this section provide meaningful, sometimes humorous, insights into the viewpoints and attitudes held by professionals in the legal system across the years.

226. "LYNCH MOB ACTIVITIES"

I'm writing a book about an interesting episode that happened in Murray in 1917. In summary, this is what it is all about. Guthrie Diuguid was a former town marshall in Murray—a white guy. The Diuguid family was a rather prominent family in Murray. This guy was a kind of renegade, though. He was shot and killed by a black man by the name of Lube Martin for messing around with Lube Martin's wife. The killing actually took place back in December 1916. A lynch mob got together, and Circuit Judge Bush ordered that Martin be ordered back to Hopkinsville for safe keeping. Well, a big lynch mob got up and threatened to hang Judge Bush, so they held Judge Bush and the common-wealth attorney hostage over there in a Murray hotel until the judge ordered that Lube Martin be brought back to Murray. So he then ordered that Martin be brought back to Murray.

By that time, the sheriff was in Princeton on his way to Hopkinsville with Martin, so he turned around and started to bring him back to Murray. Governor A.O. Stanley got wind of it while he was in a legislative session in Louisville. Somebody made an anonymous phone call to him, said, "Somebody is about to hang the judge down at Murray if he doesn't bring this black prisoner back."

A.O. didn't have any state militia. He didn't have any national guard. They were all down on the Mexican border fighting Pancho Villa, so he had no means by which to do anything about it except get on the train himself and come down here to Murray.

It just happened that they were meeting at the Seelbach Hotel at the same time that the Transportation Club was having their annual dinner there, and had all kinds of big wheels of the railroads present. They said, "Hey, no problem." So, they rigged him up a special train and got him on his way out of Louisville about midnight.

He got in at Paducah just after Lube Martin had got back there, but the last train to Murray had already left. So the sheriff put Lube Martin up in the McCracken County jail, and A.O. Stanley went on to Murray. That was about 5:00 or 6:00 A.M. when he got there. The mob was gathered around the hotel there in Murray, threatening Bush and Smith.

So Stanley went in and got everybody up to the courthouse and made this unbelievable speech, saying, "I'm here to make sure the law is enforced. Before you can hang the judge, Lube Martin, or anybody else, you are going to have to hang the governor of Kentucky."

Basically, that dispersed the mob. And they had actually man-handled Judge Bush a little bit while he was trying to make his way from the courthouse to the hotel. They'd pushed him some around the courthouse. It was a real tense situation. Back at that time, a lot of lynchings were taking place. A.O. Stanley became an overnight hero in the national press. He was a southern governor who did more than give lip service against a lynching.

Bill Cunningham, Eddyville, January 21, 2002

227. "POLITICALLY SAVVY COUNTY JUDGE"

I recall that one time the county judge that was in office lost his health and wasn't able to serve, and I had to go to his home and tell him it was time to resign. And I got a friend of mine, who was the county commissioner, not a lawyer, appointed as county judge. Then, I had to educate him as to his duties as county judge.

During that period, we had a state trooper and a state tax collector here in Maysville, and they proceeded to get a warrant for one of the richest men in Maysville, charging him with hauling steel-sheet blocks from river barges up to the Carnation Company, where they used it to make cans for Carnation milk.

I didn't want to prosecute that fellow, as he was the father of a fellow that graduated from high school with me, and also in college. But I prosecuted him and of course the politically savvy county judge just laughed at me and acquitted him.

John H. Clarke, Maysville, February 20, 2002

228. "Witness Won't Swear to Tell the Truth"

Grady Ruff was a good friend of mine from Hopkinsville. He died not long ago. He was an old marine—built like a fireplug. He was commonwealth attorney when I first started trying cases. He later on became a district judge. Grady was a great guy with a big heart, but he was kind of rough. You never knew what he was going to do. He'd just do what he wanted to, basically.

A pretty well-documented story claims that when he was a district judge over Christian County, he had the standard revolving door that defendants came through into court. He was trying a case one day and this old boy came in to witness. Well, all the times before, this guy had been in court as a defendant. He was always getting charged and convicted with stuff. But he was to be a witness this time!

So he comes in, and Judge Grady Ruff raises his right hand to give him the oath. Grady asks him to raise his right hand while taking the oath, but this fellow won't do it. Grady says, "Why aren't you going to take the oath?"

This fellow answered him, said, "Well, Judge, every time I've come in here I'd swear to tell the truth, and I'd tell the truth, but I'd end up in jail. So this time, I'm not going to tell the truth."

So Grady, who was quite a character, said, "Well, all right, just get on the stand and lie then."

So the guy gets on the stand and testifies without taking the oath.

Bill Cunningham, Eddyville, January 21, 2002

229. "Judge's Decision Reconsidered"

We had an old lawyer here, Earl Rose, and he's been dead a long time. He was a good lawyer. He told me this story. He appealed one of these claims, either black lung or Social Security, against the federal government. He had a client that wanted to repeal it. Of course, the Third Federal Circuit in Cincinnati heard it.

Rose said that he went up there and this three-judge panel read over what the case was about. They told him, said, "Now, Mr. Rose, we want you to understand that we think a lot of District Judge Ford." Ford was the district judge that he had appealed the case from. "We think a lot of Judge Ford. We think a lot of his decisions, and we don't like to overrule his decisions, but you filed this case."

Earl said that he reached and picked up his hat off the table. He said, "Well, that's all right with me. I live next door to Judge Ford, and we visit one another. I think that we're good friends. We have a chat about twice a week. But if this is offensive to Judge Ford, then I'm getting out of it. Tell my client to get somebody else if he wants to go through with this."

They said, "Well, we'll hear it and decide." He said that just as he expected they got a decision that gave him his verdict and so on.

He said that was the funniest looking bunch of men. He said, "I always thought that you could appeal any case, and I've appealed many, many cases. I always thought a judge understood that it wasn't offensive to him, that it was just a matter of law of facts to be reconsidered by somebody else."

Edward Jackson, Beattyville, July 20, 2001

30. "High School Band Plays Inappropriate Tunes"

I remember an amusing story that took place when I was prosecuting attorney. I had both Warren County and Allen County. Scottsville is the county seat of Allen, and the courthouse in Scottsville was right in the middle of the square. There was no air conditioning. The courtroom was on the second floor. If they had a jury trial, they had to raise the windows so people could get some air. In the summer time it was hot.

I was prosecuting a man for arson. The windows were raised in the courtroom, and downstairs out front they had some sort of political meeting. And the high school band had been hired to come to the outside and play music. Well, I'm trying this man for arson, and the band all of a sudden started playing "There'll Be a Hot Time in the Old Town Tonight!"

The defense attorney in this trial accused me of plotting to have the band there, so the judge adjourned until the music was over, so he thought.

In a little while, we started the trial again, and once again the band started playing, and this time they played "When the Saints Come Marching In," just as the defendant was taking the stand. This time, I accused the defense attorney of plotting to have the band to play that song. The judge laughed at both of us.

Morris Lowe, Bowling Green, March 9, 2001

231. "The Drunken Lawyer"

Here's one of the stories they tell about motion hour in McCracken County many, many years ago. During the war, or right after, many people didn't have automobiles. Back then, it was a tradition that a lot of lawyers on Thursday afternoon, after work maybe if they took off a little early, would take the train over to Cairo, Illinois. There was always plenty to drink there in Cairo, and also a few games to get into. Friday was going to be an easy day because they had motion hour in the morning, and usually on Friday afternoons you didn't have a whole lot scheduled. They didn't schedule trials on Friday. So they'd take the train over to Cairo and have a good night out. And depending on how much of a night out, take the train back to Paducah sometime late Thursday night or sometime early Friday morning.

After having a motion hour one such night in McCracken County, Judge Price, who was presiding then, had this lawyer, who was still under the effects of the night before, to stand up in the back of the area where the lawyers were seated. The lawyer mumbled something. Judge Price said, "Speak up, I can't hear you."

Supposedly, this lawyer responded, "Hell, Judge, that's nothing. I can't even *see* you."

Richard Roberts, Paducah, November 2, 2001

232. "Lawyer's Awesome Fees"

Fees are always good for a story. We had a lawyer here in Paducah named Joe Grace who was an excellent criminal lawyer. He was known to be pretty good at opening a pocket to collect his fees. Well, Roy Vance had just come to practice here at that time. Roy is now retired from the Kentucky Supreme Court. At the time Roy began practicing law he was the youngest lawyer to have ever been licensed in Kentucky, and I suspect he still holds that distinction, but I don't know.

When Roy came back here to practice, people from the end of the county where he was reared asked him to defend this case. Well, they also wanted some experience, so they hired Joe Grace, who was older than Roy, along with him. Joe called Roy and said, "Mr. So-and-so is coming in this afternoon. I'll come by and we'll meet him, and I want you to let me do all the talking about the fee. I've got everything worked out and I can make some money for us."

As a matter of fact, Roy was in my office last week, and I always nudge him a little bit to get him to tell this again. Anyway, he said that he went over there and this man came in and Joe began by telling him that this was a serious charge and that he had been wise in hiring two lawyers to represent him. Of course, two lawyers would cost him more money in building him up for it, and that his defense was going to cost two hundred dollars.

Well, as Joe was telling him that, this man reached in his bib overalls and was pulling out a big wad of bills. Joe didn't even miss cadence in his speech and said, "*Per count*." So it came out that the fee would be two hundred dollars per count!

Richard Roberts, Paducah, November 2, 2001

233. "CASH, CHECK, OR SEX?"

In the early 1960s, the economy in eastern Kentucky was suffering from a decline in the coal market. Among those affected with the downturn were the lawyers. One such lawyer was asked by a friend, "How is law business these days?"

The lawyer sadly replied, "I'll tell you how business is. It is so bad these days, I've begun to take some of my divorce fees out in money."

Anonymous contributor

234. "OLD FELLOW'S FIRST TIME IN COURT"

An old fellow from Clinton County went before Judge Swinford in federal court over in Bowling Green. He was sort of a foolish man who had never been anywhere to speak of outside of Albany. Judge Loveless tells this story, and he declares it's the truth.

They brought this old man to court and had him charged with several things. He was supposed to have appeared beforehand but hadn't shown up at court in Bowling Green. Judge Swinford gave him an awfully firm lecture, then just told the marshall, "Get this man out of my way. Take him over to the jailhouse. He'll be there when we need him, and we'll just keep him until I try him."

As they were going out of the courtroom that old fellow said to the bailiff, "That old white-headed son-of-a-bitch in that raincoat up there is mad today."

The old fellow had never seen anybody in a robe before.

Robert L. Wilson, Jamestown, April 19, 2002

235. "Lawyer Improperly Addresses Female Judge"

This is about a case I tried years ago, probably in 1982, involving John Y. Brown Sr. He was one of the premier trial lawyers of his time. He was the father of John Y. Brown Jr., who is also a lawyer. John Y. Sr. had run for a lot of offices, but never got elected to a statewide office. I'm told that one of the reasons that John Y. Jr. ran for governor was because his father wanted him to, and he did, and he was a good governor.

Close to twenty years ago, I tried a case for Kentucky Fried Chicken in Jefferson County. John Y. Brown Sr. was on the other side of the case, and Bill Boone and I represented KFC. One of the other lawyers was John Y. Sr.'s son-in-law at the time, Bill McCann.

We had a good female judge, whose name was Olga Pearce. She was originally from somewhere up in New England. She still had a New England accent, and she had been on the Jefferson Circuit Court bench for eight or ten years, or more. And during the course of the trial, John Y. Sr. continually referred to her as "honey." He would say, "Oh, I'm sorry, honey," or "I didn't understand that, honey." After about the eighth or ninth time he did this, she said she would hold him in contempt if he used the word again.

Well, the next day during some interchange, he used it again. And she told him she was going to hold him in contempt. He apologized and laid himself on the mercy of the court, saying that he was sorry but that it was a phrase he had always used. When he was a youngster, his family had a maid whose name was Honey, which made it worse with the judge. It made it all the worse, because here it is he is trying to justify his conduct and his use of the word "honey," and he is now equating the judge to a maid whose name was Honey.

So, he went through this whole rendition and finally the judge just looked at him, shook her head, threw up her hands, and said, "It's obvious you are hopeless. I just give up. Please try not to use that word anymore."

That case lasted for about two and one-half months. I was a relatively young lawyer at the time, and I cross-examined one of their first witnesses. We were defending, and we ultimately prevailed in the case, but it was a very difficult case. One of the first witnesses was one whom I cross-examined. When we were finished, we went out to lunch, and John Y. Sr. walked up to me and put his arm around me, and said, "Richard, I see you try a case more by ear than by note."

I said, "Pardon me?"

He said, "Well, the way you handled that witness, I see you try a lawsuit more by ear than by note."

I was puzzled at first as to what he was saying. When I looked at him, he said, "You listen to the witness; you don't take a lot of notes. You listen to the witness."

I realized in a moment that he was paying me a high compliment. He went on to say, "For a young lawyer, you do quite well. You've learned something a lot of lawyers never learn throughout their career. That is, to be a good cross-examiner you should listen and not make so much reference to the checklist."

In other words, even some experienced lawyers do the same. They'll have a little checklist, and they are more intent on getting through the checklist and asking the questions on it rather than listening to what the witness says.

As an early instance for me as a young lawyer, I've never forgotten it, and I've even told John Y. Brown Jr. that story. Even in his mid to late seventies, John Y. Sr. was one hell of a good trial lawyer.

Richard Getty, Lexington, April 30, 2002

236. "LAWYER WITH AN ACCENT"

Back in the '30s, a Harlan lawyer who was originally from the Virginia Tidewater, and thought to be practicing under his brother's license, was appointed to defend an indigent in a criminal case. After declaring his client guilty, this lawyer addressed the jury with these words, uttered with a broad Tidewater accent, "Please ladies and gentlemen of the jury, don't send my client to the penitentiary. He just got back from there."

Eugene Goss, Harlan, May 22, 2002

237. "Lawyer Jokingly Misinforms Judge"

In the 1930s, a couple was divorcing in Harlan Circuit Court and the case was being heard by Judge James S. Forester. The parties had settled all of their property rights except for their Fostoria stemware, but found that they could not agree as to which one of them would get that item of property.

The husband decided to take it to the judge and let him decide which one should get it. In the course of the hearing, the parties kept referring to the stemware as the "Fostoria." Each time that it was mentioned, the judge would look at them quizzically. Soon, he abruptly called a recess and motioned Daniel Boone Smith, the wife's attorney, to come up to the bench. He leaned over and whispered, "Boone, what is this Fostoria you all keep talking about?"

Boone, who was a well-known jokester, whispered, "Why, Judge, it is her undies, step-ins, and things like that."

Judge Forester banged his gavel on the bench and stated emphatically, "I am going to give the Fostoria to the wife. She is the only one I know who would have any use for it."

Eugene Goss, Harlan, May 29, 2002

238. "Sexism and Other Misconduct in Court"

When I started practicing law in Louisville in 1973, there were not many women who were practicing law at that time in Louisville. The ones that did weren't usually seen in court. I was one of the few women attorneys. I knew one woman that did estate practice. There were a few there—Olga Pierce was one of the judges, but there just weren't many women. We would have motion hour, and there might be fifty attorneys in the courtroom waiting for the motion, and I would be the only woman. And when you consider that I'm only five-feet tall, and at that time I looked very young, it was a rough time. A lot of people didn't want to accept me as an attorney, and they had these ridiculous benches.

There were several courtrooms, and I literally could not see over the bench. I would take a volume of the *Martindale-Hubbell*, which is the directory. In one courtroom, I had to take a copy of that to stand on in order to be able to see the judge. The benches were just ridiculous back then, but I don't think they make benches that tall now.

There was a lot of sexism: a lot of comments that I shouldn't be a lawyer, or just disrespect—thinking that they could intimidate me, or just treat me like a child, or not treat me as an equal attorney. There was still a lot of sexism and a lot of racism in the bar. I think it's a lot better now, but it was a pretty hostile environment in which I started practicing law.

In addition to that, I was really appalled at some of the things I saw happen on the bench, primarily in district court. I did a lot of housing law, and we had one judge who would just sit there and rattle off all these names and just not wait to see if anyone was going to respond. I can remember people standing up and shouting, "That's me, that's me! Stop! Stop! Stop!" so they could have their case heard. One day this judge got to a name he couldn't pronounce, and he just skipped over it. I don't know whether or not that poor person was in the courtroom that day or not and had their case heard. Probably not; they probably got evicted without notice.

Another judge that was sitting on the district bench then owned a bunch of rental property, and he would hear his own cases. He would be lawyer and judge, all in the same case—in his own cases. And he would rule on his own eviction notices concerning the property that he owned. Of course, that was back in 1973–74, thus before the Judicial Reform Act that went into effect about January 1978.

In reference to that same judge that would hear his own cases, one time I was entitled to a jury trial under the statutes, and he said if I wanted a jury, I'd have to bring my own jury. Admittedly, that had a certain amount of appeal to it! I figured I could take some sprint, but I knew that really wasn't going to work, so we did not have a jury trial in that case.

Forrest Roberts, Owensboro, June 7, 2002

239. "Blatant Sexism"

When I was practicing for Northeast Kentucky Legal Services, there was one district court judge that had in his office—I guess it was supposed to be an Indian princess—a drawing of a young Indian woman, and she was naked from the waist up. He also had a water pitcher; it was in the shape of a woman's breast, and the water came out of the nipple. He would have this pitcher back in his chambers, and if you ever went back to his chamber, you had to sit there and look at this stuff.

I never had any clients who had any conferences in the chambers, but I think it would be pretty upsetting to look at. By that time I was pretty hardened to things like that, but that was the most blatant form of sexism I ever ran into anywhere.

Forrest Roberts, Owensboro, June 7, 2002

240. "Judge's Sense of Smell"

I wasn't there, but my husband told me about this. It was a possession of marijuana case—the question of lab, lab results, chain of custody, and whether or not it was in fact marijuana. The defense was trying to raise the issue that there was no way to prove identity.

The judge says, "Bring the substance up here." They do, and he takes a great big sniff of it, then says, "The court will take judicial note of the fact that this is marijuana!" He then proceeded with the trial. Believe me, he knew what marijuana was! I think he used it.

Forrest Roberts, Owensboro, June 7, 2002

241. "Judge Favored Local Lawyers"

When my father started out as a young lawyer in the 1920s, he said that he was called to go up to court in Leslie County. They had a judge up there whose name, according to my father, was Lou Lewis. Father didn't know what to expect, so he went into the courtroom there in Hyden. Judge Lewis came out and sat at the bench. Of course, they didn't have robes in those days to speak of. Well, Judge Lewis came out onto the bench in overalls and bare feet. He was just completely barefooted. He had a motion there to make, so Judge Lewis said, "Now, before we hear from the out-of-town lawyers, I want to go around the room with all the Leslie County lawyers to see if they have cases to be heard."

As he went around to each lawyer, my dad said he'd ask, "Have I ruled in a case in your favor this month?"

The lawyer would say, "No, Judge, you haven't."

Then Lewis would say, "Well, draw me up an order. You'll win your case today." He'd do that with all the local lawyers, then he'd start on the out-of-town lawyers.

After hearing that, I said, "Well, I know how he got re-elected."

Eugene Siler Jr., London, June 20, 2002

242. "A JUDGE MAC SWINFORD STORY"

This is an early case that we had when I was U.S. attorney. We appeared before Judge Mac Swinford, who was from Cynthiana, and he had a lot of great stories he liked to tell. During the Vietnam War, in all draft evader cases he would give everybody five years if they were convicted of draft evasion. That was the maximum and that is what he gave them, because he said, "Well, you'll be eligible for parole after two years." So he did that in all those cases.

One of my early cases to prosecute was a draft evasion case in Covington. When we got in court there in Covington, Judge Swinford wanted us to come to the bench. The defense attorney was arguing the case, and he wanted it dismissed. Judge Swinford was a little piqued because the court of appeals had reversed him in a couple of cases because they said he hadn't given each case individualized sentencing. He'd given everybody five years, and they would send some cases back to him to make a new sentence. Well, in this particular case, Judge Swinford was getting kind of angry. The defense counsel said, "This case needs to be dismissed, Judge."

Judge Swinford said, "No, I'm not going to dismiss it. You're going to have to go to trial."

The lawyer said, "Well, I'm going to take an appeal."

When he said that, Judge Swinford just kind of blew up. He said, "Well, you just go ahead and take an appeal. Take it across the river to Cincinnati. Those judges over there can't get any other kind of a job, but they reverse me all the time anyway."

And here I was prosecuting, and it was all going on the record, so I said, "Now, Judge, we don't need to put this on the record do we?"

He said, "No, take it off the record," but I knew it was on there.

Eugene Siler Jr., London, June 20, 2002

243. "SHYSTER-LAWYER QUESTIONS FORBIDDEN"

Judge Mac Swinford was a colorful man. In a couple of other cases he was questioning the jury. And the lawyers often times liked to ask the jury lots of questions, and Judge Swinford asked his own. After he got through, he'd expect that you wouldn't have many questions to ask.

There was a lawyer in Newport whose name was Morris Weintraub. He's now deceased. He was a good lawyer, and he had been Speaker in the House of Representatives and was a state senator. He also appeared often in federal court. Well, he was in this case and was asking the jurors all kinds of questions. Judge Swinford just broke in. I was on the other side, but I didn't object. When Judge Swinford broke in, he said, "Now, Senator Weintraub, just ask them if they'd try the case on the evidence. Ask them if they can be fair. Just don't ask all those shyster questions that you see on TV."

Of course, the jury heard all that, and I was trying to get it erased from the record.

Eugene Siler Jr., London, June 20, 2002

244. "A Rural Mailbox Episode"

We had a prosecution case one time before the late Judge Moynahan from Lexington and Nicholasville. He was arraigning people in a case that we had, and the charge was that of knocking down a rural mailbox. It doesn't sound like too heavy of an offense, but it was a felony, and still is a felony. So, this defense counsel was from Winchester, and he came up to the bench and said, "Now, Judge, my client is charged in this, but I'm sure we can work out some arrangement, as this is not a very serious offense. It's just that of knocking down a mailbox."

In court that day, Judge Moynahan had dark glasses on, which was strange for him. He pulled his dark glasses down and set them on the bench, and said, "Well, look at my black eye. I'll have you know that I think it's a pretty serious offense. Somebody knocked my mailbox down just last week, and I was trying to straighten it back up and hit myself in the eye with the mailbox."

So, I knew that my client and I were in pretty good shape since that had happened to the judge when trying to get the lid back in place.

Eugene Siler Jr., London, June 20, 2002

245. "Judge Swinging on a Rope"

This is a story about Old Judge Will Rose from Barbourville, who was the father of William Rose, circuit judge. My father said that Judge Will Rose was a little bit eccentric. What he would do when he went to hold court, instead of staying in a hotel, he would just stay in his chambers in the courthouse. Father said that Old Will Rose was over in Knox County holding court and sleeping in his chambers, and some people heard this bell ringing right in the middle of the night. People got up and looked out, and there was Will Rose pulling on the bell rope. People wondered what he was doing, and they asked him why he was ringing the bell. He said, "Well, I was just trying to see if I could get out of here in case of a fire." There he was, swinging down on a rope on the outside of the building in the middle of the night.

So that was sort of an eccentric activity on his part.

Eugene Siler Jr., London, June 20, 2002

246. "JUDGE INITIATES HUMOROUS CORRESPONDENCE"

There's a circuit judge in western Kentucky to whom I had mailed a copy of a pleading. My copy machine was kind of on the blink. The copy I sent him was kind of faded, and he sent a letter back on his circuit court letterhead with a one dollar bill attached. He sent the pleading back, saying that he couldn't read it, and that "here is a dollar donation toward getting you a new copier."

So we replaced the cartridge in our copying machine and I had my secretary type a letter in large caps—all caps in bold print. The large caps made the sheet of paper look like a little sign. I sent it back to him along with a two dollar bill, along with the letter that said, "Dear Judge, please find enclosed herewith two dollars toward the purchase of a new set of glasses."

I called his secretary, and when I identified myself, she just busted out laughing! She thought it was a hilarious thing.

Ken S. Dean, Madisonville, April 15, 2002

20

Sexual Charges and Sexual Abuse

⚖

Lawyers and judges prefer not to tell stories that relate to sex, sexual abuse, and sexual charges. Due to the offensive nature of the bulk of these sexual charge and sexual abuse accounts, the author suggests that they be read, if at all, only by persons who feel they can cope with the contents. The various themes range all the way from bestiality to rape and incest; often, the victim is a girl or young woman and the abuser is a member of the family or the surrounding community. In one case, the victim slays her abuser.

247. "The Melvina Law"

This is a hand-me-down story. I wasn't present when it took place. They had these two fellows living up the hollow here in Menifee County. They shared a little old cabin. And there was this woman here in Frenchburg, who was kind of the town clown. I don't know whether or not one of them had taken her up to the cabin and had sexual relations with her, but she accused one of them for doing that and got a warrant issued. Maybe he was indicted, but I don't know. Anyway, they were trying him in court, and this fellow that was sitting there in court listening to it told me that the accused man's buddy came in through the main door.

This woman that had brought the charge was on the witness stand, and she looked back and saw him, then called his name and said, "I want you to do something with him."

They said, "Now wait a minute. We're not dealing with him, we're dealing with this other man that you claim raped you, so what does this man that just walked in have to do with it?"

She said, "Well, he hasn't done anything yet, but he's fixing to." It sounded as if she thought *he* was going to seduce her the next time. See, these two men lived together up there, and they both may have had her up in the cabin. Her name was Melvina, or Elvina. Now then, if somebody is about to start to do something, they call it the Melvina Law—they're fixing to start.

Asa R. Little Jr., Frenchburg, November 26, 2001

248. "MAN HANGED FOR RAPE"

My uncle retired as Commanding General of the Northern Division of the Mississippi National Guard, Columbus, Mississippi. When they named the armory for him, my mother and I went down to that ceremony. Uncle Bill got to reminiscing that back when he was a young man there had been a black man accused of raping a white woman in Vicksburg. They were scared of his being lynched in Vicksburg, so the national guard had to escort him over from Vicksburg to Hinds County, for trial over there.

Uncle Bill was talking about some of the difficult times he had had in the national guard, and here he was escorting this very unpopular black person, and his friends and neighbors hooting and hollering at them, saying, "We'll *get you*, Bill Roberts," and other things like that. But Uncle Bill concluded by saying, "We took him to Jackson where he got a fair trial and they hanged him." So his eye was always on the justice.

Richard Roberts, Paducah, November 2, 2001

249. "FAMOUS LADY OF ILL REPUTE"

There was a very interesting place in Bowling Green back before and during World War II. It was commonly referred to by the good people of Bowling Green as "Pauline's." She ran a house of ill-nature, of bad repute. And she brought in young women from in and out of town, wherein they served her purpose. Her place became widely known in a big area, but it never caused anybody in Bowling Green any particular trouble, at least as far as I know. Things changed, however, in 1943 during World War II.

A colonel from Ft. Campbell came to town, and at that time I happened to be city prosecuting attorney, which meant I had to prosecute all cases that came to trial in Bowling Green Police Court. I was called in to consultation also, and I was advised, as was the chief of police, that Pauline's establishment must close down. And, if it did not close immediately, Bowling Green would be out of bounds for all the soldiers in Ft. Campbell and Ft. Knox. So the chief of police and I notified the police to go by and notify Pauline that she must close, and to do so immediately.

Well, driving by the place about a week after that would indicate whether or not it was closed, and it very obviously was not closed. In view of that, I went to the city judge and got a search warrant. Then I went down to the police department that night about nine o'clock. I got four or five policemen and a patrol wagon that was jokingly called "Black Mariah," and I told them to follow me to Pauline's.

They followed me down to Pauline's place, and I put some officers at each door, and another officer with firearms and I went to the front door, rang the bell, and presented her with a search warrant. We went in and promptly arrested those who were there, both women and their male clients. There were a number of young ladies there, along with several soldiers, and a farmer from a neighboring county and his two sons, which I thought was a little unusual. Everyone was taken to jail.

Pauline immediately called Attorney Rodes K. Myers, and within thirty minutes he had somebody to execute a bond for her. These soldiers were released. We made the man and his two sons pay a fine of ten dollars each, then they were also released.

Now, all that was left was the girls. At that particular time, there was a medical doctor in Bowling Green who had been sent here by the United States Department of Health in Washington. He was a very intelligent young man and apparently had all the potentials for being a good doctor. He came to us immediately after those girls were locked up in jail and told me, said, "The government has a rule that if the police lock up a girl from a house of ill repute, she cannot be released and she cannot make a bond until she has been certified as to her clean health by the U.S. Government."

I'd never heard of such a rule, but it did exist. So the girls stayed in jail for a couple of weeks before they were released. I'm certain that for at least a short time after that the house of Pauline ceased to exist. Now as far as Pauline was concerned, when her case came up in court, she paid a fine of forty to fifty dollars, something to that extent, and went on her way. But the truth of the matter is, she operated her house of business in Bowling Green for several years after that before she retired. There's no doubt about that. The police didn't really bother her— maybe just occasionally, as necessary. After she quit matters here in town, she and her second husband, a man named Webster, moved to a farm out in the county. I don't know how long she lived, but she got to be a tremendously large person. To my knowledge, Pauline herself never took part in what the women did. She was just the boss in her house.

The establishment she had in Bowling Green was on Clay Street— a brick house. That house was torn down later, and the people that tore it down auctioned the bricks as being "bricks with great history." They sold for two to three dollars apiece, and a good many people were presented with bricks, and I was made beneficiary of a couple of bricks myself!

Jo T. "Top" Orendorf, Bowling Green, May 3, 2002

250. "Tired, Hungry, Innocent Man Surrenders to the Law"

Here's a story that has both some serious stuff and some funny stuff in it. Before I was county attorney, I was defending a boy named Jamie Pennington. At that time, I was doing a lot of defense work in this county and having a lot of success with it. Jamie Pennington was accused of rape first degree. He was originally indicted by the Floyd County Grand Jury. After I was hired, the case got off to a bad start for the prosecution in that case, because when we got a copy of the original indictment, essentially the very words of the indictment said, "Jamie Pennington committed the offense of rape first degree. He had sexual intercourse with ———— ———— [name withheld]." That's all the indictment said. That's not a crime. The indictment was so obviously defective that I filed a motion to dismiss the case. Essentially, the argument before the judge at that point was that it was obviously not a crime to have sexual intercourse with the young lady. In fact, I think I told him at a hearing that I was confident at that point in time that I told the judge that if this was a crime, he'd better call the jailer to come and build a bigger jail, because a lot of people would go to jail.

Well, that case got tossed out, but they re-indicted Jamie. That one claimed that he had sexual intercourse with this lady by forceful compulsion, which is a crime, if by force.

I went into this case without a doubt in the back of my mind but that I was going to win. . . . This young lady who had accused my client of rape had been at a party with my client, my client's girlfriend, with several other people at this party. They smoked a lot of marijuana, drank a lot of alcohol. This young lady, my client, and his girlfriend, in front of several other witnesses had an ongoing conversation about having a threesome together. This young lady left the party with my client and his girlfriend, presumably to engage in that threesome activity at his home.

Well, this young lady ultimately alleged to the police that she had gone to sleep on my client's couch and that she woke up with my client on top of her having sex with her. She had not given him permission, obviously. As a result of those allegations, he was indicted.

When we went to trial, what witnesses told us about what happened up to a certain point what she testified to was that in spite of all this evidence of smoking marijuana, drinking alcohol, talking about having a threesome, they had abandoned that plan and that she was sleeping on the couch and my client and his girlfriend were sleeping in the bedroom, and that she had woke up with him on top of her having sex with her. But she said on the stand under oath that he had taken her panties off while she was asleep without waking her up; that he had taken her sweatpants off one leg while she was asleep. Of course, the obvious question was, "Unless you were wearing your panties on the outside of your sweatpants, how could a person take your sweatpants off over the leg and leave them on that way without taking your panties completely off?"

She wasn't a very credible witness. But anyway, she testified to that. Going into the trial, the commonwealth attorney, who probably had not done enough work to know the truth, had offered us a plea in this case—absolutely, we'll take anything less than a plea of rape with first degree, which is the highest level of rape in Kentucky—and offered us twenty years in the penitentiary. That's all he offered my client. It was that or trial. We laughed at that. Said, "No way."

After she testified before the commonwealth attorney, I didn't get to cross-examine her yet. We took a break in the case and went back to the judge's office. The judge was just shaking his head. He calls the prosecuting attorney, says, "You did not want that woman to be cross-examined."

Of course, I'm biting at the bits. It's just like shooting fish in a barrel.

The commonwealth's attorney reduced his offer from "rape first degree" for twenty years to "sexual misconduct," which is a violation in Kentucky at thirty days.

Here's where the case got really interesting. I'm sitting in the judge's chamber having this conversation, and the commonwealth's attorney is all but admitting defeat at this point. You've got twenty years or thirty days, and the only person who has testified is the remaining witness, thus you don't have much of a case. . . .

Well, my client did the most stupid thing I've ever seen a person do. In a case where we couldn't lose, and in a case where the commonwealth has all but admitted defeat at this point, my client *left*. He fled. He ran. He was chased by police. They had a manhunt for him in two different states: Kentucky and West Virginia. . . .

This was a case we couldn't lose, but because he fled and ran, he ended up spending a lot of time in the penitentiary.

He was scared, obviously nervous. He made arrangements for his girlfriend to pick him up. . . . I actually went looking for him myself, because we had a good case. I was hoping to find him and get him back there real quick, but we didn't. He eluded the police for the better part of a week. Had a manhunt in the hills of Kentucky and West Virginia. They never caught him, but he walked himself back into the jail and said, "I'm here to turn myself in."

In a case that we couldn't lose, I think he ended up with five years in the pen. I think he turned himself in because he was tired of hiding; he was hungry and discouraged.

That case actually made Paul Harvey's "Top Ten News of the Weird."

Keith Bartley, Prestonsburg, November 10, 2000

251. "Abused Daughter Kills Her Father"

There is so much incest and improprieties that take place that it's hard to remember them all. Anyway there was this fellow out here at Minerva who came in here from somewhere in the mountains. About twenty-five to thirty years ago, he was raping his daughter, and the daughter finally got tired of him doing that to her.

She shot him once, and he raised up in bed and said, "Sissy, don't do that anymore." But she shot him again and killed him, and in court they let her off. Didn't send her to the penitentiary. I defended her.

His wife didn't seem to have all her buttons, but this daughter is still living around here as far as I know, somewhere down toward Charleston Bottoms.

John H. Clarke, Maysville, February 20, 2002

252. "Little Girl Sexually Assaulted by Mother's Murderer"

There's the case of the little girl over in Owen County whose mother was raped and her throat cut. The little girl was six, seven years old and she was sexually assaulted by this guy. . . . She laid there for twenty-four hours or so before they found her next to her dead mother. They were able to save her, and she did live after she had surgery. She was later adopted, as there was nobody in the family capable of handling her.

The mother's boyfriend is the person who did this. He got life in prison, charged with two murders and raping the little girl.

Stan Billingsley, Carrollton, March 20, 2001

253. "Elderly Man Wants to Plead Guilty to Rape"

We had this girl in court who had mental problems, but she was okay if she took her medicine. And she was awful bad to fight people. Anyway, she rented off this old man. He was about eighty-eight years old at that time. He rented to her, and they had a falling-out—a fight.

So she comes over to my office. She was in her right mind when she came in, but she said she wanted to get a warrant for this old fellow. So I asked her, "What for?"

She said, "Well, he tried to rape me."

That was a little bit hard to believe, but still if she wanted to make an affidavit to that effect, it was my duty to write the warrant. So, I finally did write the warrant for her.

So they brought the old man over to me. When they brought him in, he was the happiest man there ever was because of that attempted rape charge! So it was about all we could do to keep him from pleading guilty, because that charge had made him feel so good.

Finally, me and the judge and two or three others finally talked him out of pleading guilty.

I suppose she wanted to file that charge just to hurt him, because they'd had this falling-out over fighting and quarreling with each other.

James Bates, Hindman, December 18, 2000

254. "Deaf Mute's Rape Case"

I was defending a young man charged with raping a deaf mute. This deaf mute weighed about four hundred pounds and was not very pretty. And he was charged with raping her.

His defense was that the sex was consensual, that he had been invited by a form of sign language that signifies sexual intercourse, and it is exactly the same sign language that every teenage boy has used all his life to signify that act.

In this trial, he testified that their sexual acts had been with her permission. And he was a country boy—very likeable and believable. He looked right at the jury and said, "The first time me and her done it, I leaned her over a chicken tepee."

And I said, "What?"

He said, "A chicken tepee!"

I said, "What in the world is that?"

He said, "You know, it's one of them little tent-looking things that you put out in the yard to put fighting game roosters in."

In the mountains, fighting chickens is a big sport, and you can see barrels or pens of chickens everywhere.

He said, "A chicken tepee is one of them tents." Said, "I bent her over one of those tents, and we did it."

I looked at the jury and I said, "I always wondered what they were for!"

In that case, the deaf mute testified that the defendant had gained entry to her home while her daughter was watching television.

I then asked her why the daughter didn't notice him.

She testified that the TV was up real loud, and she's a deaf mute.

The young man was acquitted.

Lawrence Webster, Pikeville, November 9, 2000

255. "Rough Woman Accuses Man of Rape"

There was a lady over in Clinton County whom I shall simply call Aunt Jane so as not to truly identify her. She was known in her community as Aunt Jane. Her reputation was such that she was pretty rough. She had several children with different fathers of each child. Naturally, her reputation was that she was quite a loose woman. That was before the time that the judge had to be an attorney before becoming a judge. He was county judge, and he tried small matters in cases that come before him.

Aunt Jane came before this county judge once and wanted to get a warrant for a local man—a fairly prominent man—for rape. The judge knew it wouldn't amount to anything with her reputation being what it was. So, he was trying just to ease things down so everybody could get along. He tried to talk her out of it, so he said, "Now, Aunt Janie, the raping twarn't too bad wuz it?"

She said real loud, "Good God almighty, it was the worst raping I ever did have."

Robert L. Wilson, Jamestown, April 19, 2002

256. "Rape, Rape, Rape"

In Clinton County, there was a young woman who charged her boyfriend with rape. They broke up and she went in before the jury and got him indicted for rape. It came to trial, and Senator Jimmy Hicks, who had been commonwealth attorney over there for many, many years, was defending the case. Eddie Loveless was commonwealth attorney. Jimmy was trying to prove his client's alibi. Well, the indictment says that the rape happened on the blank day of July of that certain year.

Senator Hicks was cross-examining the witness, trying to pin her down as to the date the rape took place. "Well, did this raping happen during the first part of the month?"

"I don't really know," she responded.

"Well, toward the middle? Or the latter?"

"I don't really know."

Hicks says, "Well, ma'am, I have to have some kind of date when this happened. My client might have been in St. Louis or somewhere when you claimed he raped you. In all fairness, you've got to give me a date. I have to have a date, so give me at least a week's leeway."

She got mad after Senator Hicks cross-examined her for quite awhile. She said, "I don't know, Jimmy, when it was. It was just rape, rape, rape all summer long."

Robert L. Wilson, Jamestown, April 19, 2002

257. "The Pikeville Madam"

O.T. Hinton was from Paris, Kentucky, then lived down where John Fox Jr. was raised, and spent most of his professional life in Pikeville.

He claims he was drunk one night in a whorehouse and wrote "Melancholy Baby" with somebody else.

One of the true stories that he tells is about this very famous "madam" of Pikeville, who claimed that she had made a deposit at one of the local banks. O.T. Hinton was hired by the bank to represent them in that case, and he had the lady on the witness stand and was questioning her about the amount of her deposit.

She claimed it was fifty-three dollars and some odd cents. Mr. Hinton then asked her in what denomination the bills were. She told him that it was several one-dollar bills, some twos, some fives, and a couple of tens.

Mr. Hinton proceeded with his examination and asked, "How did you get this money?"

Her reply was, "I earned it."

He then asked, "Then, how did you earn it?"

She said, "You ought to know, Mr. Hinton, you've been there often enough!"

Lawrence Webster, Pikeville, November 9, 2000

21

ILLEGITIMACY

⚖

Like stories regarding sex crimes, those about illegitimacy are seldom shared by lawyers and judges; only six were obtained for inclusion herein.

258. "When a Mother Is Not a Mother"

One of my most interesting cases is about the case in which I was involved after I had been a lawyer for only about fifteen minutes. A young man walked into my office and said, "My father died without a will. I'm one of his illegitimate children, and I would like to inherit from his estate."

At that time, which was in 1975, Kentucky statutes said that an illegitimate child could inherit from the mother but not from the father. Obviously, it's a little easier to show who your mother is than it is your father.

Being a brand-new lawyer, and not having any cases to do anything else with, I thought, "That doesn't sound fair to me," especially since he'd been raised by his father in his father's home. He actually had his father's name, and he was a junior. Robert Rudolph was the man in this case. So I said, "Robert, you don't have any money, and I don't have anything else to do, so we'll try the case." Sure enough, we lost at the local circuit court level. That had been the law in Kentucky for one hundred years.

We appealed the case to the Kentucky Court of Appeals, and while our appeal was pending there, the United States Supreme Court in a case that originated out of Illinois ruled that an Illinois statute that was identical to the Kentucky statute was unconstitutional.

So we happened to be in the right place at the right time, and our court of appeals followed the United States Supreme Court decision and ruled that the Kentucky statute was unconstitutional and held that he could inherit from his father.

He probably didn't inherit $1,000 or $2,000 worth of property, which was totally inconsequential. Fifteen years later, Robert Rudolph finds himself back in my office, and he says that his brother so-and-so died without a will. He owned about $150,000 worth of rental property around here. A lady has shown up claiming that her son is the sole illegitimate son of Robert's brother. So the very law that he had changed as unconstitutional was coming back to bite him in the rear end on this one, because if that child could establish that he was the child of the decedent, he would inherit the entire $150,000 to the exclusion of my client, because the child would be closer kin.

The only problem was the mother of the child that was claiming paternity didn't raise her head for two years and eleven months after the brother died. So it made it a little bit difficult to get a blood test since he was already dead, buried and gone. And the statute at that time said that you can only bring a paternity suit within three years following the death of somebody. So they got in just under the window.

All this pre-dated DNA a little bit, so I'm trying to figure out if I could get a blood test from a brother that might be reliable enough to find out if this two-year-old child really is the surviving kin.

While we were looking for that, they said, "Well, there's a guy over in jail that we believe had visitation rights with the mother and we think he's the father."

So I got a court order to have blood tests from the mother and the baby and this jailbird. When it was all done, I got a call from Dr. Kawas, who was the pathologist at that time. He said, "Well, I'm sorry to tell you that the jailbird is not the father of the child," and he said, "But I'm also surprised to tell you that the mother is not the mother."

Of course, that had created a lot of controversy at the hospital because they thought that maybe they had a switched-baby situation. This happened to be a black couple, and there were no black babies born within four days of the date of this one, so that wasn't the case.

What had happened is this mother had just grabbed a neighborhood kid and had taken that kid out to the hospital for the blood test without knowing it would exclude her, too.

So we went back and, without revealing what the blood test disclosed, I told the judge that I needed a second blood test since we didn't have good results on the first. Then we had photographers out there, and we fingerprinted and footprinted everybody, and she apparently showed up with the right child at that particular time, and the guy in jail still wasn't the father. We entered into an agreed order finding that the child was in fact the sole surviving child of the decedent, so he would qualify for Social Security benefits. His mother on his behalf disclaimed any claim against the estate. So my client ultimately received his share of his brother's estate, and the child wound up getting supported by the taxpayers.

Joe Evans III, Madisonville, July 28, 2000

259. "Checking on Illegitimacy"

A social worker up in the mountains went to interview this mother about her kids not going to school. The social worker said to her, "Now, you have this one child that was born out of wedlock."

The mother said, "Well, what do you mean?"

The social worker said, "Well, the child is illegitimate."

The mother said, "No, no, he's not illegitimate. His dad and I got married when he was in the fifth grade."

Ken S. Dean, Madisonville, April 15, 2002

260. "Who the Fathers Were"

This woman was on the witness stand and the attorney was trying to attack her character. He said to her, "Isn't it true that you've got four children and you don't know who the father of any of them is?"

She said, "That's a lie. I do have four children, but the youngest one belongs to the Baptist preacher, and the next youngest one belongs to the Methodist preacher. But you're right about those first two. I don't know who their daddy is because, you see, that was before I got saved."

Lawrence Webster, Pikeville, November 9, 2000

261. "Twin Babies with Different Fathers"

I had this divorce case once with a woman with twins. Well, it turned out that the twins had different fathers, and they were brothers. Her husband was the father of one twin, and his brother was the father of the other twin. They were born at the same time. She apparently got pregnant close together.

The divorce came about because of her affair. Her husband found out that she was having an affair with his brother, thus he was suspicious whether the children were his or not. They did paternity testing on both twins and it turned that one was his child and one was not.

Ultimately, the husband had to pay child support on the one, but not on the other. His brother had to pay child support on the other. That was truly an unusual case with the twins having different fathers.

Sue Brammer, Maysville, February 20, 2002

262. "LADY WITH THE SHORT, SHORT SKIRT"

I have a client that I know screwed at least two people in Hopkins County, and I was one of them. You never know what clients are going to wear into the courtroom, and what they wear may influence the outcome of the case. This fellow came to me and said that he had been sued on a paternity case. Well, I asked him about it, and he swore that he'd never had sexual relations with this lady, period.

I said, "Well, fine, but let's just get a blood test if that's the case and we'll be in good shape."

He said, "No problem. I'll get a blood test."

He got the blood test back, and there was a 99.987 percent probability that he was the father. Well, I called him up and said, "Well, congratulations, I've just met the second immaculate conception, so now do you want to tell me the real tale?"

He said, "Well, I don't care what the blood test says, I didn't have sexual relations with this lady."

I said, "Well, fine. We've got two options. First, we can go to trial and just challenge the accuracy of the test, or second, you can have a second test run, but I don't recommend that you do that, because if it comes back 99.987, your goose is cooked."

So he said, "All right, I'll take your advice and we'll go to trial."

Well, the mother had moved away, and she was flown back in for the trial. Well, she came in the courtroom wearing the shortest skirt of any woman that I've ever seen inside the court or outside the court. I don't know how she even sat down. But even if you believed her version, she said that they'd had sexual relations only on one occasion.

She'd flown back into town to go to a funeral related to the Wheatcroft mine disaster eight or nine years ago that killed ten or twelve miners. She didn't have a place to stay, so she stayed at this guy's house even though she didn't know him before then. According to her, they slept together one time and that was it.

So, my client says no times, and she says one time.

Well, we had a six-woman jury. Well, they flew in the DNA specialist from North Carolina, and she testified that there was only a one in eighty billion chance that he was not the father of the child. Nevertheless, the jury came back and found that he was not the father of the child.

The trial judge in the case called me from his office and congratulated me on the outcome. He called me Joe Paterno from then on.

Joe Evans III, Madisonville, July 28, 2000

263. "A PATERNITY CASE"

I've always been amazed at how many clients will lie to their attorney. I don't know if they think they can bamboozle their attorney and they can then bamboozle everybody else, or if they truly believe in what they are saying. I think it may be the latter. I think they really think they can bamboozle you into thinking that you're going to stick to their story.

I had a paternity case one time, and this one client totally blew me away. This client was fighting very hard to have this guy declared the father of her child. But when the blood test came back, he wasn't the father.

That just blew me away. I don't know if she didn't know for a fact, but surely thought it. He had a better position in the community than she did, and maybe she could get some support for the child that she couldn't have gotten otherwise. But it really blew me away when she came up to me after the case and said, "Thank you for believing me." I don't know if she truly thought he was the father, or just didn't know. But I really did think that he was the father until the blood test came back.

Forrest Roberts, Owensboro, June 7, 2002

22

JURY JUSTICE/INJUSTICE

⚖

Lawyers who must try their cases before jurors hold diverse opinions as to the fairness of the jury system. One lawyer, who recalled a time when indecisive jurors "would pitch a coin up to determine whether to find the defendant guilty or not guilty," told me that the jury system safeguards the public against overly zealous judges. Another believes that juries, which sometimes include at least one of the accused's friends who "can hang the jury," are too lenient. A third lawyer told me that juries often act on their belief of what should be done, rather than the facts, which leads many professionals in the legal field to "complain about the decline of the American justice system." However, this same lawyer believes that in "99 percent of the cases, the judge supports the jury's decision." Read on to see whether or not you agree or disagree with the jury decisions described in the following stories.

264. "JURY INJUSTICE"

I tried a case not too long ago in which a man had shorted out the electric system. He'd put a coin in behind the fuse. He was apprised of it, and one tenant in his apartment took the coin out. Apparently the owner had put it back in, for the next tenant that came along burned up his house and the neighbor's house.

I sued for and in behalf of the insurance company of the neighbors, and the jury just laughed me out of court. They couldn't find anything for the benefit of an insurance company, regardless of what the fellow did.

When the jury comes up with a verdict that is different from what you are defending, you've had it! Generally you are stuck with whatever the jury says.

John H. Clarke, Maysville, February 20, 2002

265. "Prisoner's Escape Attempt"

A little guy named Steve Martin was in the prison system at Eddyville when I first got to know him. He is real small, something like four feet, nine inches. In fact, he is so small that his nickname was Jock, or Jockey. Like a lot of other inmates at that time, Steve got the idea that there were tunnels beneath the prison at Eddyville. It was believed that if you got into the tunnel, it would lead you into a cave that led to the outside. And there was a cave in old Eddyville that led up underneath the penitentiary, but as far as anyone knows, there was never a passageway up into the penitentiary. But there were some manmade tunnels under the penitentiary for their ductwork for their heating system. They had these old boilers that provided steam heat. And those tunnels were pretty small. If a person got in there he could walk around, but it wasn't very comfortable. Of course, when the steam was being used out of the tunnel, these big pipes took up most of the space and were pretty hot. Because of their size, Jock got the idea that he could get into that tunnel and go looking for the passageway that led to the outside. He got in there and started looking for it, but he couldn't find it. Back then, the criminal law of escape didn't require that you had to leave the penitentiary. If you were in an unauthorized area, you could be charged and convicted of escape. So they put out a manhunt for Jock stating, "Jock has disappeared. We don't know where he is." And they searched for him for two days or so, and he was down in that tunnel.

Jock said that the guards would come in there with their flashlights looking for him. Well, he was small enough that he could hide underneath the pipe. He said that one guard came by— almost stepped on his hand. The guard looked around while he was shining his flashlight, then said, "Well, one thing is for sure, the little son-of-a-bitch is not down here."

Anyway, it was so hot in that tunnel that Jock almost dehydrated. He was down there for two or three days. He finally had to come out, and they had to give him some medical treatment.

They tried him here in Eddyville for escape, and I represented him. Well, there wasn't any question about the evidence. It was an open and shut case, but the jury acquitted him. I think they did this because they determined that three days in the sauna of those steam pipes was punishment enough. I guess that comes under the story category "Jury Nullification." This means that the jury will hear the evidence, they'll hear the law, then they'll do what they want to do. I've seen that take place a lot of times. As a judge, I have to say that is totally inappropriate because when you swear a jury, you swear them to try the evidence, then come back with a verdict based upon the evidence and the law. However, the jury is also given the option of believing or disbelieving all witnesses. But you can never question them, for they could just say, "Well, we didn't believe anybody." But where you get a lot of jury nullification is when you have a bad victim, and I've had that several times.

I always thought that was an amusing story about an escape attempt.

Bill Cunningham, Eddyville, January 21, 2002

266. "MONROE COUNTY JURY"

Going to court in Monroe County was always a very interesting experience. Of course, the Carters were very much in control. Jimmy Carter was the circuit judge, and if you had a case, you always got one of the other Carters to help you with the jury and set counsel table with you.

Paul Carter was sitting at the counsel table, and my partner, Wayne Priest, was with me. We'd filed a suit for Earl Payne Comer, who was an insurance agent and lived in Gamaliel—an agent for a life insurance company that had been acquired by an Indianapolis company. When his company was acquired by the Indianapolis company, they terminated Earl's agency relationship wrongfully. So we filed suit for the premiums that had been vested in the life insurance policies against the successor company, and it was being tried in Monroe County. They had the Kentucky counsel and also sent down an in-house lawyer from Indianapolis. We tried the case, and Earl put on a good defense case, and it was tried in the usual Monroe County style. Of course, back then they had a water bucket and dipper there in the courtroom that you could go up and get a drink of water from.

I was making my closing argument to the jury, and was bearing down pretty good on it. Right in the middle of the closing argument, the lawyer from Indianapolis, who hadn't said anything, jumped up out of his chair and yelled, "Don't do it!"

I was totally offended by that, so I went over to the water bucket and got me a drink of water with the dipper and set down at the counsel table to regain my composure. Then I went back to talk to the jury, and after that the jury came back with a good verdict for us. After that, I was leaving the court, going outside, and one of the members of the jury called me over and said, "I just want you to know, we reached a verdict to give Earlie Payne the amount requested, and we recalled that fellow standing up calling you a liar, so we put fifteen thousand dollars more on the verdict for him."

Charles English, Bowling Green, May 27, 2002

267. "Shot and Killed"

Once I had this old black fellow in court in Princeton. He was a bootlegger in Bootsville, the black section of town. But everybody liked him, as he was a very likeable old man. And there was this young, twenty-two-year-old black guy who was a big bully. Everybody despised him, as he was a nuisance to everybody. He kept threatening to go up there and take money away from this old bootlegger. He'd push him around, take money from him, demand money. It got to where he didn't even have to push him around. So he came up there one time and told the old bootlegger that he wanted money—threatened him, then went walking away. As he did that, the old bootlegger pulled a gun, pointed at him and shot him dead.

There wasn't any question. Legally, it was a case of cold-blooded murder. The old man was no longer under threat—no longer under immediate threat of bodily injury. The guy he killed was basically walking away.

We tried this case, and I was the prosecuting attorney. The victim's reputation was so bad, and the defendant's reputation was so good, that we moved the trial out of Princeton and tried it down here in Lyon County. And even the Lyon County jurists let him go because they said the guy [he killed] deserved to be shot. We have a lot of that in criminal justice.

Bill Cunningham, Eddyville, January 21, 2002

268. "Is Killing Justifiable?"

I had a case in Cadiz. There was a filling station there on the edge of town, and this young boy, who was all hyped up on drugs, went into the filling station. Well, the guy who was running the filling station was a great big old boy, who was about twenty-five years old, was about six-foot-four or -five, and weighed 240 or 250 pounds. He had a .45 pistol strapped on his side. Well, he knew this kid that come in there hyped up on drugs and was demanding some money. This big fellow said, "I ain't going to give you no money."

"Well, I'll just take it myself," the boy says, then goes over to the cash register and takes out some of the money. The owner says, "Put that back. Put that back."

"No, I need this much money," and he just walks out of the filling station. He starts walking across the driving area, passes by the first pump, then gets to the second pump, which was almost out on the highway. At that time, the manager of the filling station pulls out his .45 pistol, shoots, and kills the boy.

Well, we tried that case and got a hung jury each time. We finally had to dismiss the case. There was no question, given the fact that the boy was already out and away from the filling station. Also, the owner knew the boy, and there was no reason whatsoever for him to shoot the boy. The jury thought, "Well, he deserved to be shot and killed."

In my opinion, he didn't deserve it. But the jury based their decision on the evidence as they saw it. The problem I had in that case as prosecutor is it was back when the jurists decided the question of guilt or innocence, and they also sentenced [the accused] in the same proceeding. We didn't have a bifurcated proceeding like there is now. Bifurcated means two different proceedings. Today, in a case like that, I would probably have got a conviction because they go out and decide guilt or innocence. They come back into court, and then you go through the second stage, then they learn for the first time, "Well, the penalty for this is bla, bla, bla. . . ."

Well, I tried to get a decision on reckless homicide, or a manslaughter, or any kind of decision to get that sentence down. But the judge wouldn't give it to me because there wasn't evidence to support it. And there really wasn't. I mean, this was premeditated: intentional shooting. The owner was no longer under immediate threat of bodily harm. This fellow was not reckless. It was just plain murder, or it was nothing. So, I think in that case if the jury had an option whereby they could convict him of something where he wouldn't get twenty years to life they would have convicted him. But knowing they would have to give him twenty years to life they wouldn't do it.

I feel that jurors come back with good verdicts. Ninety-five percent of the time, they are good. You'll find a jury occasionally that really gets off, but that is truly unusual.

Bill Cunningham, Eddyville, January 21, 2002

269. "Was Only the Man Guilty of Adultery?"

An example of jury justice happened in the circuit court in Breathitt County at Jackson. I don't remember the nature of my business there in court, but I had a job to do. When I walked in, the jury was trying a couple on the old charge of adultery.

At that time, I don't remember, but I think they could be fined up to five hundred dollars in a class A misdemeanor. The commonwealth put on its proof; the defendant put on their proof. The man and woman were both charged, of course, since it would be hard to see how one person alone could commit adultery without some consenting other individual. The commonwealth showed that under his proof the defendant came to this lady's house every afternoon after work, took his lunch box in, and was often seen in the yard mowing, setting flowers and shrubs, and doing other things, and he would be observed leaving the house in the morning to go to work.

Well, the defense seemed to me to be fairly weak. They simply said, "We didn't do it." The lady did not put up too vigorous a defense either. So after the arguments of counsel, the jury went back in the jury room. They were gone for some forty-five minutes I'd say, then returned into court. The judge asked them if they had reached a verdict. The foreman said, "We have, Your Honor."

The judge said, "What is your verdict?"

The foreman said, "Your Honor, we find the defendant, the man, guilty of adultery, but we find the defendant, Emily, not guilty."

So, in the wisdom of the jury, one of them was found guilty, but the other one wasn't!

John L. Cox Jr., Stanton, November 26, 2001

270. "Jury Justice in a Wrongful Death Case"

I like our jury system. Even when I've lost a case in court, I like our jury system. I can't think of a case, based on the evidence the jury had at a trial, where the jury made the wrong decision. Although they may have just as easily decided in my client's favor. This is not to say that I'm not disappointed at times. I always want to win my case, but sometimes you're trying a case in which you know you shouldn't win, that you should lose. But by the time you psyche yourself up to try that case, even though you know that, you somehow get to thinking that you can win this case. But if I can't say that the jury did the right thing, I can never say they did the wrong thing, given the evidence, even though I may be disappointed. A positive example of jury correctness involves one of my cases.

I had occasion to represent a widow in a wrongful death case against the CSX Railroad. . . . This case was tried in federal court action because so many of the railroads have federal laws. In fact, what happened was that the railroad sued my client. Her husband was operating a coal truck in western Kentucky and was hauling about eighty tons of coal. As he approached the crossing, he couldn't see a train because of the overgrowth of trees on the railroad's right-of-way. The crossing was equipped with a flashing light, but the flashing lights didn't come on. They'd been shot out by a prankster, but they'd been shot out a long time. The railroad would have had occasion to inspect it, and should have by its own policies to inspect it several times since they had been shot out. We were fortunate to be able to prove that it had been some time since they had been shot out, because the inside workings of the light had wasps' and dirt daubers' nests in them. Worse than that, just three days before my client's husband was killed, there had been another accident at the crossing. The train had clipped the tail end of a different coal truck as it traveled through. Thankfully, that fellow's wife called the railroad yard and said, "There's something wrong with your lights. They don't come on at this crossing."

So the railroad sends their signal man out with no more description of the problem than "We've got a short start out there on Highway 814."

There's a standard amount of time that they provide for the lights to flash before a train comes through, because obviously if you're traveling fifty miles an hour and you're a hundred feet from the crossing and the lights come on, you don't have time to stop. So those lights have to come on for so long a period of time in advance of the train's actual crossing, given its speed.

Well, the signal man interpreted the bolt short start to mean that he needed to increase the amount of time to twenty seconds, to twenty-five, or twenty-eight, whatever it was. In the meanwhile, he doesn't learn of the problem that the lights don't operate, period, regardless of how long the signal is set for it. If you don't have a working bulb, it's not going to flash. That was the problem, and that was the problem that he didn't discover. So three days before my client's husband was killed, the railroad had notice of a problem but failed to fix it.

Well, if a train hits a Volkswagen, there's no problem. It's like a bug hitting the windshield. Likewise, it doesn't do any damage to the train. It has left that Volkswagen off the tracks, but the train is going to keep going. But when a train hits an eighty-ton coal truck, it hurts the train. Well, with misinformation, this railroad decided that it sure would like to be the plaintiff and sue somebody for once, instead of always being sued. So what do you think the railroad did? When they hit that coal truck, the train still slung that eighty-ton coal truck like a rag doll, but it derailed the train and did about three-quarters of a million worth of damage to the train and the track.

The railroad sued Rhonda Parker as the executrix of the estate of her husband. And boy I killed them with it! The railroad came in here before there was even a good stand of grass on her husband's grave and sued her.

A lot of different proof factors went on in the case, but by the time we got to the end of the case, that jury did not like that railroad. And as much as they apparently hated to, they concluded that Rhonda's husband was at least a little bit at fault and had contributed to the cause of the collision, that maybe he should have been going a little slower and looking a little harder before he got to the crossing.

What we have in Kentucky now is comparative negligence, or the apportionment of fault between the parties involved. Used to, we had contributory negligence. If the plaintiff, by his own negligence, contributed to the cause of the accident, then he recovered zero. Even if you could look at a circumstance and say, "Well, the defendant is 90 percent at fault here, but I think the plaintiff did contribute some to the cause of this accident," then the plaintiff recovered zero due to contributory negligence. Twelve or fourteen years ago, that law changed to where you now have comparative fault between the parties. Thus, the jury is permitted to assign a percentage of fault to the parties involved. If I have a one hundred thousand dollar claim against you for damages and I sue you, and it's determined that you were 90 percent at fault causing the accident and I was 10 percent, then my damages are reduced by the percentage of fault attributable to me, so I would recover 90 percent instead of 100. Well, the jury apportioned the fault as 96 percent to the railroad and 4 percent to Parker.

Parker's claim for wrongful death was made on what we call a counterclaim because the railroad sued her, the widow, before there was grass growing on her husband's grave. She then countersued on a counterclaim for the wrongful death of her husband. So there was not only a competing issue on the amounts of fault between the two parties, there was also an issue of the competing damages. Suppose the jury says fifty-fifty, and if we prove the destruction of the estate is worth $1 million, we recover $500,000. But under that circumstance, suppose the railroad's damage was $1 million also. Then, under a fifty-fifty case, we'd get a judgment for $500,000 and they'd get a judgment against us for $500,000; you'd have a complete offset, and we'd thus get zero dollars. That would be the bottom line.

So because 4 percent of the fault was placed on Parker, the jury had to give the railroad a judgment against Parker's estate for four percent of the railroad's damages. I didn't understand why at the time, but the jury awarded more than I asked for. I asked the jury for $883,000. That was the value as proved by our expert economist of the destruction of this young man—twenty-nine years old—of his anticipated earnings over the course of his lifetime. And the jury's verdict came back for an odd figure—$900,000, plus some. That was an odd figure. Why didn't they pick a million if they wanted to award more and they wanted to burn up that railroad? Why not a million dollars? Or why not $950,000, some odd figure?

Well, the paralegal working in the law office where I was working figured it out. Not being mindful of the liability insurance that the trucking company had to satisfy any judgment that the railroad might obtain against his estate, or his employer at the time, the jury apparently got to thinking, "We don't want Rhonda Parker, the widow, to have to pay this railroad anything."

Thus, the odd amount—the excess in the judgment or verdict over what I asked for—was 4 percent of the railroad damages. That was the jury's response to all of that. They did the right thing. It took mathematical ciphering to figure it out but in the end that's exactly what happened. It figures to the penny. They gave to her every dime that we asked for, plus they gave her 4 percent of the railroad damages to use to pay the railroad back. In other words, they added another 4 percent to that to offset the railroad's damage claim against her.

Peter Ervin, Louisville, April 26, 2001

271. "Nancy Wabner vs. Ron Black, et al."

George Tapp was an old man, a widower without children. He was a member of the Garvinwood General Baptist Church in Evansville, Indiana. Eight years before his death, George was courted by the General Baptist Foundation, which was represented by its director, Ron Black, asking him to leave a portion of his estate to the foundation and church. Mr. Black met with George in his home and learned that George had substantial assets. Black wrote to George reciting the identity of his assets and suggesting that he should "Do the Lord's work" with some of them. When George acquiesced to include the foundation in his will, Mr. Black referred George to a lawyer who prepared George's will. George, who owned a residence in Evansville, a farm in Webster County, Kentucky, and had about $250,000 in cash, left a one-quarter share of the residuary of his estate to the foundation and a one-quarter share to Garvinwood. The will appointed Ron Black as executor.

George had a niece, Nancy Wabner. She was his only lineal descendent. George and Nancy were very close. Two years after the will, and six years before his death, Nancy moved from Louisville to Webster County to be near and care for Uncle George, her aunt Leona, and her mother Chelsea. George cut out a parcel of his farm for Nancy to build a home on. In the months before his death six years later, George moved from Evansville to Poole, Kentucky, so that Nancy could better care for him. He gave Nancy his power of attorney [POA] with the express power to "change and re-designate" the ownership of his certificates of deposit. When George gave the POA to Nancy, he instructed her to move his accounts from Evansville to the bank in Poole and to put her name on his accounts with his. This Nancy did. After an intense battle with cancer, George died some eight weeks later at home with his sister Leona and with the loving care of Nancy.

When the Baptists assumed executorship of the will, they learned that substantially all of George's assets went to Nancy under the survivorship bank accounts. Their share under the residuary was not what they expected from the plan they had laid in George's will. They thought Nancy had taken advantage of Uncle George and committed a fraud on the estate. They argued that Nancy's conduct amounted to a gift to herself (or self-dealing with her principal's money) and that no gift was authorized in the POA document. The Baptists thus filed suit against Nancy to recover the money.

This should be enough to follow the argument. I thought it was pretty good. The verdict was eleven to one in our favor [i.e., in favor of Wabner]. (Civil cases require at least a nine-member majority.) Most of the jurors would have been Baptist. Incidentally, Nancy's husband is

Jewish and Nancy is a converted Jew. The Baptists attempted to bleed these facts into trial, but no apparent prejudice resulted. Even when the odds may seem stacked, the jury does the right thing.

Peter Ervin, Louisville, April 26, 2001

272. "Jury Justice"

In referring to jury justice, it was once called "do-right instruction." There is a case in the court book that says that this judge, after the trial was over, instructed the jurors as follows: "Now, listen, you go out there and you know what's right, so you do what's right."

Not many judges ever went as far as that one did. Basically, however, the jury did it on their own a lot of times. We had a lot of good jurors in this country. They took their job seriously, and they'd do what was right. A lot of times, maybe they didn't want to, but they'd do it. That's the way it was with me as circuit judge. A lot of things I had to do as circuit judge, I didn't want to do to people I knew. But I couldn't let them go without penalty, and somebody else not go. It had to be done. And I made a lot of people mad over what I did, but I did it exactly the way my daddy did. People had nothing but praise for him.

B. Robert Stivers, Manchester, July 19, 2001

273. "Jury Selection"

We don't have many black people here in Grayson County, but in Breckinridge and Meade counties they have a pretty substantial black population. After I became judge, I knew that sometime or another before computer selection of jurors took place, the judge appointed three commissioners. These commissioners went to the tax rolls and registration books and selected names and put them in a jury wheel, and I drew from the jury wheel. When I became judge, I always instructed the commissioners when I went there to divide the potential jurors into five groups: 18–30 years old, 30–40, 40–50, 50–60, and 60 and over. Half of them were to be men, and half were to be women. That's what I always told them, and that's what they did. But I knew that sometime or another, somebody would raise the question that the blacks didn't have any representation. So, I made the point to put a black commissioner in service every two or three years. So, instead of having all whites on the jury commission, I'd put a black person on the list.

After I did that, I was trying a case in Meade County one day, and this black lawyer there happened to be the head of the NAACP in the state of Kentucky. He approached the bench, and says, "I demand that a certain percent of this jury be black."

I responded, "I'm treating you better than that. One third of this jury was selected by a black person." Well, he couldn't believe that! It had just happened that I had a black person serving as a commissioner.

So, he went out and talked to himself, says, "I never have heard of a black person being on a jury commission."

Kenneth Goff, Leitchfield, May 8, 2002

274. "Jury Injustice"

I've had a lot of serious cases in court. One that comes to mind was back when I was commonwealth attorney—I'll get on a soapbox a little bit here. This is somewhat about the Vietnam War that lasted twenty years. This shows you how people get their thinking out of kilter. Within that twenty years, they say there were sixty thousand people killed, and that fact tore this country all to pieces. But the sad thing about it is that in any one of those twenty years, there were sixty thousand people killed on the highways here in the United States. But nobody thought a thing about that.

I tried a case in Meade County halfway through the Vietnam War. A motorist had run over a child and killed the child. Now, understand, people were marching in the streets over the Vietnam War, but this man killed a child and the jury found him guilty but just gave him a five-hundred-dollar fine. That decision was truly a jury injustice decision. Even today, if you'll look at the records, you'll find that happening all over the United States.

Kenneth Goff, Leitchfield, May 8, 2002

275. "Women on the Jury"

I tried a case in Meade County one time when I was commonwealth attorney. I wasn't judge then, so I didn't pick the juries. However, the judge back then didn't demand that one-half men and one-half women be on the jury. But we'd always have two or three women on the jury.

Meade County is wet, and they had roadhouses. Some people got into a fight, I think on the inside of a roadhouse, and these fellows went out and when the man came outside, they shot him right in the face with a shotgun. Didn't kill him.

Well, we had a couple of women on the jury and the rest of them were men. I tried that case as commonwealth attorney, and I was vigorous in my prosecution. The jury went out, then came back and gave him a little fine. Of course, I didn't like it, but there wasn't anything I could do about it.

The next morning I went into court in Meade County and one of the two ladies that sat on the jury asked me, "Mr. Goff, what do you think about our verdict?"

I said, "Well, I know what it costs to shoot a man in the face in Meade County."

She said, "Oh, you didn't like it?"

I said, "No, I didn't."

But I learned that when a half-and-half jury decides on a case, they all have the responsibility along with everybody else, and they can't be compassionate. The monkey is on their back, too. And when women got their fifty-fifty, we had better juries.

Kenneth Goff, Leitchfield, May 8, 2002

276. "First Word from the Lord"

This was a case that came out of the Whitley County Circuit Court, as it was told to me what a jury down there did at one time in years past. As it is now, the jury sets the penalty in a case, and in those days the penalty for carrying a concealed weapon was two to five years. So this jury got a case involving a person carrying this concealed pistol. The jury carefully considered it, and the judge told them to go out and think about what the others say about it before they make a decision.

So, they all went into the jury room. Then, in electing a foreman, they elected a preacher. He said to the other jurors, "Now, wait; before we do anything about what the judge said, I want all of us to get down on our knees and pray about this before we make a decision." So, he made all the other jurors get down on their knees, and then he started leading the prayer. He said, "Lord, give us guidance and tell us what we are supposed to do here. Amen."

He jumped up and said, "Let's give her five years." He didn't give time for anyone else to consider a decision!

Eugene Siler Jr., London, June 20, 2002

277. "Prejudice against Women Jurors"

Years ago, we had a fellow in Lexington who had sort of announced to the world and announced to the newspapers there that he knew a way to get out of paying your taxes. He had done it for years. Of course, it wasn't very smart to tell the newspapers about that, but they published a big article about him in the paper—about how he hadn't paid his taxes for years, and wasn't going to. I was U.S. attorney at the time, and I said, "Well, I guess we'd better investigate this fellow."

The IRS checked on him, and sure enough it was just like he said. We wouldn't have known about it if he hadn't gone to the newspapers. So, he got arrested and was brought in before Judge Moynahan, who was supposed to try him. This fellow's name was Sam Straface, and he decided he wanted to represent himself. Judge Moynahan said, "Well, I'm going to let the standby counsel be here."

The first bad mistake Straface made was the fact that he failed to file an income tax return, which is only a misdemeanor. And in a misdemeanor, you only get three strikes at the jury instead of ten that you would get if it were a felony charge. Well, Judge Moynahan called the jury up and had them seated. He said, "Now, Mr. Straface, since you are representing yourself, you can strike the jurors that you don't want."

Straface stood up, and instead of writing them down like most lawyers do, so the jurors won't know who struck them, he stood up big and said, "I strike all the women on this jury because they are inferior to men. I want them all off."

Well, the problem with that is he only got three strikes, and there were about seven women on the jury. So, the judge says, "You can't do that. You are going to have to accept some of these women."

Well, already the women on the jury were prejudiced against him because of what he said. So he was found guilty very quickly in that particular case.

Eugene Siler Jr., London, June 20, 2002

23

DISORDER IN THE COURT

⚖

Seldom are there contemporary episodes of physical conflicts in court. However, verbal disagreements are still very common in some instances, especially in the hallway or other areas outside the courtroom. When lawyers and judges were asked about physical conflicts in or just outside the courtroom, a few stated that they or their colleagues experienced a desire to become physical on occasion, but common sense, accompanied by the need to maintain respect for the legal system, prevented any physical response. Thus, as the first two stories in this category indicate, most physical conflicts in court are initiated by the accused.

278. "COURTROOM: THE ARENA OF HUMAN TRAGEDY"

The Kentucky State Penitentiary is located in my circuit. I grew up close by and actually wrote a book about it called *The Castle*. I've known inmates all my life. Albert Jones, my good friend in Paducah, called the courtroom "The Arena of Human Tragedy," and I've always thought that was a very apt description. He called it that because nobody wins; everybody loses—at least there aren't many victories. People can't talk about victories and defeats when you're dealing with human tragedy. That's the way it is when you're dealing with the penitentiary. Consequently, it's like the solemnity of church services. When something funny or unusual happens, it is kind of emphasized in an arena where things aren't supposed to be funny.

We have a courtroom at the penitentiary. We meet there on the first Friday of each month and deal with non-jury matters. Over the years, some interesting things have happened. In fact, about two years ago, I got attacked by this inmate who came over the bench after me. Generally speaking, inmates are well mannered and are respectful of the court just as much as are people outside the penitentiary. The reason for this is because we treat them with respect. They are entitled to the same rights and benefits as anybody outside, with the exception of that one that came over the bench after me.

He did this because he'd made some threats toward me in the mail in letters he had written, and he was tried in my court several times. He wanted to go to KCPC, which is the Kentucky Correction Psychiatric Complex, but everybody that examined him said that he was sane, that he was just kind of mean. But I think he leaped at me in order to get attention, and maybe to try to convince people that he was mentally off—so mentally off that he goes over the bench after the judge. I think that was why he did it. Of course, he might have done this because I had denied many of the petitions he had asked for.

I kept him off of me until the guards got on him, and that was only about a split second! They subdued him and took him back to prison. . . .

Bill Cunningham, Eddyville, January 21, 2002

279. "BIG FIGHT IN THE COURTROOM"

I resigned from the United States attorney's office after three years. I'd had enough of that prosecuting, and just day-in and day-out and gone all the time, so I thought I ought to be with my family more. So we quit and moved to London.

I was defending a fellow there one day in a state circuit court—a belligerent sort of fellow. I think it was over a stolen vehicle, but I'm not sure. The deputy was on the witness stand testifying and the jurors were right there in the box, and they were sitting right in front of the judge, and the witness, and everybody else. All of a sudden, my client hollered at the deputy, "You are lying," and he jumped right up and went running up there and grabbed hold of that fellow.

The circuit judge started hitting the table and said, "Get him, get him." They were fighting all over the place. Other deputy sheriffs came in and they were fighting all over the place. They were fighting over on the jurors. On one woman's lap they were fighting.

I just sat still. I let it go. I thought, "Well, this is pretty funny here, what's going on." The judge was still hammering the bench, "Get him, get him." That's all he was hollering, all he could think of, "Get him, get him."

It took about five deputies to down him right in the middle of that floor. They finally handcuffed him and took him out of there.

The spectators in the courtroom were enjoying that fight, too.

B. Robert Stivers, Manchester, July 19, 2001

280. "JUDGE STRIKES THE LAWYER"

This is a story about how grabbing a lawyer by the collar resulted in a judge being removed from the bench. It's sad because, in fact, the judge was having serious mental problems as it ultimately turned out. And there are stories about judges that became so enraged over a lawyer's behavior that they would reach around there and grab them. The judge does the grabbing. That's the part that I'm talking about; it's very uncommon, but I know of three or four incidents where it happened.

The one I started to describe was in a court situation where the lawyer was objecting, and the judge just summarily ordered him back to his chamber. And as he walked back, the judge grabbed him by the lapel and started shaking him, said, "You can't do that to me."

That was a bad situation. The lawyer filed a complaint with the governing body relating to that particular judge, and the governing body censored the judge and jerked him off the bench for a short period of time.

So there are few, but some, stories where in the heat of a debate the judge decides to get up and leave. He orders the lawyer, rather than stay in the courtroom, to come back to his chambers, and in the process of going back there, there becomes a confrontation that results in the exchange of blows between the lawyer and the judge. That happens maybe once or twice a year in the Kentucky area.

Boyce Martin Jr., Louisville, December 7, 2001

281. "PHYSICAL CONFLICT BETWEEN LAWYERS"

I'd heard this story long ago, but didn't have any details until our local newspaper had an account of it about three weeks ago. They have articles that took place thirty years ago, forty years ago, and on and on. I forgot when this happened but I think it was back in the 1940s. There was a lawyer here in Greenville named Hubert Meredith, who at one time was the attorney general for the state of Kentucky. Well, in the courtroom he got into it with another lawyer—a real verbal confrontation. The other lawyer's name was C.A. Denny.

The news article that was in the paper supported what I'd always heard across the years, and that is they got into a fight, and one of the lawyers, I think it was Lawyer Denny, pulled a knife on Attorney Meredith in front of the jury. The sitting judge at that time, whose name was, I think, Doyle Willis, held them both in contempt of court and threw them both in jail.

That was the story that was reported in the paper, which is called *The Leader News,* and it was a reprint from an old edition, which was in the *Greenville Leader.*

David Jernigan, Greenville, May 17, 2002

282. "Courtroom Encounter"

Judge Joe P. Clark down here in Simpson County, he always had a running battle with Roy Steers. They got into some sort of hot argument in court one day, and Roy made a remark to Joe P. that was not particularly complimentary. The story has it that Joe P. pulled his pocketknife out on the bench and chased Roy out of the courtroom.

That's a story, but it may have really happened.

Charles English, Bowling Green, May 27, 2002

283. "Women Fight in the Courtroom"

This is just about the most extreme courtroom dispute I ever heard of. It started in an area in Perry County which is particularly backward. It is called Forge's Branch, and both the accused and the accuser were from there. Actually, the two families lived right across the road from one another. That's not uncommon around there. They were always disputing something among themselves, such as whose child had done something to the other one at school, or whatever. One of these gentlemen's wife left him and took up with the man on the other side of the road and his family. That act brought on trouble, and they had a general altercation, which was marked initially by a fistfight between some of them, or some rock throwing, and harsh words. Finally, guns were brought to bear on the subject, and then they shot, as we might say, a lead mine at one another. In the midst of all that, one fellow got wounded, so he was taken to town to the hospital, and recovered. He then indicted the fellow he believed had fired the shot that injured him. Under the old penal code, the old crime code was called "shooting and wounding with intent to kill." Of course, that's an archaic charge now.

I heard that the trial might have a certain amount of amusement in it, so I went to the courthouse just to see what happened. I was watching the trial. The commonwealth attorney had told me that there was one weapon on the side of the injured party, the accuser, who was demanding to make a witness in the case to be sworn and tell what she knew. But as far as the commonwealth attorney could ascertain, she knew nothing whatsoever about what had happened, and was probably not an eyewitness to it. . . . But he went ahead and put her on the witness stand and figured it would come to pretty short order. Well, he was wrong because he got her name and where she lived, then asked her what she knew about the shooting. Then, she looked straight out over the jury's head and into the audience and pointed at the woman who had left her husband for the other man and said, "I know there would be no goddamned case here if that slut hadn't caused it all."

The accused, having heard her good name ["slut"] used in that highly insulting way, came right around the jury and crossed the bar, and the other lady came right off the witness stand, and they began fighting right there between the jury and the judge. The bailiff at that time was an elderly gentleman who was a very big and heavy man, but he wasn't about to get in between them. He was just standing there saying, "Quit, quit." And the lawyers, especially the ones who were spectators, were way too smart to get into it. The only way these two women got separated was when the accused and his accuser had to pull them apart.

I thought that was quite an amusing incident!

Asa "Pete" Gullett, Shelbyville, June 3, 2002

284. "Two Opposing Lawyers Sent to Jail"

One time I saw two lawyers who called each other bad names in court and came to blows. They got into it there in the courtroom, and the court put them both in jail. In my opinion, they both were slightly, if not more, inebriated. They used some real rough language toward each other, called each other some bad names, and finally got into it physically. What started it was when one of them walked over to the other lawyer and shouted, "You know that's a lie, you so-and-so and so-and-so," and stuck his finger out toward the other lawyer's face, stuck it into the side of his nose and made the blood come out. It cut his nose a little.

The other lawyer got up and they got right into a fight. The judge did the only thing that a judge could do. He sent them both to jail.

John L. Cox Jr., Stanton, November 26, 2001

24

PRISONERS

Many stories in this book tell about court cases in which the guilty persons were sent to prison. However, few accounts were recorded that featured individuals who were actually in prison at the time. Perhaps it is a truism that once a trial is completed, lawyers and judges seldom have contact with those persons who go to prison.

285. "PRISONER ATTITUDES"

I always emphasize in court to these defendants that they're never going to straighten up until they take the full responsibility for their conduct. You blame Mama, you blame your wife, you blame your defense lawyer, you blame this, you blame that. I get one or two letters a day from prison or jail. I can read that letter and tell you right now where this guy is going, because if he is still blaming other people, he's not going to make it until he accepts full responsibility.

There was this old convict that I ran into once in the penitentiary. I was doing some investigation on a case and this convict was a witness. He wasn't being charged. He was just a witness. I called him in to talk to him, as I always do. I enjoy talking with those old cons—just sit around and shoot the bull. We were sitting there talking, and he got ready to leave and got up, said, "You know, I'm not guilty for what I'm serving this time for. But, you know, I've gotten away with so much in my life, who am I to complain?"

Yeah, he said he wasn't guilty but that he wasn't complaining. He figured that he had it coming after all he'd done and got away with.

Bill Cunningham, Eddyville, January 21, 2002

286. "More Power to Inmate Headed for Chair"

These two guys were on death row for a long, long time, and both were facing the electric chair. For years and years they talked back among themselves on death row. They'd get out and walk the prison yard an hour each day and talk. They got to be good friends, and finally it came the day for one of them, and as they were leading him to the electric chair down the hallway, they went past this other guy's cell, and the fellow in the cell leaned out and said, "Ol' buddy, more *power* to you."

Ken S. Dean, Madisonville, April 15, 2002

287. "The Three Jones Boys"

I was judge in a case that involved these three Jones boys from McCreary County. They lived right in the middle of the national forest; had a little tract of land in there. They were all bachelors in their thirties and forties. They lived in an old shack that didn't have any running water. They had to go down to the creek to get their water. They didn't have any electricity, and they had to go outdoors for toilet purposes. One day, they were cutting some wood for firewood for use in their cabin, and they cut it from timber there in the national forest.

When they were brought into court, you could smell them clear across the room because they hadn't had a bath in a long, long time. They were arraigned before me in court, and I said, "Well, how do you gentlemen want to plead?"

Their lawyer said, "They plead guilty, Your Honor."

I said, "Well, it isn't too serious of an offense. You were cutting this wood for firewood, but you can't do it without a permit. And you can't cut live wood anyway. We're going to give you a short sentence. It's not going to be too bad because what you did is not a malicious crime."

At that time, we had a halfway house up here at Livingston that was a former motel. So it wasn't too bad. I said, "We're going to put you in this halfway house and you'll have to stay there for sixty days, and during that time, if you want to go home you can't. But after sixty days, you'll be put on probation, and that's all the sentence you will get for cutting the wood."

They were taken to the halfway house. It had hot and cold running water, and had a TV, and had inside restrooms and all that kind of thing. The probation officer came to me just before their term there at the halfway house ran out. He said, "Judge, I need to talk to you. Do you remember the Jones boys that you sent up to the halfway house? Well, they've been up there, and they've had such a good time that they asked us if I could come to you and ask if they could stay just a little bit longer."

I use that story sometimes to illustrate the fact that sometimes people don't catch on to what is supposed to be punishment.

Eugene Siler Jr., London, June 20, 2002

25

MISCELLANEOUS

⚖

Most stories in the miscellaneous category are closely related to themes found in the regular story categories in this book, but not really close enough to be assigned to one of the various other categories. Nevertheless, some of these miscellaneous stories, such as those about the TVA dams and the famous fiddle are among the more interesting accounts in the entire book.

288. "COMING OF THE TVA DAMS AND LAKES"

There were a lot of cases taken to court when the TVA started buying up the land between the rivers [now called Land Between the Lakes, except by local people]. There were very hard feelings. Actually, I'm a third generation that has been displaced because of the lakes. My grandfather, my father, and mother were displaced because of the coming of Kentucky Lake. Then my parents and I were displaced with the coming of Barkley Lake.

There are people here over the past fifty to sixty years that have been displaced because of the lakes; displaced because of the relocation of roads, relocation of highways, construction of new highways such as interstates. There's hardly anyone around here that hasn't had land taken against their will. I've never heard any bitter resentment expressed in my family, but there are a lot of people that feel a lot of bitter resentment, especially the people between the rivers. Their land was taken even though they feel that it wasn't necessary for the coming of the lake. But I tell them that in a way they may be blessed, because at least they can go back to their home places, their cemeteries, because they are all still there. Their houses aren't there, but everything else is, and someone else is not living on the land. But there were a lot of lawsuits in the land between the rivers, and those people have a lot of bitter resentment. There were a lot of lawsuits as a result.

There was one man that they let stay over there. He lived down in the Tennessee portion. He was a World War shell-shocked veteran who was mentally disturbed. Well, everybody around there were afraid of him. He got to stay there, and he stayed there until the last ten years until he finally got placed in a rest home in Benton, Kentucky. The house is still standing down there around the Buffalo Range, but the TVA owns the land. The last time I was down there they had a big old fence around it to keep people out of there.

Bill Cunningham, Eddyville, January 21, 2002

289. "EMOTIONAL COURTROOM EXPERIENCE"

I was judge when this happened. This boy over in Trigg County had been drinking, and he got out in his car and ran into this couple and their two young children. It killed the couple, but their two young children survived. They prosecuted this guy, Stephen Brown, that did the driving as a drunk driver, and he was convicted.

The mother and father of the deceased husband were grief stricken but not vindictive. The mother and father of the wife, who was their only child, were very, very bitter. When it came time for sentencing, the defendant got on the stand and made this very sad, passionate plea for forgiveness. He told them he was sorry. And the father of the dead mother said, "You did the crime. You have to live with it." However, the father and mother of the children's dead father got up and said, "Stephen, we forgive you." They brought the children up and they all embraced before he went off to prison. There wasn't a dry eye in the courtroom.

That's what Albert Jones meant when he described the courtroom as "the arena of human tragedy."

Bill Cunningham, Eddyville, January 21, 2002

290. "BASKETBALL RIVALRY"

Kentucky is a big basketball state. I had a basketball case one time in which I represented the Mason County School Board. We got into a dispute with the Kentucky High School Athletic Association about where the tournaments were to be held. We filed a case asking the judge to rule on whether it was permissible to have our district tournament at Mason County High School every year. Mason County has this great big gym.

At that time there were about five schools in the district, and the gate cash receipts were split among these schools. Some of the smaller schools like St. Patrick and, at that time, Tollesboro, had its own gym. They liked for the tournament to be held at Mason County High because the gym here would seat more people, more people attended, and they got more proceeds out of it.

Fleming County had a basketball team that was more of a rival to Mason County, and they didn't want it played on Mason County's home court every year. And the Athletic Association said you had to switch it around, even if the majority of schools in the district wanted it at one place. We filed a suit on that but we lost. And I have to go to Fleming County about every night this next week to basketball games!

Sue Brammer, Maysville, February 20, 2002

291. "Inmate Has Crush on Female Judge"

We had this fellow that used to be here in Hindman. It was about the first year when I was county attorney that I became acquainted with him. He was a big old guy in his late thirties, and in the wintertime, he would pull his shoes and clothes off, except for just a jockstrap, and walk up and down the road, barefooted. He'd do this during the winter, no matter how cold it was. Occasionally, this would stir people up. They'd call the sheriff, and finally they'd lock him up in jail. I don't know why he wanted to be locked up like that. But he'd take spells. He'd just want to be in jail.

I could always tell pretty well if he had one of those spells actively at work on him. He'd come down to the corner there at the courthouse and leave his shoes setting there. So I could tell every time when I saw those shoes setting there that he was acting up!

I remember the first year. The county judge had just about had enough of him. So the judge was talking to this fellow. This fellow said to the judge, "If you'll give me eight dollars to buy a car battery, I'll leave and never come back."

The judge said, "We'll do it. I'll give you the eight dollars."

Well, he gave him the money, and this fellow went away, but not for long. He finally came back again.

That took place about the second or third term after they reformed the courts. All assault cases were to be tried in the district court instead of the county court. And at that time, we had a woman judge. Well, for some reason or another, this fellow that acted up all the time got struck on [got a crush on] this woman judge.

He'd come up there to the courtroom and come up to try to get the law enforcement officers to take him to jail. But they didn't much want to because they knew this was just an expense to the county. And they wouldn't want to refer him anyway. But he kept on disturbing the court. He was known as Speedy to everyone around here. So finally, this woman judge told him, said, "Speedy, if you don't quit, I'm going to hold you in contempt of court."

He got up, shook himself around, sort of dance-like, and said, "Judge, honey, you can hold me any way you want to."

He really said that.

He had a father that was a strange-acting person, too. At one time, the state police had tried to arrest the father, and he had cut one of them with a knife. So, the state police didn't care much for him.

Of all things, this fellow carried this cloth bag around his neck with a string, and the bag had two live copperhead snakes in it. He carried that bag everywhere he went. One day he come to the court-house with the bag around his neck. The circuit court clerk was talking to him one day, and he took this bag of snakes off and laid it on this guy's desk. The clerk told him, "You get that off from there. I want nothing to do with those things!"

He left the area. After awhile, the law was looking for him. Over near the Litt Carr community, here in Knott County, on top of the hill was some caves. And these people that lived in the valley there were bothered by some fifteen to twenty dogs that would come down of a night and get into the garbage and scatter it all over the place. These people wanted something done about it, so somebody, probably a law enforcement officer, tracked these dogs back there to this cave. Well, this fellow was there in the cave, living there with those dogs.

Sometime after this, this fellow run off with a sixteen-year-old girl. Her parents came into my office and told me that this fellow who had taken their daughter had her put a copperhead snake down inside the front of her dress. They said, "The law will have to watch her and be careful if they catch her, because she's got that snake in this bag down inside her dress."

I think that this guy went off to North Carolina because the law was looking for him. He died there. I don't know whether the girl went with him or not. I think the parents got her back.

James Bates, Hindman, December 18, 2000

292. "Lawyer Cites the King Edward VIII Defense"

This is a true story of what happened in a trial. This young school teacher, who was very inexperienced in teaching and in the ways of the world, took up with a young student who knew more about the ways of the world than he did. As a matter of fact, she was a wolf in sheep's clothes.

He was going to the high school guidance counselor because he had a lot of guidance problems. He got in his car with the student, went across the state line, and was then charged with kidnaping. Well, he was very much in love with her, and when I *voir dired* [examined preliminarily to determine competency] the jury, the first thing I did was to look around. It was an all-woman jury, and the first thing I did was to start out by *voir diring* them. Then I asked the jurors, "Have any of you ever been in love? Raise your hand." A lot of them sheepishly raised their hand and smiled, and I asked, "Have you ever done anything stupid because you were in love?" They just kind of sheepishly raised their hand.

Well, we went through the trial, and it lasted all day. When it came time for the closing argument, I stated to the jury, "This man has already lost his license to teach, and he's been punished enough. King Edward VIII gave up the throne of England for the love of a woman, and that's what's happened here. He's already been punished enough." The jury acquitted him after I made this Edward VIII statement.

The young lawyer who was with me didn't know of any way that this man could ever be acquitted, because he had a gun and he allegedly forced this girl into the car at gunpoint.

Anyway, after the jury came out and acquitted him, we were walking down the sidewalk and this young female lawyer with me said, "Oh, I see it was the old Edward VIII defense that caused him to be acquitted."

Ken S. Dean, Madisonville, April 15, 2002

293. "Government Didn't Pay Adequately for Land"

They had a fellow from Russell County by the name of Elzie Brummit. He lived in a remote section of the Jabez community. When Lake

Cumberland come in, the government condemned part of his property and flooded it. Of course, the good part of it was creek bottom fields and a lot of timberland. He never did go along with the TVA. He wouldn't sign anything. In fact, the government put their money for him in escrow, but he would never go pick it up. They supposedly had court to make a deed to his land, but just a few years ago I hunted for it but never could find the deed. But whether they had a deed or not, at least they claimed the land. The government surveyors marked the boundary along the lake with red paint on trees. That indicated the government boundary. Well, the government protects that very strictly. You can't even cut a little bush on government property.

What Mr. Elzie would do, and I've defended him a couple of times on these charges, he had a bad habit of cutting timber and wasn't too careful about where he cut it. In fact, on the government line, he'd just go get him some red paint and go down and paint below the line. The government indicted him in federal court for doing that, for selling government timber. He wouldn't show up for court. They sent a summons after him, and finally after he didn't show up for a couple of cases, they sent the U.S. Marshall after him. The marshall came and picked up Mr. Elzie and took him to Bowling Green to federal court—took him before Judge Mac Swinford.

Well, Judge Swinford was mad, so he just gave him the awfullest lecture for not showing up for court. He said, "I'm going to hold you here in jail to decry. I sent you notices, but you didn't appear—had to send a U.S. Marshall after you to escort you over here. So what do you have to say for yourself?"

Mr. Elzie said, "Well, I can explain this whole case to you, Judge."

The judge said, "No, you can't. You've got to get you a lawyer first. Have you talked to a lawyer?"

Of course, Mr. Elzie was dressed in overalls. He was a very poor man, and he was dressed more poorly than he was in reality.

He ought to have had plenty of money from the timber he sold, but he never had the appearance of having money. Mr. Elzie would always hold his hand up like he was swearing. Everything he'd say, he'd always do that. He stood up and said, "Judge, if you'll listen to me, I don't need a lawyer. There is something wrong here."

After he said that three or four times, Judge Swinford was just exasperated with him and said, "Okay, Mr. Brummit, tell me what's wrong."

What Brummit said was the best legal defense I've ever heard. He said, "Well, Judge, I had this little farm over there that I bought off of Daddy's heirs. I heired my part, then bought the rest of it out. I've lived there since I was a young man. I've got old now. I was minding my own business and then here comes the government and they just took my land. Just took it away from me. Paid me nothing for it. They say they've got twenty-five hundred dollars over here for me to pick up, but I ain't going to pick it up. They say they paid me twenty-five hundred dollars for my land. They say that's what it was worth. But Judge, listen to this. They now say that I've cut ten thousand dollars worth of timber off of my twenty-five-hundred-dollar land. So, there's something wrong here, Judge."

Judge Swinford looked to this attorney and said, "Is that right?"

The lawyer said, "Why, I don't know what they paid him for the land."

"Well, you go look and report back to me if this old man was telling it right." Judge Swinford then looked at Mr. Elzie and said, "Mr. Brummit, you're right. Something is wrong. This case is dismissed. The government has charged you with cutting ten thousand dollars worth of timber off of land for which they paid you twenty-five hundred dollars."

What a wonderful defense that old man came up with.

Robert L. Wilson, Jamestown, April 19, 2002

294. "Illegal Drugs Dispensed by Local Physician"

This happened in McLean County, and the way this all ended up in the court system is that there is a man down there by the name of Dr. Smith [pseudonym]. He lives there in McLean County and just recently retired. Dr. Smith had a family practice down there. He was well thought of and had a big practice. But he had a wife, and he believed that his wife was having an affair with a man down there, and he wanted something done about it. Well, Dr. Smith had a female patient from Madisonville who came to him on a periodic basis, which is the subject of the second part of this story. Anyway, Dr. Smith wanted this boyfriend of his wife to be beaten up, and he asked her if she knew of anybody that could do this for him. And she said, "Yeah, I've got a relative over in Madisonville that I'll get to do it."

Well, they were supposed to make arrangements and she'd report back. Well, she reported back that she couldn't get a certain guy she had in mind, but that he had a nephew in the army, and that nephew had a buddy, and both of them were on a furlough from the army, and they would do it for hire. So, that's what happened. They hired these two guys.

Dr. Smith's wife's supposed boyfriend was at his place of work there in this McLean County town, and it just so happens that a constable was there visiting this guy when this nephew soldier and his soldier buddy showed up. A fight broke out, but the boyfriend and the constable ended up whipping these two young soldier boys. So the girl who had arranged all of this was there and witnessed all that happened. She then reported back to Dr. Smith in his office what had happened. Then he asked, "Well, did they beat my wife's boyfriend up pretty good?"

She said, "Naw, just in fact it's the other way. If that's the best we've got fighting for our country, we're in a lot of trouble."

So anyway, the guy that got attacked and the constable, they pressed charges. This soldier and his buddy testified that they'd been hired. So the police said, "Well, if that's true, we've got to get some evidence. We can't believe Dr. Smith would do something like that."

So they agreed they'd put a recording device on the woman whose name, I think, was Cathy. She was to go back to Dr. Smith and talk about it some more and get some admissions. And they figured they could use that and charge Dr. Smith.

She got to telling some more stories about Dr. Smith; how he gave her drugs for payment of all of this. Dr. Smith not only wrote prescriptions, but he also had a dispensing license, and he dispensed his own prescription medicine. He was his own pharmacist. They couldn't believe that, but she said, "Yes, and he gives me drugs."

They said, "Well, why would he give you drugs?" Of course, in this case, it was for her to arrange that fight intended to beat up his wife's boyfriend. And it was also for sex. They said, "You've got to be kidding."

She says, "No, I'm not kidding."

Well, she was an overweight gal—not very attractive. She told them that she used to be pretty good looking as a younger girl and that Dr. Smith liked to have sex with her. That's how it started, but as she got more unattractive, she started recruiting some of her better looking girlfriends who also wanted drugs. Wow, this story is really starting to grow, and nobody could believe this was going on. He could have sex with them, and they could get their drugs.

Anyway, the police said that they wanted to know about the fight—

that they wanted to put the tape-recording device on her—but if drugs were involved in it, they wanted to work on that also. They went on to tell her that she couldn't use any drugs and that she couldn't have sex with him. She told them, said, "Well, now he may ask for some sex."

They said, "Well, you can't do it if you're working for us. You'll have to make up a story and turn him down, but try to get as much incriminating evidence as you can on this tape."

So, she went back in under the authority and the direction of the police. And she got a pretty good tape recording. He got indicted for trafficking in drugs. People think that trafficking is someone who sells for money, but it is also defined as giving, transferring—otherwise as dispensing of drugs illegally, including for sex, or whatever. So he got indicted for all that, and I tried him and the jury convicted him. It wasn't easy to find jurors in McLean County, because everybody down there in his town just loved him. The courtroom was packed day after day. We tried him for about three days. A lawyer from Owensboro represented him.

This tape that she recorded is one of the best tapes you'll ever hear. She goes into his quiet office, and you could hear every word. Sure enough, he propositioned her for sex, but she claimed that she had a headache and couldn't do it. But some of the language on the tape is very good, and he gave her some drugs. She was nervous, and before she left she said, "Dr. Smith, I need to use the bathroom."

You've got to envision that we're in a courtroom and as quiet as can be. Twelve jurors are sitting there, and the judge is up there, and Dr. Smith is sitting next to his lawyer, and I'm there. The courtroom was packed with people, but you could plainly hear on this tape the woman say, "I've got to go to the bathroom." You could hear a door shut; you could hear clothing rustling, and could even hear her sit down, and all of a sudden, you could hear the unmistakable sound of her urinating in that commode. Well, everybody was just sitting there in the courtroom waiting for this woman to finish. My judge told me later on, said, "I know you're not supposed to discuss the evidence with me before a trial, but don't you ever present a piece of evidence like that again without telling me what's coming up!" He said, "I almost fell off the bench!"

The follow-up on all that is that the medical licensing board had some say-so in what to do, and they took away his right to dispense certain drugs. They had a big hearing up in Frankfort, and even after that trial in McLean County in which he was convicted, people from his hometown fully supported him and they loaded up buses and went up to Frankfort to be present at his hearing. He got suspended for just a brief time.

Dr. Smith just recently retired, and they had a big deal at his church and everybody came in and praised him. I read in the paper that said, "If anybody has any memories, or anything you want to write, or show up, in honoring Dr. Smith, bring it." So I thought about going down there with that tape, but I didn't do it!

David Jernigan, Greenville, May 17, 2002

295. "World's Most Famous Fiddle"

This is a true story involving Marion Sumner. He was called the Fiddle King of the South. He fiddled for Cowboy Copas and Johnny and Jack, and was a tremendous fiddler. He was the fiddle player who taught Kenny Baker and his brother to play, who was Bill Monroe's fiddle player.

This story involves the most famous fiddle of all time. There is a legend in America about a southern boy in Georgia who made a bet with the devil who could outfiddle the other. That story is the basis for Charlie Daniel's song "The Devil Went Down to Georgia." That story is about Lowe Stokes, who was a fiddle player with the Skillet Lickers, the greatest of the old-time bands during the '20s from north Georgia. Lowe Stokes is considered by many to be the best American fiddler who ever lived, and he was the person about whom that legend grew up.

Many years after Lowe Stokes' death, Marion Sumner ended up with Lowe's fiddle. Marion was a poor man, but he liked refreshments, which is typical of fiddlers. He hired me one time to file a bankruptcy for him.

In a bankruptcy, you have to list all your assets. Well, he had the most famous fiddle in the history of the United States as one of his assets. And you have to list everything, or you face bankruptcy fraud. So we couldn't tell any lies about that fiddle. So we put it down on the schedule as "one fiddle." When we went to the first hearing, Willard Hamblin, from down around Williamsburg, Kentucky, who was a retired military man, and who was a lawyer, and kind, good, and generous to the poor people. He was a trustee in bankruptcy who understood poverty and who understood mountain people and loved them and would do anything to help them.

It was his duty to collect all the assets of Marion Sumner and sell them for the benefit of the creditors. So, he was questioning Marion about his assets, and he looked on there and saw that notation that said "one fiddle." He said, "Well, Marion, tell me about that fiddle."

Marion said, "Well, it's old."

And Willard said, "Would you give fifty dollars to get to keep it?"

Marion said, "Yeah, I reckon I would."

So for fifty dollars, Marion Sumner bought back Lowe Stokes' fiddle—probably worth fifty thousand dollars—without ever telling a lie.

Lawrence Webster, Pikeville, November 9, 2000

296. "LITTLE BOY TIED TO POST"

I got a call from an exasperated young woman one time, who sounded really intelligent. She said, "Mr. Webster, I know this is going to sound awful, but we've only lived in Pike County for about a month, and we rented a house that sets upon like a cliff. Well, about twenty feet out the back door is a cliff. We have a child that's about two years old, and we can't let him go outside and play because he'll fall over that cliff. The only way we can do it, and we've been doing it this way, is to tie him to the clothesline post so he won't fall over the cliff. And we hadn't done that but one week until the neighbors called the social workers. These social workers are coming out here and accusing us of child abuse for tying that child up. They just don't understand that's the only way he can play."

So I explained to her that I didn't think she needed to worry about it, that the people would understand, and to just relax. She thanked me and was very relieved. As she was hanging up the telephone, I said, "I do have one piece of advice for you. Be sure to put his water bowl close enough to the post that he can drink."

Lawrence Webster, Pikeville, November 9, 2000

297. "MOST DESIRABLE QUALITY OF A FENCE"

There are three really serious things in Kentucky that people will really file suits over. One is running around with someone else's wife, another is property line dispute, and the third is killing a dog. Those are the three areas where matters really become heated. I recall years ago having a property line dispute, and I asked this woman what kind of fence it was that she wanted built between her property and the other property after this property line dispute had been established. She answered by saying, "I want one bull high and hog tight."

That's a pretty good description of a fence—bull high and hog tight.

Charles English, Bowling Green, May 27, 2002

298. "POOR NELL"

This is a story about Judge Pleas Jones. He and I were very close friends. When I first began practicing law, he got me into his office and said, "You know, there's this woman in town and her name is Nell. She's always hit me up for money, so we need to get her on some sort of pension, or some kind of a draw."

I said, "Well, I agree with you because she's always hitting me up for money—also hits my dad up. We've always helped to support her."

He said, "Well, I'm going to tell you what we should do. I want you to represent this woman, and we'll try to get her on welfare."

I said, "Well, okay, but I don't know exactly what I can do."

He said, "I'm going to appoint you in this case, so you just take it and go. We'll have a conference with her, and you set it up and I'm sure we'll get the money for her." So, we were trying to get this poor woman on some sort of welfare benefit. He told her, "Now, Nell, Gene Siler is going to represent you, and we're going to set it up for you to go up to Danville to the mental hospital, and you can take this test. And after you take this test, we're sure that you can start drawing a welfare pension."

Pleas Jones had it in his mind that this woman appeared not to be very intelligent, and she couldn't read and write. So, we shipped her up to Danville to take the test, and she came back home and went to report to Pleas Jones.

He said, "Well, now, how did that test go?"

She said, "Why it was great. I passed it just like a top. They told me to put these square pegs in the square holes and the round pegs in round holes. Well, I did it all, and I answered all their questions."

Pleas said, "Oh, Nell, you're not supposed to do that. You're supposed to fail the test."

She answered him, "Well, Pleas, if you had told me in advance, I'd have failed it."

So, she came back as "not incompetent," so we had to go through another hearing. And I had to go before a state hearing examiner. He started questioning Nell. He was rather dignified, and he was asking her questions. I could see that we weren't doing too well, so I finally said to her, "Nell, you've told me about women's problems that you have, so go ahead and tell this hearing examiner exactly what you've told me."

She said, "Oh, I'm just plumb rotten inside. I'm in awful shape."

After she said that, he granted her the pension. So, I guess that Pleas and I kind of ganged up on the state to try to get this poor woman something that she deserved.

Eugene Siler Jr., London, June 20, 2002

299. "Back When Times Weren't So Fast"

Tom Waller, who was my early law partner, said that one day in a land dispute they were taking depositions on a Saturday at the courthouse in Marion, Kentucky. They did it on Saturday because that's when people weren't working, and most of the witnesses would be hanging around the town square anyway. So they would be in a law office there on the town square and finish with one witness, then somebody would go out and walk around and find the next witness and bring him up. They'd be passing time while they were waiting.

This one witness had just finished testifying. One of the lawyers turned to him and said, "You must be awful proud. Now they've cut a new road out where you live, and you can get on that road and from there go to the main road and go anyplace in the whole world."

The old fellow said, "Yeah, I guess that's right, but I'm not sure that it's a good thing. Sunday used to be a day of rest, and I'd get up of a morning and put on comfortable clothes and sleep a little late. Then go in and sit in an easy chair next to the raddeo [radio], listen to a church service and I'd hear a great organ, a wonderful preacher, and a wonderful choir. But they cut that road in, and the next thing I knew my wife was getting me up just like on a workday, except I couldn't wear comfortable clothes. I had to put on a celluloid collar and hook up a team just like on a workday. She told me we was going to church. Well, I got there, but didn't have no easy chair—sat on a hard pew. There was no great pipe organ, just an out-of-tune piano; a person with a screechy voice was singing, then here comes the preacher. And when he finished he run around out front to shake everybody's hand to make you brag on him. He asked me if I liked his sermon, and I didn't want to tell no lie in God's house, so I said, 'I've heard better.'

"The preacher said, 'Well, that may be, Mr. Jones, but folks like you are the hope of a country church.'

"I told him, 'Well, preacher, the raddeo [radio] is going to do to the country church what the automobile did to the tumblebug.'"

Back then we had time, or at least we took time to get to know people better. That's not a story about a lawyer, but it arose from the context of practicing law at a more relaxed pace back then.

Richard Roberts, Paducah, November 2, 2001

300. "AT THE MERCY OF THE COURT"

This is a true story and it is about Judge Lawrence Jordan when he was on the bench down at the district court. I remember this from one of my early years. The judge was trying to take a plea from this big heavyset fellow, or was trying to figure out what had happened. I think this fellow had watched too much television. He felt like he could get a better deal if he used the words, "I throw myself on the mercy of the court." Judge Jordan couldn't get him to respond to his questions because this fellow kept saying, "Judge, I throw myself on the mercy of the court." He had picked up on that phrase and thought it would bring him good results.

Finally, Judge Jordan said, "Would you quit throwing yourself for just a minute and listen to the questions I'm trying to ask you so that you can tell me what I need to know?"

That's a true story.

Randy Teague, Madisonville, July 28, 2000

301. "DIFFERENT LAW IN FLOYD COUNTY"

We had a lawyer here in town named Thurman Hibbits, and he's always good for stories. He liked to tell a story about the time a fellow from down in Floyd County came to see him about a matter, wanting legal advice. And the fellow didn't really want legal advice. He wanted somebody to agree with him. And whatever he told Mr. Hibbits, the law didn't help it any. So Mr. Hibbits explained to this guy what the law was, and it didn't suit this fellow at all. So the guy turned to go home, then turned around to Thurman and said, "By God, that ain't the law in Floyd County."

Lawrence Webster, Pikeville, November 9, 2000

302. "Disbelief of Client's Testimony"

O.T. Hinton had a lawsuit for a man they called Big Ed Venters here in Pikeville. That distinguished him from a shorter fellow who later became judge with the same name. This particular lawsuit was what we would call a "swearing contest." In cases like this, one side said one thing and the other side said the other thing. Big Ed was a local car dealer and he was fairly used to having his ways—a powerful man in town.

So they tried the case and they lost it. On the way out of the courthouse, going down the stairs, Ed Venters looked up to O.T. Hinton, his attorney, and said, "O.T., I would like for you to tell me how in the hell you lost that case."

O.T. replied, "It was easy, Ed, the jury didn't believe a goddamn word you said."

Lawrence Webster, Pikeville, November 9, 2000

303. "House on Fire"

These stories come from my memory. Lawyers share these accounts with other lawyers. I don't know whether you'd call this a lawyer story or not. It involved a prominent client in Pikeville by the name of Oliver Anderson, who is now dead. He was one of these persons who was a little bit on the shady side, but everybody liked him. He had a tremendous personality.

One time he hired somebody to burn his house down, and in order to provide himself an alibi, got up a bunch of people and went down to a high school basketball game. There came a lull or quiet time in the gymnasium during the ball game. All of a sudden, the public address announcer said, "Paging Oliver Anderson."

Oliver jumped up in the midst of all those people and hollered, "Oh, my God, my house is on fire!"

That's a story that we lawyers like to tell each other.

Lawrence Webster, Pikeville, November 9, 2000

304. "Judge Gets Even"

There was this man that went into the judge's courtroom, then just stood there and said, "Judge, you remember me, don't you?"

The judge said, "No, I don't guess I do."

He said, "I'm the one that introduced you to your wife twenty years ago." When he said that, the judge picked up the gavel, whacked it on his desk, and said, "Life in prison."

He said, "But Judge, I just run a stop sign."

The judge said to the bailiff, "Take him away."

Ken S. Dean, Madisonville, April 15, 2002

305. "THE POMPOUS LAWYER"

There was a lawyer in Glasgow, [name withheld], who was a very good lawyer, also a very self-assured person, also very opinionated. Somebody might call him a pompous lawyer. He was always very proud of his automobile. He had a new Cadillac and was going to court over in Edmonson County years ago. He was traveling along right on the other side of Rhodi when an old farmer pulled out of a side road and caused [the lawyer] to lose control of his car and hit a fence post.

[The lawyer] was infuriated about it and filed a suit against the fellow in the Edmonson Circuit Court. [The lawyer] told his version of the story, and was being cross-examined by Bev, or Beverly, Vincent, who was another real "distinguished character." In court, the old farmer testified that when [the lawyer] got out of the car he literally jumped out of the car, then ran back and shook his fist in this fellow's face and said, "My God, man! You know what you've done? Here you've torn up the biggest car in Barren County and almost killed the smartest fellow in the state of Kentucky!"

Charles English, Bowling Green, May 27, 2002

306. "OUT-OF-STATE DRIVER"

A Harlan city policeman saw this fellow run this red light with his car. The policeman whistled the driver down, then asked him, "What do you mean running that red light?"

Trying to excuse himself, the driver said that he was from Philadelphia and that he hadn't noticed the red light. The officer looked at him rather sternly and said, "Well, if you are from Philadelphia, what're you doing with that Pennsylvania license tag on your car?"

Eugene Goss, Harlan, May 22, 2002

307. "The Man with a Funny Name"

When I was living in Morehead, there were about six months when there was no public defender, so what the bar did was to say that everybody was going to be a public defender. They were just going to divvy up the defense case cases, so for six months there I was doing criminal defense work. I had never none it before, and never wanted to do it since then.

My husband, who did a lot of criminal defense work, said, "Listen, if your defendant tells you that somebody with a strange name did it, the person who says this is guilty."

Well, I had this guy and he was supposed to have stolen something, but he couldn't remember. He couldn't remember it, he said, but said he didn't do it. He didn't do it, but somebody else did it, he said. But he just couldn't remember this guy's name that did it. Well, during the morning on the day before the trial, he came in and said, "Oh, I remember the guy's name. His name is Goose."

My husband says, "He's guilty, if the guy he mentioned is somebody else with a funny name." And, yes, he was guilty.

Forrest Roberts, Owensboro, June 7, 2002

308. "Lawyer Allegedly Called Wife a Cheat and Sneak"

A fellow came to me whose wife had signed a note with her daughter and son-in-law. At that time, the statute didn't provide that a married woman could be surety on a note by herself. But she had signed it at this store, and the store had taken judgment against this couple. So they put a lien on this old man and woman's bank account that had signed as surety. So he came to me, and I filed a motion to dismiss the lien and served a notice on the other lawyer. In the meantime though, this old fellow had told me how mean this lawyer had talked to his wife. So I asked him, "Who is the other lawyer?"

Well, he didn't know his name. He thought he was from Mt. Sterling, and he just talked and talked. I kept inquiring if he could tell me the physical description of the lawyer. And he finally came up with the description of a lawyer that to me was probably the most polite lawyer in Mt. Sterling. This fellow said that the lawyer called his wife "a cheat and a sneak."

We had the hearing in court, and the judge sustained my motion. We got the court order to give to the bank to release the funds. The old fellow got his money out of the bank. He was talking to me a little later, and I said, "I'm surprised that this lawyer would have said anything to your wife. He's about the most polite lawyer in Mt. Sterling."

Well, he said, "I know he did it, because I was right there and heard him."

So I said, "Well, if you were present, why didn't you call his hand and tell him that was your wife?"

Well, he said, "He wasn't talking to me though."

Asa R. Little Jr., Frenchburg, November 26, 2001

BIOGRAPHIES OF STORYTELLERS

Prepared on the basis of information received at time of the recording session.

Keith Bartley was born in 1966 in Floyd County. He graduated from Pikeville College, then attended Salmon P. Chase College of Law, Northern Kentucky University, from which he graduated in 1991. He has practiced law in Prestonsburg since then and has served as Floyd County Attorney since 1996.

James Bates, a native of Floyd County, graduated from Eastern Kentucky State College, then enrolled in the Detroit College of Law, now Michigan State University, from which he graduated in 1960. He has practiced law in several eastern Kentucky counties and has served as County Attorney, Circuit Court Master Commissioner, and District Court Trial Commissioner.

Stan Billingsley was born in Wyoming. He graduated from Western Kentucky University and then from the University of Kentucky College of Law in 1971. He worked as an attorney in Carrollton, as City Attorney in Carrollton and Warsaw, and as a judicial officer; since 1984 he has served as District Judge.

Sue Brammer was born in Maysville in 1959. She graduated from Xavier University, then from the University of Kentucky College of Law in 1984. She has practiced law since 1984 in Maysville, where she has also served as Assistant City Attorney and City Attorney.

John H. Clarke was born in 1918 in Maysville, where he graduated from high school. He graduated from the University of Kentucky, where he also attended and completed law school in 1942. Having been a practicing attorney in Maysville since then, he has also served as State Legislator for one term and as Mason County Attorney for eight years.

Lige Coffey, who was deceased at the time this manuscript was prepared, was a Russell County native. He began legal practice in Jamestown about 1958. His stories were recorded by the author and his students on July 11, 1988.

John L. Cox Jr., born in 1921 in Powell County, attended the University of Kentucky for six years, graduating from the College of Law in 1948. He practiced law in Stanton, but served primarily in public office as Powell County Judge, 1950–1954, and County Attorney for eight terms, 1958–1990.

Bill Cunningham was born on land that is now inundated by Lake Barkley. He graduated from Murray State University in 1966, then from the University of Kentucky College of Law in 1969. He was in private law practice from 1974–1992 and has served as Circuit Judge of the Fifty-sixth Judicial District since January 1992. He served in various other legal capacities prior to that and has won national acclaim for his work and for the various books he has authored.

Kenneth S. Dean was born in 1941 in Alexandria, Louisiana. He graduated from the University of Arkansas in 1965, received a doctorate of education from Northeast Louisiana in 1971, and graduated from the Salmon P. Chase College of Law, Northern Kentucky University, in 1980.

Charles English was born in Smiths Grove, Warren County, in 1935. He graduated from the University of Kentucky in 1957 and from its law school in 1960. English served as President of the Kentucky Bar Association from 1985–1986 and is presently Kentucky State Delegate to the American Bar Association. In 1998 he and ten other ABA lawyers were invited to go to China to meet with various Chinese lawyers.

Peter Ervin graduated from the University of Louisville in 1980 and from its law school in 1983. He has been in private practice since then, both in Louisville and in the western portion of the state. He is a member of the Kentucky Bar Association and has been affiliated with other relevant agencies during his professional career.

Joe Evans III, born in Maryland in 1950, graduated from Western Kentucky University in 1972 and from the University of Kentucky College of Law in 1975. He is a member of both the Kentucky and American Bar Association and currently practices real estate, mineral, domestic relations, and probate law in Madisonville.

Richard Getty was born in Pennsylvania in 1946. He graduated from the University of Kentucky in 1971 and its law school in 1974. He has served on the United States Court of Appeals and on the United States District Court in Kentucky, Michigan, and Ohio. He has co-authored a book and served as a temporary faculty member at the University of Kentucky.

Kenneth Goff was born in Grayson County in 1926. After serving two years in the military, he graduated from Western Kentucky State College in 1949 and from the University of Kentucky College of Law in 1951. He served as Grayson County Judge Pro-tem, 1951; County Attorney, 1953–1966; Commonwealth Attorney, 1969–1975; and as Circuit Judge, 1975–1992.

Eugene Goss, born in Harlan County in 1928, graduated from Eastern Kentucky State College, then from the University of Kentucky College of Law in 1959. He has been an attorney in Harlan since 1959 and has served as Kentucky's Secretary of Transportation, 1970–1972; as Commissioner of Economic Security, 1970; as a trustee of the University of Kentucky, 1972–1976; and as a member of the Board of Trustees, Kentucky State University, 1984–1986.

Asa "Pete" Gullett was born in Hazard in 1946 and graduated from Centre College in 1968. He received his law degree from the University of Kentucky College of Law in 1971. Gullett practiced privately, 1971–1999, and served as Hazard City Prosecutor, 1973–1976, and as City Attorney, 1977–1984. He is presently Chief Operating Officer of the Lawyers Mutual Insurance Company of Kentucky in Louisville.

John O. Hardin III was born in Caldwell County. His family moved to Hopkinsville, where he graduated from high school in 1947. In 1951, Hardin graduated from the University of Kentucky before serving four years in the military; he then graduated from the University of Louisville School of Law in 1961. From 1968 to 2000, he practiced law in Hopkinsville, and from 1962 to 1972, he served as State Representative.

William R. Harris was born in Simpson County in 1943. He went to the University of Kentucky in 1961, where he earned both his undergraduate and law degrees, completing the latter in 1967. After a brief period in the military and two years of practicing law in Bowling Green, he returned home to Franklin, where he was an attorney from 1971 to 1989, then was appointed as Circuit Judge for the Forty-ninth Judicial Circuit.

Byron Hobgood, a native of Hopkins County, graduated with honors from Western Kentucky University in 1969, then enrolled at the University of Kentucky College of Law, from which he graduated in 1972. As an attorney since then, he has held several public offices, serving as President of the Hopkins County Bar Association and as a member of both the Governor's Task Force on Judicial Reform and the Governor's Task Force on the Criminal Justice System.

Edward Jackson was born in 1917 in Lee County. He attended Eastern Kentucky State College, enlisted in the army, attended the University of Kentucky College of Law, and graduated with a JD degree. Re-entering the military, he attended the University of Virginia to study military law and was then sent to the Pentagon, where he worked in the Judge Advocate's office. He returned home to Beattyville, where he has practiced law since then and held many public law offices, including Circuit Judge for eighteen years.

David Jernigan, born in Muhlenberg County in 1949, graduated from Western Kentucky University in May 1971 and from the University of Louisville School of Law in the spring of 1975. He returned to Greenville, where he worked with two law firms for brief periods before joining his current law firm in 1976. He has served as Circuit Judge for the Forty-fifth Judicial District since August 1997.

Asa R. Little Jr., born in 1927 in Menifee County, served for a brief period in the army after graduating from high school. He then attended Morehead State College and the University of Louisville. Subsequently, Little graduated in 1961 from the University of Kentucky College of Law. After serving briefly as an attorney in Flemingsburg, he moved to Frenchburg in late 1961, where he has practiced since that time. He served as County Attorney for eighteen years, 1965–1983.

Morris Lowe was born in Warren County. He attended Vanderbilt University as an undergraduate and as a law student, graduating from the law school in 1951. He practiced law in Bowling Green for a few years, then was elected Commonwealth Attorney, a position he held for thirty-two years. He retired from that position in 1990 and is now in private practice once again.

Boyce Martin Jr. was born in Massachusetts in 1935. He grew up in Louisville, the son of a college professor. He attended Davidson College and graduated in 1957. After a period of military service and bank employment, he enrolled in law school at Washington and Lee, in Lexington, Virginia, and graduated in 1963. He served as an attorney briefly in New York, then moved to Louisville, where he practiced law for two years before returning to the United States Attorney's Office. He served in various judicial positions over the years and is now Chief Judge, United States Court of Appeals.

Keith McCormick was born in Iowa and attended elementary school in Minnesota and high school in Lexington, Kentucky. He graduated from the University of Kentucky in 1975 and from the University of Louisville School of Law in 1980. He first practiced law in Louisville, and then in Morehead beginning in 1984. He has served as Director of the Public Defenders' Law Office and as Assistant Commonwealth Attorney.

Sam Boyd Neely Sr. was born in Calloway County in 1915. He attended Murray State College, then enrolled in the University of Kentucky College of Law, from which he graduated in 1942. He served as City Attorney for both Hazel and Mayfield, Kentucky. He stopped practicing law in 1997 and was awarded the Liberty Bell Award upon retirement at age eighty-three.

Jo T. "Top" Orendorf was born in 1910 in Lexington, but his parents moved to Bowling Green, where he graduated from Ogden College High School. He attended and graduated from Centre College, then graduated from Tulane University Law School in 1933. He practiced law in Bowling Green until retiring in the mid-1990s, but also served as a teacher at Bowling Green Business University and as a banker.

Forrest Roberts was born in 1948 in Atlanta, Georgia. She graduated from Centre College in 1970 and from George Washington University's National Law Center in 1973. She worked for the Legal Aid Society in Louisville from 1973 to1977; worked briefly for Team Defense in Atlanta; served as Director of Northeast Kentucky Legal Services, 1979–1985; and then moved to Owensboro to engage in private practice. Her primary client is the River Valley Behavioral Health Program. She is married to attorney Allen Holbrook.

Richard Roberts was born in 1937 in Paducah. He graduated from the University of Kentucky, then enrolled at the Yale University Law School. After six months of military service, he returned to Paducah and has practiced with the same law firm for the past thirty-nine years.

Melanie A. Rolley was born in Madisonville in 1967. She graduated from Western Kentucky University in 1989, then attended Salmon P. Chase College of Law, Northern Kentucky University, graduating in 1993. Since then, she has practiced as an attorney in Madisonville and served as Treasurer of the Hopkins County Bar Association (1996–97) and as President (1998–99).

Eugene Siler Jr. was born in 1936 in Williamsburg, the son of a lawyer/judge. He graduated from Vanderbilt University in 1958, then, after two years in the U.S. Navy, from the University of Virginia Law School in 1963. He practiced law in Williamsburg with his father beginning in 1964. He was appointed as a United States Attorney in 1970, then served from 1975 to 1991 as a District Attorney. He became an Appeals Court Judge in 1991, and at present is a United States Circuit Judge for the Sixth Circuit Court of Appeals, Cincinnati.

B. Robert Stivers was born in 1922 in Alabama, where his father was stationed in the military. Robert attended Sue Bennett College, served in the army during World War II, then graduated from the University of Louisville School of Law in 1952. He was then appointed as Clerk of the Supreme Court of Kentucky. He was subsequently appointed as Assistant United States Attorney for the eastern half of Kentucky. He practiced law primarily in London, Kentucky. Both his father and his grandfather were attorneys, as are his two sons.

Daniel P. Stratton was born in 1953. He graduated from Eastern Kentucky State University in 1975 and from the Salmon P. Chase College of Law, Northern Kentucky University, in 1978. He was engaged in private practice in Pikeville for approximately five years, then served as In-house Counsel and in other positions at the Citizens Bank of Pikeville for fifteen years. He retired in 1998.

Randy Teague was born in Madisonville in 1947. He graduated from Southern Methodist University, Dallas, in 1970 and from the law school at the University of South Carolina in December 1976. He has been in law practice as an attorney in Madisonville since 1977.

Cass Walden was born in Monroe County in the early 1900s. He attended law school at the University of Kentucky, then finished law school at the Jefferson School of Law in Louisville in 1933. He practiced law in Edmonton, beginning in 1934. Across the years, he served as State Representative, District Senator, member of the Public Service Commission, and as Circuit Judge (1964–1984).

Lawrence Webster was born in Shelby County in 1945. He graduated from Transylvania University and the University of Kentucky College of Law. He has practiced law in Pikeville since 1971. He was Republican candidate for Lieutenant Governor in 1987. In addition to his legal practice, Webster is a journalist who writes columns for a local newspaper and one for the *Lexington Herald-Leader.*

Robert L. Wilson, born in Russell County in 1944, is the son of a lawyer and Circuit Judge. He graduated from Western Kentucky University in 1965 and from the University of Kentucky College of Law in 1968. He served as County Attorney for eighteen months; was appointed as District Judge in 1999, after thirty years as a lawyer; then was named Circuit Judge for Wayne and Russell Counties on April 1, 2002. His father served as a State Representative, County Attorney, and Circuit Judge.

Woodson Wood was born in Maysville in 1928. He graduated from the University of Kentucky College of Law in 1950, then returned to Maysville where he has served as a lawyer since that time. In 1957, he was elected as Commonwealth Attorney and served for thirty-seven years. His father served as Circuit Judge, his son as Commonwealth Attorney, and his brother as a local attorney.